Praise for *Midlife C*

"*Midlife Crash Course* ha
the menopausal woman.
award-w
 ...ᴋ,
 ...ɪssonance.

"I inhaled this book in oɪ ...ɪɡ! From one of the lowest points in my life, *Midlife Crash Course* brought me guidance and renewed energy. Every woman who has ever had a broken heart, a physical illness or a lost relationship must read this guide to maintaining a woman's health, joy and essential beauty over her whole life span."   —Leslie Acoca, M.A., M.F.T.,
executive director, National Girls Health
and Justice Institute

"*Midlife Crash Course* is the *real* story of one woman's journey— and no passport is required. It's the perfect book for the woman who has lost her faith in *Prayer*, her trust in *Love* and her appetite to *Eat*."   —Gloria Hillard,
former CNN correspondent
and a contributing correspondent for NPR

"In this wonderful story of midlife transformation, Gail Feldman tells, with honesty, humor and humility, how she learned to practice what she coaches—to be resilient in the face of unimaginable events. *Midlife Crash Course* gives us actions that heal and outcomes that inspire."   —Dr. Suzanne Lopez,
author, *Get Smart With Your Heart: The Intelligent
Woman's Guide to Love, Lust, and Lasting Relationships*

"This is the most complete and accessible antidote to psychological pain I've ever read. Gail Feldman has a graceful respect for the struggles we all face—both inevitable and unexpected —and she offers practical solutions that I'll refer to every single day. Every woman I know—my sister, my mother, my friends and colleagues, are all looking for balance, and trying a hundred different therapies and religions and gym memberships to find it. Here it is, distilled into this little book of wisdom. I'm thrilled to have read it. I plan to buy several copies: one for beside my bed, one for my bookshelf, and a couple to have on hand to give to people who need it. Bravo. Just a masterful work."

—SARA VOORHEES,
syndicated film critic, author of *The Lumiere Affair*

"I read this compelling book in one sitting. Gail Feldman's new book is like an intimate conversation with a very experienced, very wise friend. Gail shows how friendship, women's gatherings, and faith can provide life-affirming choices in the face of personal trauma. Gail's story of resilience provides a beacon for all who find themselves on a difficult journey at mid-life—or any stage of life.   —MARILYN O'LEARY, M.A., J.D.,
co-author of *Keep Choosing, Keep Living*

"Dr. Feldman has guided and consoled many thousands of people during her career. Now, this moving account of her personal journey to find healing and wholeness in her own life will be a blessing to every woman who takes the opportunity to read it."

—LOIS DUNCAN,
award-winning author of more than 30 books, including
Who Killed My Daughter? and *Seasons of the Heart*

"*Midlife Crash Course* is an honest account of one woman's journey to find inspiration when life unravels at the seams. It unveils new lessons when least expected and those that can only be learned after we have truly grown wise. It is a compelling story about love lost and a new self gained."   —DIANE DENISH,
Lieutenant Governor, State of New Mexico

"*Midlife Crash Course* is the story of one woman's journey to a state of grace and wisdom through the experience of physical pain and trauma. Gail's spiritual transformation spirals throughout every facet of her life and provides healing insights for all of us who have experienced "crashes" on some level. This book is a breath of inspiration for all women."

—DEANNA MINICH, Ph.D.,
nutritionist, author of *Chakra Foods for Optimum Health*

"As a survivor and thriver of open-heart surgery, I resonated with Gail's challenging journey to wellness. Gail tells her story with insight, self-discovery, and compassionate self-care—this book will serve as inspiration for us all."

—MAGGIE LICHTENBERG,
author of *The Open Heart Companion*

"Dr Feldman, through her journey to the depths of depression and then back to a happy, productive life, shares the power of using courage and honesty as our guides as we evolve toward wisdom and struggle on our own heroic journey."

—BARRY M. PANTER, M.D., Ph.D.,
director, The American Institute of Medical Education;
former clinical professor of psychiatry, USC School
of Medicine; training and supervising analyst
Southern California Psychoanalytic Institute;
editor & co-author, *Creativity & Madness—Psychological
Studies of Art and Artists Volumes 1 & 2*

"We would expect a therapist to do a how-to book drawing on the stories of clients. Instead, Gail Feldman shares her own Midlife Crash with honesty and vulnerability, confirming that no amount of knowledge exempts us from life's challenges and surprises. Perhaps in her story you'll witness your own hero's journey."   —GAIL LARSEN,
founder, Real Speaking, author of
*Transformational Speaking: If You Want to Change
the World, Tell a Better Story*

"Your books are miracles of insight and healing. Thank you!"

—DEBORAH LARZARRI, M.A.,
behavior analyst

MIDLIFE CRASH COURSE

The Journey from Crisis
to Full Creative Power

GAIL CARR FELDMAN, PH.D.

VANTAGE POINT

Vantage Point Books and the Vantage Point Books colophon are registered
trademarks of Vantage Press, Inc.

FIRST EDITION: June 2011

Copyright © Gail Carr Feldman, 2011
All rights reserved, including the right of reproduction in whole or in part in
any form.

Published by Vantage Point Books
Vantage Press, Inc.
419 Park Avenue South
New York, NY 10016
www.vantagepointbooks.com

Manufactured in the United States of America
ISBN: 978-1-936467-03-7

Library of Congress Cataloging-in-Publication data are on file.
0987654321

To the overwhelwing mystery and magic of the Life Force, the Spirit, that impels us to self-discovery and the healing possibilities in Awareness, as well as to all my companions on this sacred journey. Thank you.

CONTENTS

9

VICTORY OVER THE PAST   179

Releasing the Past · Magical Flight · Refusal to Return ·
Master of Two Worlds · Red Resilience · The Ultimate Boon

10

FINDING THE FREEDOM TO
FLOURISH   201

The Keys to Transformation · The Power of Self-Care · My
Own Crone · Abundance · Snake Medicine

11

SUPREMELY SUPPORTIVE SELF-CARE
FOR THE JOURNEY   221

Power Yourself with Prayer · Breathing Healing · Grieving Feel-
ings · Meeting Your Ogres · Gentle Self-Coaching Along the
Way · Guiding Metaphor—Becoming a Warrior for Your Life ·
Rainbow your Life · Meditation I

12

MIGHTY WOMAN UPDATE   257

Format for Mighty Women or Women of Wisdom · Sharing
Circles

INTRODUCTION

THIS BOOK IS is about a personal healing journey. It came from a need to understand and integrate the trauma and sense of desolation I experienced following a divorce after 35 years of marriage, a subsequent relationship that left me broken-hearted, and an accident that resulted in broken bones and a head injury. I fell into deep and hopeless depression during this time and began to have startling panic attacks—the same uncontrolled and disorienting emotions that so many of my women patients suffer during their own variations of life change and debilitating loss.

While I am an expert in the area of psychological trauma and the grieving process, that knowledge did not prepare me nor diminish the impact of "losing my life," as it were, to pain, medical appointments, social isolation, depression, and fear that the future would only bring more of the same. One of the first saving graces was learning that I would be helped. If I asked for help, I would receive it, even when I didn't ask nicely, like the time I screamed obscenities at God and the response was a loving, divine visitation.

My wish in writing this book is to provide an inspirational missive for women in transition—women who have been stopped, stunned, left, lost, wounded—women who wonder, *What's next. How will I cope? Can I get through this? How will I create a new life, and if I do, what might that life look like?* While this story is mainly my own, it mirrors the climactic endings and struggle for new beginnings that all women experience following divorce, death, physical injury, and the additional losses, large and small, that accumulate in midlife.

I've placed the story in the context of the "heroine's journey," where, from ancient mythology, we learn that the higher purpose for life's inevitable suffering is the growth of the heart, mind, and spirit. As part of the journey, we encounter our inner demons of fear, battle old patterns of dependency, and learn to balance and assert both masculine and feminine energy. Ultimately, the journey leads us to acceptance, compassion, and love for self and others. The inner strength and spiritual awareness discovered along the way dissolve the misery, bring hope, and propel us toward a self-expression that is fearless, joyful, and authentic—our wisdom in full and vibrant bloom.

The concept of being on a heroic journey reframes the experience of life crisis into an ongoing set of courageous acts—every action reflecting the determination to overcome obstacles along the way. Our mission is to seek meaning, understanding, and connection to community. The mythological terms used to describe the heroine's journey also provide guideposts that normalize the post-trauma reactions of depression and anxiety. The "descent into darkness," "the road of trials," "the belly of the whale"—these designations lessened the feeling that I was defective somehow in my ability to process grief. In truth, I was on a profound and arduous journey. And so are you, dear reader. From this perspective, we can be respectful and nurturing—even view our healing as a mystical and sacred process.

On the heroine's journey, we're assured that help will be provided, even supernatural aid and magical assistance. I received everything that I needed through the promise of prayer, dreams, the right body or mind therapist appearing at the right time, and surprising visits from animals like the snake in my bedroom and the hawk on my front porch.

Midlife is a time of crisis for millions of women. Because we're living so much longer, the "new" midlife is now three decades long—our 40s, 50s, and 60s—with many women juggling the care-needs of four generations—parents, children, grandchildren, spouses, and lastly, ourselves. In our culture, simply losing our youth can be a difficult passage, but losing health, love relationships, and the communities we've been part of for so long turns the landscape of our lives to lonely, desolate, and surreal. For women to know they're on a journey of great significance, not the dead-end road of life brings hope and awareness of the ways a woman can empower herself to create the last chapters of her own story.

While many books for women in midlife are written from the expert's view and provide information from academic, research and clinical perspectives, my story is a deeply personal, painful first-hand account of trauma and healing from a psychologist's own experience. My hope is that you, the reader, can identify with and draw inspiration from someone who might be seen outwardly as invincible, but who, like everyone, suffers and recovers.

The placement of midlife crises in the context of the mythology of the heroine's journey brings meaning and purpose to experiences of pain, loss, and impairment. Mythic tales are about trials and travails, but also excitement and happy endings. My travels to Thailand and Vietnam were part of a happy ending. Exotic experiences in foreign lands added spice to the inherent magic and mastery of both the worlds of light and darkness. The boon, the great gift of the heroine's journey is transformed awareness. This evolution of consciousness, which is crucial for our world today, allows us to live from the heart, with compassion, love and renewed purpose.

"Stay in the Spiritual Fire
Let it cook you
Be a well-baked loaf
and lord of the table
You've been a source of pain
Now you'll be the delight"

Rumi

"In the midst of conscious suffering, there is already
the transmutation. The fire of suffering becomes the
light of consciousness."

Eckhart Tolle

.1.

TOSSED
ON THE PATH

Broken Body, Broken Heart

On Valentine's Day, 2004, Colorado called. Instead of staying home in Albuquerque nursing my nostalgia for flowers, chocolate, and lost love, I thought this February 14th I'd lose myself skiing in the winter-white peaks of the Rockies. It had been four years since my divorce, but only one month since the ruin of my relationship with the man I thought would be my next life partner. Losing my marriage of thirty-five years had felt like a slow, limb-by-limb amputation. But I'd grown a new limb, as it were, in the form of a life with Ben, a man who said he wanted to marry and bring my Southwestern art to blend with his New England antiques in a rambling territorial-style house he planned to build for us surrounded by huge cottonwood trees and ancient vineyards. He offered to design one room as a studio, where I would develop my newfound fondness for drawing and watercolor painting. I would cut down my psychology practice in order to continue writing. We would travel, and we would also fulfill a dream of mine—to establish an educational foundation for underprivileged children. Instead, I'd learned that Ben was unreliable, unpredictable, and, most important, married.

My friends, at first supportive of my relationship with Ben, slowly became alarmed at my growing depression in response to his last-minute cancellations and callous accusations that I was only with him for his money. They urged me to commit to my own care, and, finally, after two years of feeling misunderstood, unwanted, and tossed about like a rag doll, I'd found the strength to end the relationship. I knew it was the right thing to do, but no amount of logic could comfort my heart, which felt like it had been smashed by a giant sledgehammer. It felt broken, its jagged edges poking and cutting me each time I moved or allowed my thoughts to train on Ben. Plus, I seemed unable to get a clear picture of my life and where I was now heading. That's why I knew that surviving this Valentine's Day would require getting as far away from home and hurtful memories as I could.

I flew to Denver, and then drove the short distance to Copper Mountain, a local Colorado ski resort. The day looked promising, I thought, as I stepped into my bindings. It was clear and sunny, crisp but not too cold. The snow was hard-pack, but not slick or icy. I loved skiing in these conditions, and I remember thinking that the true proprietors of this place, the forests of fir trees displaying their sparkling snowy jewelry, stood like proud hosts, welcoming me like a guest to their mountain home. I acknowledged their hospitality and silently thanked them for giving me a place to enjoy the snow and the thrill of skiing, which would provide me with some much-needed distraction from my devastated love life.

I shook off the thoughts of the men I'd left behind as I got on the chair lift. As the lift carried me upward toward the top of the mountain, I imagined the excitement, the adrenaline rush, I would experience flying down the hill. The thrill of fast, downward movement would renew my love of life itself, if not my hope for my love life, and make me feel alive again.

I spent the morning skiing the steep mogul runs on top of the mountain and was on my way to meet a friend for lunch at the lodge. I stopped to catch my breath at the end of a bump run and took time to inhale a few more deep breaths. I felt the same total-body exhilaration I always experienced on a good day of skiing well on challenging slopes. The concentration required had kept me focused on skiing; I'd forgotten my problems. I felt alive and happy. The run ahead of me was broad and empty. I pointed my tips straight down and went for it, relishing the speed and the cold wind on my face.

"Why?" someone once asked. "Why risk life and limb on the expert slopes when you can just cruise and enjoy all the well-groomed intermediate runs?"

Considering that question had made me realize that skiing, along with so many things I'd felt driven to do in my life— earning my Ph.D., achieving financial independence, and booking my family on exotic travels—took me far away from my origins. If I went fast enough and far enough, the dirt road we called "Tobacco Road" in San Diego, with its alcoholics (both violent and passive), pedophiles (just one we knew of), and abandoned women (divorce cost too much and required proof of adultery), where I had grown up would recede into the distant past and maybe disappear altogether.

Suddenly, out of the corner of my left eye I noticed movement and color. The impact to the left side of my body came so quickly and with so much force that my ski bindings disengaged, allowing the skis to continue their downhill trajectory without me. I lifted off them and flew as if in slow motion through the air. Time seemed to creep to a standstill. As I turned in midair, my mind quickly flashed on a childhood memory of somer-saulting high above my friend's backyard trampoline, but I was keenly aware that I was on a ski slope sailing through the air with nothing to catch me.

The initial shock of being hit reverberated through my body a second time as I landed on my right shoulder. My head slammed down next, and then my hip hit against the hard-packed snow. I don't remember feeling my limbs connect with the ground. I was too focused on the deep terror I felt as the tree line far below swirled into view, and I prayed I wouldn't go flying into the forest.

I slid to a stop and lay there for a moment trying to wrap my mind around what had happened. Someone must have run into me. I took stock of my body. The pain in my shoulder was deep and dark, not the white sharp pain I associate with broken bones. I thought maybe I'd dislocated my shoulder since as I sat up it felt like my arm was just hanging in its socket. My head hurt, too.

Assuming—and hoping—I wasn't too badly hurt, my thoughts turned to the other skier. It seemed he had been at fault; after all, he came from behind me, and the rules of skiing follow the rules of driving—the person in front (in this case "downhill") has the right of way. But I had been skiing my entire adult life and, even though I was skiing fast (or maybe because of it), I felt I should have been able to avoid a collision. I rose, my arms feeling like dead weights. I didn't know how I could possibly get myself back up that hill to the other skier, but I knew I needed to check on him.

With dread I began to move. Each step sent waves of pain through my shoulder and head. I managed to trudge up the incline to where he was sitting, holding his arm. My heart dropped when I saw it was a boy of about twelve. He was angry and yelled at me, "Why did you do this?" The mother of two, I felt mortified that he might be injured and that he might think I had caused this accident. Even though I had no reason to feel guilty, I did.

"I'm so sorry," I said. Despite the fact that my pain made it difficult for me to stand and to focus, I noticed the conflicting thoughts swirling in my mind. "You little shit. You're the one who ran into me. How dare you yell at me?" And then, "My God, I so hope you're not injured."

His parents skied up. The father tended to him and ignored me. I could feel my cheeks turning warm with blush. The mother stood, calm, friendly, I thought, sensing her son was not seriously hurt. When the father suggested they go to the medical clinic, the boy said, "No, I'm fine."

His mother turned to me then and said, "Are you all right?"

"No, but I'll get myself down the mountain," I told her.

Sadness filled my gut with a pain almost as deep as what I felt in my shoulder and head, causing me to wonder if I'd injured some internal organ. The happy victory over Valentine's Day was lost. I felt a failure, both physically and emotionally. Here I was, divorced and brokenhearted, a middle-aged woman gazing down the precipice of old age alone, and now I had to deal with another injury. I couldn't remember what I thought this phase of my life would look like when I was young, but it certainly couldn't have been the picture before me at this moment.

I was afraid to think of what kind of damage had been done to my body. My awareness focused itself totally on the dark pain and weakness taking over not just my shoulder and head, but every part of my physical being as I began what seemed like an endless trek down the slope to my wayward skis. With a fair degree of difficulty, I managed to collect them and somehow get into my bindings. I straightened up gingerly, feeling the pain intensifying, and then began to glide very slowly down to the chairlift.

I tried not to think about anything but getting down the

mountain. The movements that I had made with such thought-less ease just moments before were now arduous. After what seemed like an hour, I reached the chairlift at mid-mountain, stopped to rest, and then tried to ski down the lower mountain to the medical clinic. After just a few yards, I began to feel light-headed, dizzy, and nauseated.

Oh God, I thought. *I just want to lie down and go to sleep.* I sat down on the snow, and seconds later a Ski Patroller pulling a toboggan came to a hockey stop next to me. I looked up, and my body sagged with relief.

"They told me on the upper mountain to come look for you," she said cheerily. "Let's get you settled in here."

She took off my skis and helped me into the sled. I felt grateful to have someone take care of me and to know I wouldn't need to get myself down to the bottom of the mountain. And, although I didn't want to admit it, I knew my body needed to be in skilled hands, and she seemed to know just how to handle its tender places. As she placed blankets over me and tightened the straps that would hold me in place for the ride downhill, I wondered if she could see the shards of broken heart sticking out from beneath my ski suit. I wondered what else had been broken within me, and if those things would heal any more easily or quickly than my heart.

"Here we go," she said, as she began pulling me down towards the clinic. "Don't worry. We'll have you there in a jiffy." Unfortunately, I knew this drill all too well, and my heart seemed to break into even smaller pieces as she pulled the sled. *This is surreal*, I thought. *This can't be happening again.*

Ten years earlier I'd caught my ski coming through the trees on a very steep chute, called "Castor," at Taos Mountain in northern New Mexico. I'd managed to ski all the way down the mountain that time, holding my poles in my right hand and moaning loudly, as if making sounds brought me more strength and focus. The doctor expressed amazement that I'd gotten there on my own. My left shoulder was broken in five places, two ribs were broken, and I had damaged soft-tissue in muscles and tendons on the entire left side of my body. I felt fine in the clinic, though, high in fact, until the pain medication wore off, and I fainted in a restaurant in Santa Fe on the way home.

It's almost embarrassing to admit that a few years later I tore the rotator cuff and the biceps attachment in my right shoulder, this time on an expert run in Santa Fe. Surgery, physical therapy, and swimming got me back into shape that time, and swimming had been the primary component of recovery from the first accident.

Now, again, I was in an acute care mountain clinic, in shock, shaking, and so cold I kept asking for more and more blankets. I felt like an inverted turtle in the tundra, wildly uncomfortable and stranded in a place I did not belong. The X-rays showed two breaks in my right shoulder.

Shit. It's definitely happening again, I thought as I closed my eyes. I didn't realize, however, that this time I would have more than just broken bones to heal. I would suffer injuries for which doctors could prescribe nothing and experts would be vague about the prognosis for curing.

ALONE WITH PAIN

THE NEXT DAY, I sat in my wheelchair at the departure gate in Denver waiting for my plane back to Albuquerque. The airport attendant had been helpful and friendly, but now I was alone, trying to remember if the pain from my previous accidents had felt this intense. I couldn't remember. I was thinking, I can't bear this. The pain was white hot, searing, and took over my mind. It drew me to a meditation technique I had learned years earlier that I called "entering the pain." I closed my eyes and concentrated on the pain. Rather than struggling against it and trying to avoid it, I moved my consciousness into the pain, stood in the pain, sat in the pain, let myself be surrounded by it and become one with it. I became a part of the pain, and experienced it as space and light. In this way, I moved beyond the discomfort to another realm, a realm of timelessness where the pain dissolved, and I could simply float and drift.

I came back into present time when the attendant called pre-boarding. Even though my upper body was injured, I felt afraid of walking by myself. I was on pain medication and felt very weak and fragile. It seemed to me that one slight jostle from an unknowing passenger might cause something else within me to shatter. One of the flight attendants helped me board and find a seat next to a window so that my shoulder would be protected from being bumped. During the flight, as well as later when I arrived back home, I tried to achieve that same meditative trance state that alleviated my pain just before boarding the plane, but to my great disappointment and despair I had little success.

My older daughter, Niki, picked me up at the airport and brought me home. She was the first of many to say, "I can't believe you broke your shoulder up again, Mom. This makes three times!" She was with me during the first accident, so I joked, "Yeah, but only two breaks. And I didn't even pass out." She and I both knew my words and laughter were empty. My face served as a transparency for my pain, and the knowledge that I would soon have to face a night with only physical discomfort for company brought with it a dark, scary feeling I did not want to face. I tried to delay her leaving with conversation, but this took too much energy. After she got me settled on my bed with water and pain meds nearby, Niki left to go home to her husband, Charlie, and their baby.

Acutely aware of being alone, I looked around at my town-house master bedroom, spacious, elegant, and replete with a Jacuzzi tub built into its own marble platform. I lay on the same bed I'd slept on for many years, but this still didn't feel like my home. It had never felt like my home. Home remained the large house my ex-husband, Bruce, and I had built further north along the Rio Grande River, nestled into the bluffs over-looking the city of Albuquerque. It had grand views from the Sandia Mountains all the way north to Santa Fe. That family home had become a social center for our extended family of friends, relatives, and neighbors, and a sleepover haven for our daughters' schoolmates.

Niki and Megan had left that nest over ten years earlier to attend colleges in Colorado. They had periodically complained about having to grow up in "boring" Albuquerque, instead of southern California where I was raised, but by the time they graduated high school they were committed, well-trained, and passionate skiers. The mountains had claimed them. I teased them during college about how their studies were seriously interfering with their skiing.

Their father and I had met on the slopes of Mammoth Mountain in California, back in the days when a lone skier would slide into a mass of people waiting for the lift line and shout, "Single." I did that, and Bruce looked over at me and then looked at his friend and said, "I'm going with her." Six months later we were married. We chose to settle in New Mexico because of the proximity to great ski areas. I think our family passion for skiing has something to do with the freedom of speed that can feel like taking flight and the mind-boggling bliss that comes from being in nature.

Pain interrupted my reverie. Family skiing was in the past now. Sadly, we had stopped skiing together before the divorce. The girls were gone, and the big house had been sold. Right now I was alone in my townhouse, and the ache in my shoulder was growing. According to the clock, I needed to take another pain pill. The thought of movement, even slight movement, was daunting. Lying there in bed, my shoulder felt like a small, dark creature, asleep in spite of the gnawing, burning, and throbbing sensations. I looked over at the pills on the night-stand. I knew I needed to take one, but I also knew that if I disturbed the creature, it would wake up and howl.

Slowly and with great effort, I sat up and shifted my weight to the side of the bed. Shooting pain ran across my shoulder and down my arm. I took the pill container they'd given me at the mountain clinic and maneuvered the top off with my left hand. There were two remaining, one for tonight and one for morning, enough to last until I saw the orthopedist the next day.

I'd been told to take the pills with food, but something like crackers would have to wait until someone could get them for me. As I lay back down, the pain creature now wide awake and, indeed, howling loudly, tears trickled down the sides of my face and into my hair. I could only wipe them away with my left hand. The ache in my heart grew deeper and larger than it had been before the accident—the shards of glass cut-ting deeply as I lay there thinking about the long rehabilitation road ahead and feeling such deep sadness no amount of crying could relieve it. Even though the road was familiar, this time I would have to travel it alone. I fell asleep in my clothes not realizing that this would become a habit. Over the next several months I'd sleep in the same shirts and baggy pants for days and nights at a time until someone could help me bathe and dress in clean clothes.

I woke up early the next morning feeling nauseated from the pain medication taken on an empty stomach and hurting in a way I had never hurt before. It took me a moment to orient myself. Yes, I'd fractured my shoulder again. Yes, I was alone in my house, not in the big one with Bruce and not in the one I'd planned to move into with Ben. A friend would be coming to drive me to the doctor, but not Bruce and not Ben. I closed my eyes again and covered my face with my one good hand. I wished I could go back in time; I wasn't sure how I was going to go forward.

The next night, my sister, Judy, called from San Diego to hear about my visit to the orthopedist. Judy was the first person I'd called after the accident, and she checked on me every day during my early recovery.

"The good news," I told her, "is that the breaks are clean, so no surgery's required to pin the bones. I just have to wear the sling and start doing the slow pendulum movements, so I don't get a frozen shoulder."

We both knew that after my first shoulder injury, the immobilization of the shoulder while the bones mended froze the joint and set me back in my rehab several months. I told her I'd be more careful about that this time. She wanted to know about the medications I'd been given, so I told her that I had Percocet for pain and an "industrial strength" muscle relaxant called Flexeril. I'd learned from the earlier accidents that I'd also require a sleeping pill during the first several weeks.

"What else is going on with you?" Judy asked. She always pressed for more details, knowing that I would tend to diminish problems in favor of keeping a narrow, positive focus on healing.

I told her the doctor wanted me to have a complete physical with my primary care doc, and he wanted me to have an MRI of the shoulder in case the repairs he made last time had come unhinged with the fall. I'd been so relieved to hear I didn't need surgery to pin bones, I'd ignored the possibility that something else could be wrong. I told Judy I hated the thought of another operation. I didn't tell her that I was terrified of another shoulder surgery. When I'd come out of the anesthesia the previous time I had no feeling at all in my right arm and hand and had thought the surgeon had accidentally severed the nerves to my arm so it had become useless. I didn't realize it would take longer for the numbness to wear off, and even though someone reassured me, fear had clawed at my stomach for the next few hours until I was sure I could move and feel my fingers. That memory and the pain of the rehabilitation process was what stayed with me, not the fact that I'd healed.

"Don't worry," Judy said. "If you need surgery, I'll fly over and help you like I did last time. What else is going on with your body?"

I hesitated before speaking. I hadn't even acknowledged totally to myself that there was anything else wrong. Yet, there were other symptoms, and each time I noticed them a wave of nausea and tiredness came over me that made me feel like I had to lie down and go to sleep rather than face the truth. "I haven't wanted to think about my head, but I think I injured it somehow," I admitted. "The vision in my left eye's disappeared and my neck feels like drying concrete and my head hurts."

"What? Did you tell the doctor that?"

"No. I can't think about it. All I can handle right now is my shoulder," I said truthfully. "I'll tell my primary care doc when I go in for my physical."

"When do you see him?" Judy asked. "You've got to tell him. You should probably have a CAT scan of your head now. You know that."

"The doctor's a her," I said to deflect her words, which I knew were true. "And I've got to get the MRI on my shoulder first and see if I need surgery. That's all I can handle. I'll make an appointment with her though, and get that scheduled."

"Call me tomorrow and let me know when that'll be," Judy said, and added, "I love you, you know, and you're going to get through this."

THE THREE DS:
DENIAL, DISBELIEF, DISSOCIATION

THREE WEEKS WOULD pass after the accident before the appointment with my primary care doctor occurred and I could share the symptoms associated with my head. Before that, I mentioned just one of my symptoms—headaches—to my friend, Jenn, an acute care physician. She urged me to call a neurologist and get a CAT scan right away. Her sense of urgency sent me into overwhelm once again. When I put her off, she gave me an article on head injuries. I glanced at the material, but it just caused me to feel more frightened than I already felt: "Over 140,000 people die annually from head injuries, and 50,000 to 70,000 persons annually are left with intellectual and behavioral deficits precluding return to regular life," it said.* I closed the folder and put it away, trying to push my terror under the cover as well. The pit of my stomach felt sick as I told Jenn if she even mentioned my brain again, she'd be banned from my house. She knew I wasn't joking and kept quiet after that.

As I think back, I'm impressed by the fierce power of denial.

---

* I've found it difficult to find consistent statistics on traumatic brain injuries, or TBIs. The Center for Disease Control's Injury Center Division reports that there are 1.7 million deaths, hospitalizations and emergency room visits related to TBIs each year in the U.S. They also state that 99,000 new patients each year are classified as disabled. Another noteworthy finding is that the rate of TBIs is rising faster (21%) than the population growth rate of 6.3%. (Medscape, March, 2010).

Unconsciously, my denial caused me to focus on the strong need to protect myself from being overwhelmed. My mind could not evaluate what I was doing, let alone comprehend the extent of my injuries or what I needed to do to care for them. Denial narrowed my sights to take on only one thing at a time, one day at a time, one thought of potential healing (or not) at a time.

I went through that time with tunnel vision, feeling as if the light could only shine around the area where I focused my attention and where I was heading. Anything beyond that, anything outside the perimeter of that narrow focus, remained dark and murky and unclear. Whatever lay outside of my tunnel could stay there; I didn't want to see it. I couldn't see it. I wouldn't see it. Not until I was ready—ready to deal with more than just my injured shoulder.

I'm a trauma psychologist familiar with what I call, "the 3 Ds—denial, disbelief, and dissociation." A variation of these cognitive and behavioral dynamics constitute the first natural reaction to every serious crisis. Most of us—myself included—simply cannot immediately accept a severe and dramatic shift in our life circumstances. Thinking about my reaction to my accident, I'm reminded of my friend-like-a-sister, Marcia, also a psychologist, and office partner for thirty years. She was given "maybe" one year to live with a rare cancer-like disease called hypereosinophilia. She closed her practice and tried to settle in with daily chemotherapy, and when she had energy enough, go for walks or to a class at the university.

"I know I can't handle the demands of a full clinical practice again," she told me, "but I could teach, and I have a paper in mind to present to the arts and psychoanalysis meeting next year in Europe."

What is she talking about? I thought. She had nearly died twice since her diagnosis, but she never spoke of death. Her husband, David, and I commiserated about how she was trying to do too much in her weakened state, and how she exposed herself to grandbaby germs, even though they could kill her.

"That sounds like a great idea," I told her. "Let me know if I can help in some way." To myself, I thought, *I'll just indulge her denial. She needs the support.*

That fall, halfway through her death-sentence, Marcia announced she was going to Vermont to the vacation house left to her when her parents died.

"What?" I asked, in a louder voice than I'd intended. "You can't do that. There's snow on the ground there, and there's no heat or water in the house. And the doctors have said you can't travel. You got really sick after just a weekend in Arizona. The airports are exhausting and full of germs. And you need quick access to a good hospital," I said, nearly breathless.

"We'll stay in a bed-and-breakfast. Don't worry, I'll be all right."

Marcia came back from Vermont and told me, "It was heavenly."

It's two years past the "one-year-left-to-live" marker, and Marcia and I occasionally have detailed talks, some serious and some hilarious, about her someday death. Over time, she began reading about and researching her illness until she became an expert on its course, how people die from it, and the possibilities for surviving. She continues her daily chemotherapy and is planning her next trip east, this time to a meeting in Toronto.

It strikes me that the flip side, or more correctly, the higher side of denial and disbelief is the wisdom of intuition and faith. When the mind shuts the door on what looks like reality, no choice in the matter remains. There's no volition. Something deeper drives the decision, and I think that something is an inner knowing that more time is needed for the mind to open to an idea of life that bears no resemblance to the life you'd been busy planning. And I believe the Higher Self, or Inner Wisdom, is choreographing the unfolding, allowing for trust to grow us in the areas of our lives that need strengthening and protecting us from the harsh pessimism of the primitive ego that would say, "Yep, it's all over. Start digging your grave." The optimism of resilience, the foundation of the Higher Self, propels us on the path toward overcoming the adversity and creating a new life.

A few years ago, I interviewed Michael Naranjo, a Native American artist, for my book, *From Crisis to Creativity*. Michael was blinded by a hand-grenade explosion in Vietnam and during his many months in rehabilitation hospitals, he refused to believe that his blindness would prevent him from creating art. He walked out of a "skills-training" class where he was supposed to learn how to make wallets and another where he was supposed to weave cloth rugs. When he insisted on attending a woodworking class, he refused to make a bench, but instead found a smooth piece of wood and began carving a bear. Now he uses power tools and knives to sculpt wood, stone, and models for his bronze statues. "Extreme denial of the situation is imperative," he told me. "Otherwise you'd be overwhelmed and unable to cope." Michael's Inner Wisdom never wavered from the belief that physical blindness would not stop him from being who he is—an artist and a sculptor.

HELPERS ON THE PATH

MY FRIENDS BECAME my heroes. Each day when they arrived at my door, I felt a wave of relief and gratitude wash over me for their presence in my house and in my life. I'd never felt so helpless—so needy and so desperate. While I always found it difficult to ask for help, I was moved to tears every time it was offered. Jenn, Marcia, Fay, Annie, all took turns preparing food for me, helping me dress, and driving me to and from my office. When I apologized for requiring their help, they would each face me directly and say, "You'd do the same for me." And Marcia reminded me that on two occasions during the acute phase of her illness, my quick interventions had saved her life. I had to acknowledge that they were right; it was time for me to be nurtured and tended, but that didn't make it any easier or more comfortable for me to accept their help and support.

My patients, many of who had suffered combinations of physical, sexual, and emotional brutality, needed to continue their therapy, so I felt required to go back to work. Intuitively, I sensed their need was saving my life by providing me with purpose and perseverance. I called upon every ounce of strength I could muster to stay upright in my office chair and focus on their pain, which diminished the experience of my own. I knew I could not let these people down—people who had already been betrayed and let down by so many others.

My secretary scheduled only a few sessions per day, so that I could lie down for an hour after every consultation. I brought pillows to the office and would lie on the sofa with ice packs arranged on my shoulder and neck, feeling at the end of just one hour of work as though it had been four. That place of dead-tired physical exhaustion was indistinguishable from depression, and from that place, I wondered if I would ever feel well again.

For those patients sent to me for hypnosis to process their trauma, I prayed beforehand. I couldn't think clearly, let alone profoundly, and I had no memory for hypnosis scripts I had used regularly for years. I called on God to flow through me and to produce the healing words appropriate for each person, and invariably, I would be amazed at the results of the session.

In response to a patient's incredulous, "Thank you so much," I'd simply say, "We had lots of help." Then I would send up a prayer for myself, that I would receive healing for my body, mind, and heart.

Giving of myself during that time made it possible for several of my patients to become healers themselves. One woman brought me a specially-designed ice pack for my neck and shoulders, and another had a large, comfortable chair delivered and in place in the office when I arrived one morning. When I called her to say I couldn't possibly accept such an expensive gift, she replied, "Look, Doc, you've saved my life. It's my turn to help you. Besides, what are ya gonna do, carry it out the building yourself?"

My commitment to my patients' healing increased their confidence, and their commitment to the process increased mine—at least for the time I was in the office. However, at the end of the day, lying on the sofa alternating ice packs with heat I became filled with the dread of loneliness. At least I had a purpose at my office, and my patients, for whom I had enormous respect, distracted me from both my physical and emotional pain.

*

Jenn took me to my appointment with my primary care doctor on March 11th. I'm blessed to count Peg as a friend also, and I have great confidence in her meticulous patient care. Peg made a sad face when she saw me in the exam room. I looked back at her with chagrin on mine. I felt embarrassed that I was hurt again and nervous about what she might say about my injuries, especially about my head and neck. In fact, I had butterflies in my stomach.

In her office, she wanted a complete update. I'd had the MRI on my shoulder the previous week, and it showed that I didn't need surgery. That was the good news. Then I listed everything else I could think of: head and neck symptoms, stabbing pain in my right hip (this was new), and I also told her that my heart rate was "all over the place." What was bothering me the most was that periodically I couldn't breathe. I literally couldn't take in a full, deep inhalation.

Peg said this sometimes happens after trauma, and she demonstrated one breathing technique she thought might be helpful. The irony of this exercise was not lost on either of us. In the past, I'd written about and taught meditation and yogic breathing as part of stress management courses. This knowledge seemed to be gone now, erased from my memory. Instead of being the expert in this area, I now felt like a small, uninformed child being told to repeat the ABCs when all the other children had already learned them. I blushed with shame.

After the physical exam, Peg said my symptoms pointed to a closed head injury, and she suspected I had several bulging, hopefully not ruptured, disks in my neck. For a moment, my mind shut down completely as if the volume had been turned down and the lights turned off. I had to force myself to bring Peg back into focus and to hear what she was saying. The term, "closed head injury," especially coming from Peg, made my symptoms real. I could no longer try to deny or resist the necessary evaluation. I noticed that the word "head" was acceptable for me to think about, but the words "brain," "bleed," and "surgery" were not. As those words came out of Peg's mouth, they evoked fearful associations to people who looked neurologically impaired and in need of a caregiver to help them eat, dress, and guide them safely through the crowds at the mall. I became lost in these mental pictures and again couldn't see or hear Peg. My body became stiff, and my stomach began to churn and my intestines to cramp.

My discomfort became so intense that I realized I might need to find the bathroom. Then I became aware of Peg saying she wanted me to have a scan of my head and neck, and also my hip and lower back. She said it was important to get this set up as quickly as possible. I nodded my head, and continued to sit there dumbly holding my stomach.

She told me my heart sounded different from in the past. Now on overload, I just stared at her, as my pounding heart joined in with my other protesting organs. I listened to it beating in my chest. It didn't sound any different to me, just more frightened in its pace than usual, if that was possible these days. Peg did an EKG there in the office, and, although it was normal, she recommended I see a cardiologist for an echocardiogram.

Peg wrote out the orders for a cardiology workup with Dr. Kathleen Blake and gave me the names of several other doctors—a neurosurgeon, a neurologist, and some kind of specialist chiropractor who worked only with the neck and head.

As Jenn and I left the building, I apologized for being so stubborn about telling a doctor earlier about my head symptoms.

"That's not a problem, sweetie. Can I encourage you to call the neurosurgeon now?" She spoke from her typical good nature, but there was seriousness behind her words.

"You can encourage me, but I won't do it. Remember the joke at UCLA about a surgeon's attitude? If in doubt, cut it out. I'm afraid a surgeon might want to operate even if it isn't strictly indicated. For now, I need to get the scans of my head, neck, and back set up," I told her. "And maybe I'll call that chiropractor."

I could tell it was with effort that Jenn kept her mouth closed and her jaw set. Maybe I was still in denial, or maybe I was simply being practical. Maybe I was being hard-headed, or maybe I was simply afraid to deal with all of this at once. It didn't matter to me. I would not contact a neurosurgeon. Consulting a neurologist would depend on the MRI results. When I got home, I took the cardiology referral slip and stuck it in the back corner of my desk drawer. I didn't need a medical doctor to tell me what was wrong with my heart. I knew it was broken.

FRIENDS AS HEROES

UNTIL THE ACCIDENT, like so much in my life, I had taken my friends for granted. Yes, they were wonderful to socialize with and always ready to lend an ear on the telephone, but now I realized how crucial friendships are in surviving the hard times. While it may sound dramatic to equate loneliness with death, that's what being alone felt like during that time—being cut off from humanity, untethered from the world, disassociated, forgotten. I'd heard the expression that no matter what happens, "Life goes on." As I sat alone in my townhouse, I felt as if everyone else was going on with their lives and leaving me behind. Yet, each time a friend called or came over, I felt hopeful. Their friendship was a lifeline of love. The human connection brought me energy to help me keep going, keep living.

I later found research to prove the powerful life support that friends provide. Two women at UCLA give us evidence of how women respond to stress quite differently from men. This responsiveness gives our gender greater strength and resiliency. For five decades, the research using men as subjects found that "fight or flight" was the normal response to stress. Professors Laura Klein and Shelley Taylor noticed, however, that when things weren't going well in the research lab, the men holed up somewhere, but the women came in, cleaned, had coffee, and talked about the problems. They decided to repeat the stress response research using women as subjects. What they found is that women have a larger behavioral repertoire than just "fight or flight."

In a woman, the hormone oxytocin is released as part of the stress response. It encourages her to tend to children and gather with other women, and when she does this, even more oxytocin is released. This hormone is the same one that is released during breast-feeding. It counters the stress response and produces a calming effect. This calming effect does not occur in men because testosterone, which men produce in high levels when under stress, seems to reduce the effects of oxytocin," says Dr. Klein. "Estrogen seems to enhance the calming effects of oxytocin."

This "tend and befriend" behavior is thought to be the reason why women consistently outlive men. Social ties reduce our risk of disease and death. In one study, those who had the most friends over a nine-year period cut their risk of death by more than 60 percent. In my case, the sense of security I felt at being able to call someone and to know they would come and help me always allowed my body to calm down and to better tolerate the inner tension of pain and the unpredictability of the future.

I knew about the Harvard Medical School's long-term study of nurses and the finding that the more friends women had, the less likely they were to develop physical impairments as they aged. Not having close friends or confidantes, they concluded, was as detrimental as smoking or carrying extra weight. Friends truly help us to live healthier, longer lives.

I understood all those facts and studies in the context of having the ability to be a friend. The idea that I was impaired and needed friends to care for me, however, felt unacceptable. Each time one of my friends came to help me in some way, I felt a huge amount of gratitude, yet I cringed at the same time. Accepting their help filled me with a sense that I was "less than" they, and less than I should be as an adult. I accepted what they offered me with some awkwardness and embarrassment, but I knew I could not take care of myself. On some level, my mind insisted that I "should" be able to care for myself, and I began to hate my weakness. Yet, I knew I had no way out of my neediness. I could not survive alone, and this knowledge left me frozen in negativity and despair.

In mythology, every heroine, at some point, finds herself on a frightening, unfamiliar path—a path that leads through darkness and fear. In much the same way, I'd found myself on a new and alien path, a path that would descend into darkness and take me through the process of dying to the past, dying to my old ways of being in order to be recreated as a more balanced woman possessing a greater ability to be receptive and cared for, as well as being the one who does the giving. At that moment, however, I couldn't see the light of re-creation at the end of my journey. I didn't even know I was on a journey. I could only see the darkness of the deep, despairing place I found myself in. I felt frozen in that emotional state.

We've learned about the "freeze" response, an actual physiological response to stress, primarily from women survivors of trauma. It occurs when a person has no ability to fight, flee, or befriend, as is the case during an accident, natural disaster, assault, or rape. One is frozen in the moment, dissociated from what's happened and from any ability to think about or plan a course of healing. We become the "deer in the headlights," or the rabbit, stone-still, when it thinks the predator's eyes have fixed on it.

I hated feeling like a victim, and yet that's what I was at those times in the dark, hopeless place I found myself. I cried, screamed, spilled and spit tears, or sank into my bed, quietly sobbing into a handful of tissues. Mentally, I knew I must redefine my notions about independence and self-care and realize that in every way that I asked for help, organized my days, showed up for rehab, prayed for strength, looked for light in meditation, I was not a victim. I was a survivor. I was in charge of my healing and with intention I would move forward on my journey. On the good days, I knew that was true, and I was inspired. On the bad days, they were meaningless words. I would cry disconsolately on my couch, scribble bitter protests in my journal, and then try to summon up the same compassion for myself that I would have for a friend or a colleague suffering a similar crisis.

.2.

THE ROAD OF TRIALS

DESCENT INTO DARKNESS

$\mathcal{I}$ moved the note with the Imaging Center's scheduling number from my desk to the kitchen counter and back to the desk, avoiding the call. The last thing I wanted was to be in that tomblike cylinder, listening to the jackhammer pounding of the machine and trying to breathe normally. I remembered the previous time. I had kept my eyes closed and tried not to think, but my thoughts kept pace with the knocking. As the machine did its work, my fears had worked on me. Panic prowled around in my chest the entire time. Afterward, when I returned home, the fear accompanied me, clinging like lint, making it hard for me to think of anything besides the possibility of another surgery.

When the call came telling me the repairs in my shoulder had held, the relief felt like exhaling air I'd held in my chest for weeks. I sat down in a chair. I felt darkness recede as though someone had found me trapped in a dungeon, slid open the door and let in the light. I whispered, "Thank you, God."

The prayers worship groups and friends had been uttering for me for weeks had been answered. Sometimes I had prayed; many times I had felt too depressed or hopeless to make a request on my own behalf. Now, the reassuring results of so many declarations of faith made me feel euphoric. But the euphoria was short-lived. With the question of the shoulder surgery handled, my relief gave way to more worry, as though one door in a haunted house had closed and a new one creaked open. I looked in at the other physical symptoms and the tests that would be required to diagnose them.

It was obvious to me, although I didn't want to admit it, that many things in my head were just not working, and this brought more apprehension. The thought that I had a brain injury scared me to the depth of my being. I still found myself unwilling to deal with that possibility by confronting it in a specialist's office. I resisted looking into the darkest, most frightening room in the haunted house—the one that held my brain. But I knew I had to do something. I forced myself to pick up the phone and call the number of the Imaging Center to schedule the next MRI.

In the meantime, I dealt with the head symptoms as best I could. I was light-sensitive and intensely sound-sensitive. My eyes would sting with pain if I tried to read, look at the computer screen, or watch television. Very often I had to close my eyes just to shut out normal indoor light. When I was on the sofa or bed during the day, I put a soft pad over my eyes, creating a darkness like black velvet—soothing to my eyes and to my head.

Ordinary sounds became noise to my ears. I used earplugs anywhere there were groups of people. My tolerance for music was reduced to ocean sounds or the relaxing music played during massage or yoga. There was one CD I played every night: *Calming Massage*, by Lifescapes, featured low, slow, flute and mandolin pieces with titles like "Balance," "Harmony," and "Transcendence." I called it my New Age lullaby, and regardless of what combination of pills I took, I couldn't go to sleep or even rest without it. The music would eventually carry me away from the pain in my body and the torture wheel of memories of Ben. It gently placed me on a soft cloud where I would drift through the night in freedom.

Long before that release into sleep, however, my noisy thoughts took off and pushed the lovely music into the background. They explored the same dark alleys each night, examined the cutting words and revisited the hurtful actions that led to the breakup with Ben—the time he sent me home in the middle of the night because he was angry for some unknown reason; the time I said we needed to talk about his moodiness and withdrawing from me, and he said, "That's your problem"; the times he called just before a scheduled trip and announced that he wasn't going. These memories felt like sharp stabs to my heart, causing me to lie there wounded, missing him.

The longing for Ben's body and touch invariably brought me back to the soothing background music, and I would open to sensations of his being there with me. I could feel his arm draped around me, as we used to sleep, with his hand resting on my stomach or my leg, as though his phantom limb had found its way through the night to my bed. At some point, I would startle to wakefulness and realize he wasn't actually there. I'd reach to his side of the bed to find it empty, the same way I felt inside.

As the music offered no consolation, I'd send a torrent of judgment on myself. What was wrong with me that I would tolerate so much disrespect? (Me, a psychologist.) How could I be so weak and so stupid? How could I humiliate myself by going back for more after the times he stood me up? *Pathetic—that's what you are, Gail.* Then I'd turn the cannons on Ben. What was wrong with him that he could behave abusively with someone for whom he professed such great love? He was a con artist, a scam man, just another guy who goes from one woman to the next, immune to the wreckage left behind.

As I lay there in the dark, my mind felt like a machine with no "Off" switch. It felt as though Ben inhabited my head, controlled the switch, and caused my angry thoughts to escalate and my emotional pain to swirl within my chest and go deep into my abdomen. With little ability to manage my thoughts or my feelings, fear grabbed my heart and held it so tightly I had trouble getting enough air.

I recalled that when my patients described the agony of compulsively reviewing the details of traumatic experiences, I would reassure them that obsession represents a normal stage in the grieving process. Now, I truly knew how awful it felt to be stuck with this repetitive churning of hellish thoughts. Nothing about this maelstrom of emotional and physical pain felt normal or like a stage I could ever move beyond. I'd calm myself as best I could. I'd tell myself that this is what we do in grief—obsess and feel hopeless. I would assure myself that "this too will pass," and each night the music would, at some point in time, do its magic and thankfully take me to sleep.

Being alone at night also magnified my physical pain. Not that the physical pain was worse at night than during the day; at night I simply had no distractions from it. Dusk, with its soft pinks and blues washing across the Sandia Mountains, had always been my favorite time of day. Now it simply signaled the coming of a dark time of loneliness.

Often, I had spent hours on the living room sofa in the late afternoon and evening with my ice packs and heating pad.

Watching the colors of the day fade and the darkness descend, I felt completely devoid of the inner joy that would typically delight me as the lights of the city began to blink and sparkle. A sense of dread took residence in my gut—dread of the coming night, the following day, and the possibility of a frighteningly limited future. Unable to watch television or read, time became torturously long, waiting the minutes and hours until I could justify laboriously moving my location to the bedroom, and once there, begin the nighttime ritual of taking pills, arranging pillows, and putting on the music to begin the long process of my mind and body settling down enough to rest.

In bed, my first awareness went to the physical pain. I would lie there, as if paralyzed—my shoulder reasonably comfortable lying flat—no movement or turning allowed, of course, so that the bones could knit. But it felt unbearable not to be able to move my head. My neck felt as though a vise was tightening around it causing waves of pain to move up into my head. Any movement made it worse. My head lay on the pillow like a painful weight, emitting deepening levels of throbbing discomfort. As my awareness of my body's distress became heightened, so would the fear that I would be in this state forever.

And this was possibly the worst part about nighttime—the hopelessness. In the black of night, I could see no future that included me as a fully-functioning human being. With these wild thoughts and uncontrolled emotions, my consciousness would return to focus upon my pain-filled head. I knew two people who'd had brain injuries. One required surgery, the other didn't, but in both cases their healing took many years, and neither recovered fully. With my eyes closed, I imagined myself living a life like theirs, requiring help to do the household accounting and being unable to ride a bike or run a mile for charity. The part of me that loved to be mentally quick and physically active would just as soon be dead. An identity as an impaired person felt intolerable.

Plus, an identity as an impaired woman, in my mind, excluded ever having a man in my life again. That image brought waves of grief rolling over me. I sobbed, loudly, deeply, fully into the darkness. I truly believed I would never again experience the peaceful physical intimacy I'd had with Ben, and that I would instead spend every night struggling with the desolation of being alone and unwanted, of having no one with whom to share my bed or my life. And with that bleak outlook, I could cry, but I could not sleep.

❦

My friend Marcia told me to call any time of the night, should I need to. I did call, but only once, around midnight when I couldn't sleep and found myself haunted by my fears. When I could stand my shivering no longer, I picked up the phone with a trembling hand. I felt small and silly not being able to get along by myself. Then, once on the phone, the words "pathetic" and "embarrassed" began ringing in my head, and all I could do was cry. I stopped crying long enough, however, to listen to Marcia reassure me. She explained that finding one's self alone and physically impaired or ill after thirty-five years of being surrounded by family would result in unexpected and devastating anxiety. I began to sob again as she finished speaking. Her words had hit home, resonating around my heart. Of course that would be true, I thought. I thanked her and felt grateful for her understanding.

And yet, the very next night I felt anxiety clutching at me when I shifted my body and the pain went deeper in my head or shot through my hip or my chest felt heavy as though threatening to stop my breathing. What if something happens to me while I'm here alone? I wondered. What if I stop breathing?

There's no one to notice, no one to help me. I could die, and no one would know.

What I would have given for someone to watch over me, someone to lie next to me or even to sit next to my bed while I slept. Instead, I was on my own. Yes, I had some help from friends and family, but for the largest part of my day—and my night—I was alone with my pain and my physical limitations.

In addition, the level of fatigue I now felt fed my anxiety. Only part of my weakness seemed related to the fact that I couldn't sleep for more than a few hours at night. I told myself that my body was working hard to heal, and it simply required more rest. But this fatigue involved a degree of weakness that could suddenly overwhelm me, causing me to lie down immediately. It felt as though my brain couldn't get impulses to my legs, or my heart wasn't up to the task of pumping enough blood to keep me moving. It frightened me to know I hadn't the stamina to make even one stop for milk or something to eat after work. If I tried, I thought the extra little bit of energy required to get out of my car, go into the store, and get back into my car would actually cause me to collapse in public. I had only enough energy to get home and lie down, breathing hard, as though I'd just finished a strenuous walk or unpacked a garage full of boxes.

Fatigue like this hadn't occurred after my other injuries. Just moving my body seemed to require huge effort. During the other recoveries, within two to three weeks I could walk for thirty minutes to an hour, use the leg exercise machines at the gym, and within a few months I could plan a trip out of the country if I traveled with a companion prepared to carry my bags. But not this time; I couldn't imagine doing anything beyond finding enough strength to stay upright for two hours at a time.

I also found it strange to be so aware of the weight of my head. It felt like an enormous task just to hold it up, and I could hear bones crunch with even the slightest turn, a sound that made me think of grinding gears in a broken-down car. I didn't want to think about crumbling vertebrae and torn tendons. My vision began to return, but the head pain didn't abate; it increased. The occipital area of my head just above my neck would hurt and swell. Strange, I thought, but obviously true as I could feel the tenderness by placing my left hand on this area. Intense pain and pressure would shoot up to the top of my head and down around my eyes.

I spoke to Marcia every day, but made no more calls to her in the middle of the night. Her constant refrain was, "You'll get through this," and each time I hung up, I doubted her words, but appreciated the love in them. I lay on my couch exhausted, my head filled with moving, shooting pains, wishing sleep would overtake me, but knowing it wouldn't any time soon. I sat with the phone in my hand staring at it, wanting to call her again, or to call someone, but I knew I had nothing to say worth listening to. I was sure no one wanted to hear about my anguish, and that was all I could think to talk about. In fact, I didn't want to talk at all anymore. I wanted to be still, quiet, free of pain, free of feelings, asleep, dead to all of this distress. Peace was what I wanted, but I could no sooner imagine what that would feel like than I could imagine feeling happy.

DISORIENTED ON THE JOURNEY

I BEGAN DRIVING myself to work and to my appointments as soon as I was able. I was scared to get out on my own, but the ability to drive relieved me of the need for so much help. I felt grateful not to have to rely on friends to taxi me around, but I was always tense. Reaching over to shift gears required cautious effort, as any quick movement could further aggravate my shoulder and my neck. And I had to take special care to use the rearview mirrors and not turn my neck to either side. I was adept, now at doing many things with my left hand (it started with brushing my teeth), but I had to move very slowly. Everything about my life seemed to narrow down to thoughts of how to make the next slow motions of carefully tending to my body.

Driving brought new issues to my awareness. I noticed that I was fearful of driving fast, which meant getting up to normal speed on the freeway. I found it more disturbing to notice that I rarely seemed to know where I was going. I would get to frequently-traveled destinations, like my office, automatically, but it seemed my internal "global positioning system" had shut off. One Friday I was driving to meet my daughter and grandbaby at Gymboree, the baby gymnastics class. Before the accident, I would take Ethan there myself, so that Niki, who was pregnant again, could have a break. Now, all I could provide was my company, but I also knew I would enjoy watching Ethan climb up ladders, roll down slides, and chase bubbles at the end of the class.

As I drove north on the interstate, I had a general idea of where Gymboree was located, but I discovered I had no knowledge of where to get off the freeway. The first time I found myself on the wrong exit I was a little flustered, but chalked it up to simply not paying attention. I got back on the highway heading south, only to get off at the next exit and have the same experience—no recognition of the location. At that point, my heart began to pound, and I began to sweat. What the hell is going on? I asked myself.

I turned the car around and got back on the highway going north a few more miles and tried another exit, but found myself still lost. I could feel my anxiety and confusion growing, my heart was now audible in my ears, and my breathing was fast and shallow. *How can I be disoriented in a city where I've lived for over thirty years?* I thought. I didn't know what to do. Just when I remembered I could use my cell phone to call for help and had begun looking for a place to stop and use it, I found myself on the right street. Relief washed over me as I pulled into the parking lot. I sat in the car with the air-conditioning turned up high until my breathing returned to normal. I tried not to consider the reasons why I was so disoriented.

That night I had the first of many disturbing dreams, dreams of being in a foreign city, lost, separated from my family, with no knowledge of the language and no memory of how to get back to the hotel where we were staying. I awoke in much the same state as I had arrived at Gymboree—sweating, heart racing, hyperventilating.

I was bewildered by my losses in short-term memory. Repeatedly, I'd be told something on the phone or in my office that I would immediately forget. I kept telling myself to write things down, but then one has to *remember* to write them down. I was in Niki's kitchen one night helping her prepare dinner, and I asked her how she'd like me to cut the vegetables. The look she gave me carried the words, "Are you crazy?" I immediately knew I must have already asked that question, and she had answered. She recovered herself and answered again, and we both laughed, making light of my malfunctioning memory. But I couldn't forget that look.

As I cut the vegetables I wondered if my brain had cracked during my accident and now little pieces were beginning to break away. The inability to function mentally like a normal person made me feel crazy. *So this is what it feels like to lose your mind,* I thought. I managed to make a joke: "Of all the things I've lost, I miss my mind the most," then I wiped a tear from my eye as I turned back to the vegetables. I wondered if I would feel crazier as time went on and how my daughter might look at me then.

My inability to remember something I'd just been told caused me to react differently depending upon who I was with: I could feel amused, feel like a lost child, feel embarrassed, or feel frightened by the prospect that my body would heal but my brain would be left with dementia. Underneath all my reactions, however, lay a fine layer of terror. I had visions of becoming one of those crazy people I'd cared for at Camarillo State Hospital in California, the ones who were left there and forgotten by their families. Women in locked wards, sitting in the "Day Room" together, unkempt, motionless hands in their laps, vacant eyes not watching the television and not seeing each other. Those visions of "a fate worse than death," as I thought of it, made me want to curl up and stay in a fetal position. But not even that was available to me since my back and neck had to be kept straight at all times.

That night after dinner at Niki's, I sat in front of my TV and squeezed the exercise ball given to me to maintain muscle tone in my right arm. Normally, I would count the repetitions. This time I kept squeezing on and on, angry tears rolling down my face, until my forearm hurt, and I noticed the fist I'd made with my left hand was so tight there were deep marks where my fingernails had dug into the skin.

RESCUE WITHHELD

I WAS DISAPPOINTED to find that it would be three more weeks before I could have the MRI on my head, neck, and back. I still didn't want to face the test or hear the results, which I was sure would not be good news, but I'd wanted it done before April 8, when I was supposed to be in San Diego for my sister Judy's 50th wedding anniversary. I wanted to know what was happening in my head and what treatment might end the symptoms. I wanted to know what could be done to realign my neck and stop the insistent pain that sat there and sometimes shot up into my head. The trip to Southern California represented something else I'd been trying not to think about. The idea of going to another city when I could barely get around in Albuquerque felt scary and impossible. With the MRI scheduled and the trip looming before me, I felt cornered, like an animal looking for an escape route.

I began to consider whether that chiropractor my doctor had mentioned could cure whatever was causing me so much pain in my head and neck. If so, I could cancel the two-hour MRI marathon before going to San Diego. And I could travel with ease. I called her office and scheduled the appointment.

❦

The young woman chiropractor had taken X-rays of my neck and head and was showing me how the vertebrae in my neck looked like blocks strewn helter-skelter. They were totally out of alignment. She also pointed out that my head was positioned 30 degrees off the center of the axis of my spine. I could see all this so clearly that I was stunned into amusement. Rather than cry at the picture of my abnormally aligned neck and head, I wanted to laugh. No wonder my neck was in total spasm and pain. And no wonder I couldn't close my mouth when I lay down to try to sleep. Even my bite was off. And that's why a cap on one of my bottom teeth had popped off. And only God could know what in hell was happening in my brain itself.

I didn't know what training made her a specialist in this sort of trauma, but the chiropractic doctor had an elegant office on the ninth floor of an expensive building, and her fees were very high. I thought she must be quite competent, and I waited to hear what she would recommend to resolve my problems.

She looked down at her notes and said haltingly, "I don't really think . . . I'm the best person . . . to help you. I have the names of several other doctors who might be able to . . ."

"But I don't understand," I interrupted. "I thought you specialized in the head and neck."

"Well, your case is one that . . . uh, Dr. Matthews or, uh, a Dr. Kellog might do better with . . ."

The corners of my mouth dropped. My amusement, which had felt like such a relief, turned to red hot anger that tensed every muscle once again. I felt a spasm in my right shoulder and reached up to massage it with my left hand. "So what is it that you think is wrong? What is your diagnosis?"

"Well, I'm not sure . . ." her voice trailed off.

I waited a moment as I stared at her in disbelief. Then I said, "Thank you," and stood up to leave.

I felt like not paying for the consultation, but I went to the outer office and clumsily wrote the check, grabbed my purse with my left hand and knocked the doctor's name placard over as I brushed past the counter on my way through the waiting room. I moved as quickly as I could to the elevators and out to the parking lot. I felt seething resentment that someone who was supposed to know how to help me and obviously knew enough about what was wrong to know she couldn't help me, didn't bother to try to tell me *what was wrong*. Had she been afraid to say the words? Was she too uncomfortable to tell me . . . that she couldn't help me? That no one could help me? That what she saw scared her? I sat in my car with anger tensing every one of my muscles, my heart racing, my breath coming in short gasps. And when the anger subsided, fear took over, and I dissolved into tears. The mantra in my mind repeated itself over and over as I drove home—*hopeless, hopeless, hopeless*, it said.

IN THE BELLY OF THE WHALE

NOTHING ABOUT ME seemed like me. The successful psychologist who'd grown a reputation for skilled crisis intervention and authored several books, one of which led to appearances on radio and television shows, including Larry King Live, seemed to have vanished. Where did that woman go? I wondered. The one with the seemingly "perfect" marriage, a physician husband lauded for his expertise in asthma and immunology . . . that ideal couple, who with their daughters had so much fun entertaining and traveling that it was not unusual for grownups to jokingly beg to be adopted by them . . . *What happened to that woman?*

She seemed to appear only at work now, able to be a competent therapist for one hour at a time in order to serve others. Outside of the office, that person became unrecognizable. The woman who looked back at me from the mirror seemed older, tired, even haggard. I'd look at couples and not be able to imagine how a man could ever love me. I'd watch my grandson and wonder if I would ever have the strength and energy to hold him and play with him again. I'd glance at the photo of Niki's thirtieth birthday dinner and be amazed that I had planned and presented it. Now, the thought of even making lunch sent me into such confusion that I'd stare at the contents of the refrigerator, dumbfounded, then close the door and eat an apple.

The formerly accomplished woman I had been certainly didn't show up at my physical therapy sessions. Maybe she thought it an opportune time to take a vacation to Italy or to go on safari in Africa. That powerfully optimistic self bailed out on me completely, went missing each time I walked into an appointment with the physical therapist. I felt so weak and fragile, like a tiny child who could fall and break if left unattended, that I wouldn't let Laurie, my PT, leave me alone for more than a minute. If she turned her back, walked away, or, God forbid, left the room, my heart would begin to race, and my breath would catch in my throat as panic set in. Whether I was working with weights, pulleys, or on the treatment table for ultrasound, heat, or traction, my mind would occupy itself with wild, irrational fears: I'll pull my shoulder out of the socket using the shoulder cycling machine; I'll fall off the treatment table and hit my head and become a vegetable; I'll be made a quadriplegic from the traction machine malfunctioning and pulling my head . . .

Fortunately, Laurie was calmness personified. Gentle and understanding, even though she'd known me to be bold and confident about healing from my previous accidents, she never commented on the difference in me this time around. She never looked askance or hinted that my fears were overblown and uncalled for. If she needed to leave my side to get more towels or blankets, she'd keep talking all the while so I could hear her voice and know she was nearby. When I would express doubts about my progress, she'd show me the numbers on how I'd increased my shoulder's range of motion or reassure me that deep muscle injuries, like those we suspected were causing the hip pain, took longer than bones to mend. And when she didn't know what to say about my head pain, she'd simply say she believed I'd eventually be okay, and that, if I wanted her to, she would pray for me. Laurie is a deeply spiritual woman, so I told her yes, to please pray for me (as often as she'd like).

None of her words eased my fears at the time, although the energy behind them helped calm me enormously. The thought that she would put me into her prayers was comforting, and I know now that her attentive and loving presence was every bit as important for my healing as her knowledge of physical therapy.

A River of Tears

In spite of the excellent care I was receiving, the small healing steps I was making, and the little ways in which my life was getting back to normal, I found myself crying on a daily basis. In the parking lot at church one day a woman greeted me and said she recognized me from a talk I'd given there the previous year. She was a stranger to me, but when she asked, "How are you?" I told her about the accident and what a hard time I was having. I began weeping and was unable to stop. I was so embarrassed, I felt myself shrinking in size.

At one of my physical therapy appointments, I met a former patient in the waiting room and did the same thing—dissolved into tears. When I apologized, she reminded me that I'd helped so many people that she felt honored that I would share my distress with her. Part of me knew that my sharing was a gift to her, but part of me also knew that I was completely out of control. In the field of psychology I would be classified as emotionally "labile," a term that denotes someone whose moods and feelings render them unstable. That was the new me—emotionally unstable. The mantra in my mind started up again—"hopeless," and I added another word, "helpless."

From the perspective of my Higher Self, the part of me that was connected to Source, or the soul, I knew I was simply temporarily lost in grief, processing the heartache over my marriage, Ben, my physical health, and the dreams for my future. I was wrapped in depression and despair. From my normal, everyday perspective, however, I questioned how I could survive this purgatory and find the key that would release me from my suffering. I wanted to cross over a threshold and move onto the next stage of my journey. I wanted a new life—a normal life, one that held a promise of happiness. The fleeting glimpses of inner peace offered to me by my Higher Self through a brief prayer or spiritual reading didn't seem to soften or dispel the grief.

ANOTHER ALLY ON THE PATH

JUDY CALLED DURING one of those late nights when I was mentally fingering my worry beads. Her voice sounded different. Her speech was slurred.

"I can't go through with this," she said.

"What are you talking about? You sound like you've been drinking."

"I have been, and I'm gonna keep on. I can't do this, this party."

"You mean the anniversary party?" I asked.

"Yeah. It's a sham, a fake. I'm a fake, and a fool, a fool to stay married this long. Vince and I just had another fight, and half the time I hate my family. The only reason I'm married this long is because I'm a coward, and I couldn't leave."

"You are so full of shit," I told her. "And you shouldn't be drinking. You *don't* drink," I said.

"Well I do tonight," she answered.

"Well, let me remind you of the reasons you stayed married," I said. I spoke of the conscious commitment she made year after year, not only to Vince, but also to the dozens of people in the family who depend on her strength and her wise counsel. I told her how important she is to her grandchildren and reminded her of the joy they bring her.

"Am I jogging your memory?"

"I guess so. But I still feel like crap."

"I know you do. You can't drink. Remember?" Judy and I both have allergies, but while mine are limited to cats and pollen, hers include nasty skin and gastrointestinal reactions to some foods, including alcohol.

I went on to tell Judy how much I respected her choice to stay in her marriage through the bad times. As I did, I noticed my guilt kicking in for having given up on my own marriage, but I reminded myself this was no time to indulge in my own feelings and regrets. I was really scared that she might do something to hurt herself. It took all of my focus and energy to speak boldly enough that she would hear me.

I nearly yelled into the phone, "You've honored your commitment to care for a very large family, and they all love you. They depend on you. You're such an inspiration to all of us . . . Are you listening to me?"

"Yeah, but I don't feel any different."

"Well, you won't right now. You'll feel awful for a while. But, guess what, you deserve to be celebrated. How rare is it for a couple to be together for fifty years?" I asked her. I felt powerful as I spoke those words, love coming right from my heart, words of encouragement to my only sister, my focus solely on her, my concern only for her well being.

"So put away the liquor and go to bed. You might have to throw up first, but go to bed. I'm going to call your friend Maggie to come and check on you, and I'm going to call you in the morning and repeat everything I've just said."

My own worries had dissolved as I talked to Judy. The fear in my gut was no longer about me, but about her. Maggie assured me, when I called her, that she would go right over and that she'd call to report to me in the morning. That night I had no problem talking to God. I asked that Judy be sent all the love and support and strength she needed to come back to her authentic self—that fierce feminine force that I experienced growing up.

For me to be telling Judy what to do was truly rare. She's four years older, but it seemed, when we were young, like she was already an adult. She bossed me around like a You-better-believe-I-know-what's-best-for-you surrogate mother. When I was twelve and she was sixteen we took the bus to downtown San Diego so we could ride the new escalator (Moving stairs! It was a science fiction phenomenon) at the Walker-Scott Department Store. In the 1950s, San Diego was teeming with sailors. This was before strip malls and shopping centers, so the only sources of entertainment—the bars, movies, and the USO—were located on lower Broadway. From the bus stop to the department store, we walked through a moving horde of young men in uniform with Judy telling me to "walk faster, don't look at them, and keep your hands up over your chest so they can't grab you." The last injunction was meaningless to me, as I didn't have anything to grab. But Judy certainly did.

My big, bossy sister ran away from home at sixteen to marry her nineteen-year-old boyfriend, Vince. Our family hated him. Even as a girl of twelve, I knew it was ludicrous that our working-class, American mongrel, Oklahoma Dust Bowl family would judge another group of people. But they did. There were dire predictions for Judy's marriage, the least of which was that it would fail. She would end up in poverty, he would abandon her, and even if they did stay together, she would be kept "barefoot and pregnant by that Wop" for the rest of her days.

For the first twenty-five years of her marriage, Judy worked fourteen-hour days at the family restaurant and raised four daughters. Now, there are nine grandchildren, four of them teenage boys. Two of them live with her. She and Vince are wealthy, and she is the undisputed matriarch of the family. Her tough, consistent love is the glue that holds an unruly tribe together. While I may be the only family member to have completed high school and gone on to college, Judy is someone I regard as being truly educated, educated in the sense of knowing people, and knowing what constitutes an exemplary life—commitment and sacrifice. I doubt she would agree, but I see her as one mighty woman. We'd talked a lot over the years about how difficult our husbands were, and how similar in temperament—quick to anger, opinionated, and judgmental. On the one hand, I envied her resolve; on the other, I couldn't imagine living in constant conflict, especially now when I felt so weak.

As I hung up the phone, I knew that, while I had hoped I could somehow avoid going to San Diego for the anniversary party, that was no longer an option. Maneuvering through airports and down airplane aisles seemed way beyond my capability, but now I felt I had to choose to be there for Judy. Like me, right now she was, in her own way, impaired. She'd always come to help me whenever I needed her. Now, in spite of the queasy feeling in my stomach, I would show up and support her. That knowledge gave me strength I hadn't had before her call, as if focusing on someone else beside myself drew on a source within me I'd forgotten existed.

I knew that by the time of the anniversary celebration Judy would recover her self-worth and her dignity, and I also knew that I would make my plane reservations the next morning. As I carefully repositioned myself in the bed, I considered what that fact meant to me. I couldn't imagine taking the trip at this point. I couldn't picture it. A small part of me resented the fact that Judy needed me right now, and that part didn't see her as my ally. She should be there for me, I thought. She's my big sister. The next morning, however, I looked up the word, "ally" in my thesaurus. I realized that a partner on the path of life would not only assist me, but also insist that I find the strength to move forward in every way possible, like a teammate who steadfastly holds to the promise of your greatness, especially when you feel anything but the ability to be great.

Judy's need caused me to rally my inner resources and focus

on helping her. And that one action took me right out of victim mode and into the knowledge that for her, and for others who care about me, I would always be a heroine. I would always do whatever would be needed to extend my love to them.

THE LAND OF PANIC

I WENT TO the airport early and parked in short-term parking. I thought it would be worth the extra expense to be close to the terminal. I took my own special pillow. I could go nowhere without it. Sitting in a chair, it would support my neck, and if I needed to suddenly lie down on the floor (as I had done recently at a meeting), I had a soft place to rest my head. I didn't feel secure about the trip in general, but having it with me gave me comfort. While waiting for the plane, I lay down on the floor of the departure area and put my legs up on the chair. With my head nestled on the pillow, the pain eased. I focused on my breathing and calmed my apprehension about the flight by counting my inhalations and exhalations.

Despite many nights and days of trepidation, the trip was not as hard as I'd expected. People were uniformly kind, and even the little old man getting on the plane behind me was more than happy to put my bag up into the baggage compartment for me. With my shoulder in a sling and holding my pillow, it seemed obvious that I was injured, and that made it easier to ask for help. But the usual excitement I had about flying and the eagerness to dig into a good book I usually brought onto a plane was missing. I just hoped the pain levels wouldn't go too high and my anxiety wouldn't have me desperately wishing for a tranquilizer. The plump, fortyish woman from somewhere in the South who sat next to me liked to talk, and I found it amusing and amazing that she could talk about her favorite recipes for over an hour.

It certainly helped pass the time and take my mind off my ail-
ments, but didn't help to decrease the worries I mulled over and
the tension in my solar plexus about whether I'd have the energy
to handle the events of the weekend.

At the San Diego airport, Judy picked me up outside the
baggage claim area, curbside. I was glad to see her looking her
usual, energetic self, but sad that instead of our usual ritual of
driving to Coronado Island for lunch at my favorite restaurant by the water, we went right to the house, where Judy had
heating pads for my neck and back waiting on the sofa. *From
one sickroom to another*, I thought. I spent the next four hours
on the sofa, visiting with two of my nieces who had driven
down from Los Angeles. I worried a little that I'd had no rest
and was looking at more hours ahead of standing, sitting, visiting, and pretending I was normal. After all, everyone said I
looked normal. I didn't feel normal, though. I felt shaky, on
the verge of losing my composure, of falling apart. I guess I felt
like Judy did when she called me, drunk. *I don't think I can go
through with this*, I thought, but I knew I had made this choice
and I would try to hold onto my resolve.

Later, at the party, I sat next to my mother, who'd turned
ninety the previous year. I tried to keep up a conversation, as
I knew she missed my regular visits, and she wanted a detailed
update on my daughters. I had to force myself to talk, though,
to find the energy. I wished that I could just listen as I had to
the lady who sat next to me on the airplane. But here were
family friends and even high school classmates I hadn't seen in
years. I needed to be engaged and happy. Instead of joy, however, my body felt tense and nervous, and I began to worry that
I wouldn't make sense as I was forced to make more conversation. I couldn't eat, not even the magnificent chocolate dessert
with raspberry cream. The concrete in my neck was moving

up into my head, and anxiety was taking over my body. How can I stay upright for several more hours? Will I make a scene and collapse, ruining this special party, I wondered, as I stood and smiled and nodded at an old friend as she talked, her lips moving—me not hearing her words.

Even though my nieces would lead the toasts, I would be expected to be the "keynote speaker," do the "roast," and provide the entertainment. I was the one who'd done stand-up comedy just for kicks, and once, I even dressed as Miss Piggy at a conference and sang, "Amazing Moi." I wondered what everyone would think if this time I stood up and simply fell over? It was starting to be hard for me to focus on anything other than what was happening with my body. And what was happening with my body was causing me to feel more and more frightened. The aching pain in my head caused my torso and extremities to feel like a growing, heavy weight would pull me right down to the floor. *What a killjoy I am*, I thought, as I finally had a chance to sit down before the toast.

Thankfully, I didn't have to perform this time. I stood up slowly and leaned against the table, and then I managed to focus long enough to do what Judy had requested. I shared some of the memorable moments from her wedding: having two flat tires on the way to Yuma, Arizona, in Vince's older brother's car; the Justice of the Peace conducting the ceremony without turning off the wrestling matches on TV; being awakened at three A.M. by a drunk pounding on the door of their highway motel room looking to kill his wife's lover; and Vince's friend, the best man, throwing up in the car on the way home. It was as if the cement in my head and neck loosened up for a time; I was aware of the pain, but my body relaxed and my mind became clear. As soon as I sat back down, however, everything solidified again, and I knew it would be a struggle to stay much longer.

By the time we got back to the house, it was midnight, one A.M. at home. I took my pain meds and sleeping pill, but couldn't imagine how I could relax enough to sleep, especially without my calming music. Just the thought of going to bed made me anxious—not a good sign, given that I needed to calm down in order for sleep to actually happen. In bed, I found no comfort. A heavy feeling of foreboding and dread began to take over. It grew inside me and sat heavily on my pounding chest until it became a dark, seizing conviction that I was dying.

Lying in my normal, mummy-like position, I became paralyzed. My thoughts raced: *I'm having a brain infarct. That's what I get for not having an immediate CAT scan. My brain is bleeding, but it might be small micro bleeds. Maybe surgery could save me. I should be in an ambulance on my way to the hospital. I don't want to wake up the family. There's a new baby in the next bedroom. It doesn't matter anyway; I'm dying. Maybe it's not the brain infarct that will kill me. It's my heart. I'm having a heart attack. I can feel it, ready to explode in my chest. It really is broken, and I didn't listen to Peg and have it checked, and it's too late now. I'm dying. I want to scream for Judy, but I can't wake up the household.*

Somehow I managed to get myself out of my frozen position, ease out of bed, and walk to my sister's room. "I need help," I whispered to her. I was trembling all over. She followed me back to the guest room, and I crawled back into bed.

"What's going on?" Judy asked, standing over me.

"I'm dying," I answered.

"You're not dying." Her words fell meaninglessly on me. Tears welled up in my eyes.

"Yes, I am. I'm having a brain bleed or a heart attack."

"No, you're not. You're having a panic attack. You're going to be fine. I want you to take another sleeping pill, and I'll get a heating pad for your chest."

I vaguely recalled Judy telling me about panic attacks she'd suffered over the years, but I could focus on nothing but the fear that I would lose my mind or my life. I took my pill, and she brought the heating pad and plugged it in, placing it on my chest. Within minutes, the warmth calmed my heart and brought me a feeling of safety, as though I were wrapped in a cocoon of cozy comfort.

"I'm leaving the light on for you. It's important that you have light," she said. And you will be fine in the morning." And, to my surprise, I was. Judy's care and belief in me had made the trip not only tolerable, but worthwhile. She was my ally in every sense. She was positive in every way, and she gave me hope. I began repeating to myself, "I'll be fine in the morning." And I began to believe it.

THE POWER OF PRAYER

WHEN I GOT back home, I put a heating pad on my chest every night. The fear that I would be like this forever, scared and impaired, would come up often, like a childhood monster hiding under the bed, but I knew I could ask for help. Rather than calling a friend in the middle of the night, I kept the number of the World Ministry of Prayer in Los Angeles, a nondenominational 24-hour prayer line, next to my bed, and several times I called at one or two in the morning after a nightmare would startle me awake. A real person would answer. It didn't matter to me that I didn't know them. Maybe it even made it easier. The most important thing was that the voice on the other end of the line would listen to me cry and try to explain my fears, and then pray for me. And I would calm down, hang up, settle into my pillows, and sleep, actually sleep.

I couldn't know at that time that my adventures on the

heroine's journey were just beginning. From the time of the divorce, I had been "tossed on the path," thrown way out of my comfort zone into unfamiliar territory. The breakup with Ben and the accident had added to my discomfort and, without my conscious knowledge, forced me to begin experiencing the sting of physical pain, fear, and loss along the "road of trials," necessary stops along the way to finding true self-acceptance and feminine wisdom.

At these times, in my bed at night, I felt far from wise and even farther from strong enough to travel a path that involved any more difficulty or pain. But there would be, indeed, many more challenges to overcome. Just as I found help and comfort from the prayer line, I would always find help, guidance, and even supernatural aid along the way.

.3.

HELP ALONG THE WAY

DISTURBING DREAMS

 $\mathcal{I}$ settled back into my routine of "rehab and wellness" appointments as soon as I returned home from San Diego. Following a massage treatment, I went home and sat in a very hot bath of sea salt and baking soda. It was recommended I stay for twenty minutes, but after about five I felt so weak I slowly got up and reached for my towel. As I stood, I felt light-headed and immediately sank to the floor. I crawled over to my bed and with huge effort climbed up and lay flat, naked, sweating. My heart pounded as though it were trying to escape the thin, bony cage that contained it. I stayed on the bed the rest of the afternoon and that night had one of my "lost in a strange land" dreams.

There were two categories for my disturbing dreams: "anxiety dreams," where I found myself alone in a foreign country with no memory of where I was staying or how to get back to my friends or family, and "total terror" dreams. In the terror dreams, I was stalked by an unknown man who intended to kill me. This night I had an anxiety dream: Ben and I were traveling together somewhere in Europe, and I was excited about sightseeing with him. As we came nearer to the city center, he walked faster and faster until he disappeared into the crowd ahead of us. He didn't return and I realized I didn't know where I was, I didn't speak the language, and I couldn't remember where we were staying. My fear grew into panic. I was stiff with tension, and I couldn't move. I wanted to cry, but I couldn't even do that. I was rooted to the pavement . . . until I woke up.

These dreams were upsetting reminders of the times Ben cancelled plans and dropped out of travels at the last minute. I knew that the deeper anxiety and despair evoked by these scenarios related to my little girl self at age eight, the age I was when my father left with another woman. I remember my mother's tears, and I remember feeling scared and lost for the next few years, skipping sleepovers to stay in my own bed at home and wondering each time I saw my father if it might be the last.

On one level I knew that my attachment to Ben was a re-enactment of being with a man like my father, who couldn't be there for me physically or emotionally. I longed for a man to be completely available and committed to me, a man who would never leave me. Freud taught us, with the concept of "repetition compulsion," that we are compelled to repeat early hurtful experiences until we master the fear and become aware that we can now choose a different pattern of relating. But the understanding that I could have a choice in this matter was barely whispered, and I simply could not hear it.

BREATHING THROUGH FEAR

IT WAS MID-APRIL, only two months since the accident, but it seemed like two years. The "marathon" MRI was scheduled for my head, neck, and lower back in a few more days, and I was feeling more and more anxious and fearful. Everyone feels degrees of anxiety from time to time. One study of average Americans found that feelings of anxiety were common enough to be considered routine, at least in our culture. There's a huge difference, however, between the normal-intense-worry-about-some-piece-of-your-life–anxiety and the shake-your-bones-heart-palpitations-inability-to-breathe-nausea fear of immediate insanity and/or death anxiety that seemed to lie in wait for me, emerging unpredictably at the end of certain days. Like the panic attack I'd had at my sister's, this type of intense fear was new to me.

So were the nightmares. They seemed to express my deep doubts about ever finding my way back to myself, to my inner strength and capacity for joy. I had three of the "I'm going to be killed" dreams the week before the MRI. Thirty minutes in that metal vault to assess my shoulder had been barely tolerable, but this time, the need to evaluate three different areas of my body would take longer. Surviving two hours in that stark chamber was unimaginable. I had once hypnotized a young woman who had failed two attempts to have an MRI for pelvic symptoms that required a differential diagnosis. Each time she had to go home, embarrassed and in a state of panic. After her successful third try with hypnosis, she wrote me a note saying that the mental imagery we'd created had gotten her through the experience with comfort and ease. She was very grateful.

While I could typically be creative with my patients, I seemed to be incapable of creative solutions for myself.

Creativity required energy and confidence, and both of those qualities seemed to have turned to ash, right along with my memory. I called a colleague and set an appointment for hypnosis. The day before my appointment, I received a call from Janet saying she had to cancel.

"I'm so sorry, Gail, but my son has had an accident, and I'm on my way to be with him."

I said I understood completely, but my stomach dropped. I think my silence suggested desperation, so Janet said, "I have a few minutes before I leave. Would you like to go over a breathing technique right now? I've found that breathing is sometimes more useful than imagery for an MRI because it focuses your attention so well."

"If you could do that, I'd really appreciate it," I said.

She recommended a three-part breath, like a pyramid. You inhale partway on the count of four, pause briefly, then continue to inhale all the way on four more counts. At the top, hold the breath for four counts, then exhale partway to the count of four, pause, exhale completely to count of four. You can also increase the count to six on the last exhale. Because of the length of time involved with this exam, she said I might want to rest periodically and breathe normally as I count to twenty, and then begin again. That should keep my mind very focused. I thanked her and asked her to repeat the instructions so I could write them down to remember and practice.

Inside the machine the next morning, I focused diligently on coordinating my breathing with counting, and at the same time I noticed I was monitoring my heart and pretending there was a heating pad on it warming and keeping it as calm as it could be in this circumstance. I'd had my choice of country, classical, or rock music being piped in to the earphones they provided. I chose country. I rarely listen to country music, so I thought it would provide the most distraction from the hammering noise of the machine. I focused all of my attention on counting and breathing. From time to time, the music would stop, and the technician would announce that one set of tests was finished, and in a moment he'd begin the next set. I tried to let the tension in my body melt away as I began counting to twenty before returning to the three-part breathing.

A big sigh of relief came from my chest when the technician announced that all of the tests were complete. He would come to get me out, he said. The microphone went silent. The music was turned off. I waited, started to hold my breath. He didn't come. I knew I couldn't communicate with the outside world and even though the lights were on inside that huge metal container, I felt trapped, suffocating. My heart began to go out of control just when the "escape hatch" was opened. Most likely, it had been minutes, but time had disappeared in my panic. The technician was very apologetic as he helped me out, and I began to breathe air like a fish gulping for water. The air was life itself, and it connected me again with the outside world.

Burning Up Grief

I once read a Buddhist saying, "When you burn, burn yourself completely." What did that mean? What was burning? Was this the grief process, burning toxic energy? Maybe I was fueling a personal bonfire with feelings that I had put away as unacceptable from the time I was little . . . a trash heap of anger, tattered boxes of resentment, deep sacks of sadness, pots overflowing with regret. How long might it take to burn all of this completely? And who would I be when that self I'd known was completely gone?

The actual sensation of burning was most intense and most persistent at the very top of my head. Sometimes I'd imagine cool water gently pouring down and dousing the flames. But this imagery only diminished my discomfort for a very short while, and then I'd retreat to my subterranean swamp of pain and hopelessness, aware that the fire had simply retreated with me, smoldering like red heat at the bottom of black coals.

When I contemplated the words "burn completely," I kept coming back to burning as transformation—a way to process deep depressive grief. But "burn in hell" and "hellfire and damnation" also came to mind. I'll never know if I heard one of my relatives swear like that, or if the tent revival preacher hollered those words in the brief time my friend Karen and I stood in the back by some empty wooden chairs, watching people moan and sway, after having dared each other to go in and see what "those holy rollers" were up to.

Maybe I'd committed some heinous crime in a past life that I was now paying for. It seemed so difficult to suffer emotional and physical pain without wondering what I'd done to bring it on. Eventually, I would regain my perspective that everyone suffers and my belief that all of life is about growth and development. And growth requires grieving, metabolizing every life crisis.

Denial and disbelief, anger and obsession, were the elements of grief that seemed most acceptable. Those emotions had energy attached to them. But depression seemed devoid of any vitality and sucked me in like a muddy sinkhole. I tried to be positive by thinking of the mental construct of dying-to-the-past. It inferred the sunlight of resurrection and rebirth, greater maturity, and creativity. It suggested the metaphor of the heroine's obligatory consummation by fire in order to burn away the small ego-self and make manifest the larger self. That larger self has a renewed life purpose, is in service to others, is able to radiate divine light. I asked God daily for patience and for faith that my personal inferno would end and I could breathe with relief on my journey toward enlightenment. But more times than not, I had to contend with just being able to breathe.

I longed for a gracious guide, a loving guru, a mentor who would pull me by the hand on a shortcut past the winding, grinding road I was on and walk me straight up to the angel of acceptance. This angel would lovingly open the door to the end of suffering, a golden light would imbue a peaceful feeling of acceptance of what is and illuminate the wonder of blessings to come. What relief it would be to relax into a vision of a brand-new self, a woman who feels good, wears a confident smile, and holds a suitcase full of fresh possibilities. Maybe, one day . . .

SUPERNATURAL AID

AFTER THE ACCIDENT I couldn't meditate. I had little ability to concentrate. I'd practiced Transcendental Meditation for twenty-five years. At the end of my meditation period, I would pray for a friend, family member, or a patient who might be challenged by illness, trauma, or death of a loved one. Now, as soon as I closed my eyes my thoughts were hijacked by the burning and aching in my head. I wondered if the pain would intensify or stay at the same level, whether it would remain in the same location or would move to slowly engulf my entire head. Then I'd notice the pain in my hip and try to shift my position in the chair to ease it. Then, the ongoing ache in my shoulder would speak up, *Remember me?*

Hypnosis for pain management was something I'd used to help patients, but I wasn't adept at self-hypnosis. "Focused concentration" and "mental absorption," those terms that define hypnosis, were now completely out of the question. I'd settle into my chair, and my mind would dart off to whatever pain or anxious thought popped up at any particular moment.

I also noticed I couldn't breathe in any kind of intentional pattern. The breathing techniques I'd used for the MRI made me even more anxious in this space where I expected myself to be able to relax. Even though I'd had two sessions with a respiratory therapist, I could only maintain consistent, even inhalations when her hand directed my attention to bringing the breath into my belly or up into my collarbones. In the MRI scanner, counting breaths in a specific manner provided a structure for my inhalations and exhalations. But left on my own, placing attention on my breathing made it more difficult to breathe. As soon as I thought about the breath, any natural rhythm would cease, and frustration and fear would take over.

How simple this normal physical process should be made me think of Ondine's Curse, the German myth about the water nymph, Ondine, who married a mortal man. With her choice to marry, she gave up her eternal youth, and as she aged, her husband lost interest in her. When she found him sleeping with another woman, she cursed him with the need to consciously initiate every breath. If he did not do that and fell asleep, he would die. It was frightening to think that in order to get enough air, I had to be consistently mindful of breathing.

One spring morning in May, I tried again to meditate. After several minutes, I gave up in frustration. I'll just pray, I thought. I'll do the five-part structured prayer I learned in studying Science of Mind. But immediately I realized I had no idea what that structure was—no memory for it at all. My mind was blank, and the blankness seemed predictive of my future— a blank mind, a broken body, a stupid and useless life.

Instead of crying this time, I was furious. *Okay, God,* I thought. *I'm told I'm a healer and that's my purpose in this life, and I'm supposed to have all these Divine Guides. Where the hell are they? And Jesus Christ! Why can't I breathe?* Then I cried and sobbed. Eventually I stopped and felt a little more peaceful. After a few moments, I heard the gentlest of male voices saying, "I will teach you to breathe."

Jesus had never appeared to me before. After my first accident, I'd asked for help to sleep through the pain at night (that time I asked politely), and an angelic Being dressed in a flowing white gown, Aimee, she called herself, took me floating with her to a place I thought of as Antarctica. We drifted above the ice floes, embraced by an icy mist that numbed my shoulder and gradually my entire body, until I felt nothing and fell into sleep. Her initial response to me, however, felt like an insult. She was laughing at me, suggesting I was taking my injury too seriously. *Only an angel could get away with that,* I thought. She told me not to worry. I would be fine. Aimee came to me each night for many weeks, taking me to the lovely icy mist. One morning as I drove to work, she appeared in my mind and said she was leaving.

"But you can't," I replied. "I'm not ready."

"Yes, you are," she said, her laughter like floating rose petals. "Goodbye."

Because the last two books I'd written were about the Goddess, I was a bit surprised that Jesus would make an appearance in my life. However silly it is to attribute human reactions to a Divinity, I guess I'd thought that he might feel betrayed or rejected, or at the very least, ignored by my moving back thousands of years in my studies to the time before his era, when God was thought of as a woman. I had resolved the issue for myself (as more powerful intellects than mine had recognized that God has no gender) by praying to Mother-Father-God.

"How can I breathe?" I asked Jesus. That resonant, loving voice said, "Just breathe in love. Let it fill your body. Then breathe out fear and anger."

In spite of my tantrum, I hadn't even realized I was angry. I settled into a calm state and began to breathe using that imagery. It became easier as I continued to focus on letting love come into my body on the in-breath, and releasing fear and anger on the out-breath. (Later, I would concentrate on sending the loving breath up to my brain, to the very top part of my head. It felt like my brain was oxygen-deprived, or maybe love-deprived, and that angry, fearful energy was smoldering there. I would imagine the breath clearing it away, and the love dissolving it.) My breathing became less jagged and more slow and regular.

I still felt the loving Presence, so I asked, "Will I get well?"

"Yes," He said. "You will be well."

"And will there be a man in my life again someday?"

"Yes, I will make sure of that." I had a sense that Jesus was smiling now.

"And will you pick him out for me? I used very bad judgment the last time."

"Yes, you needn't worry about this."

"Thank you. And can I call you Brother?" I asked.

"Of course, just as you are my sister. We are all sons and daughters of God."

"Good. Thank you." I felt lighter and a little touch of happiness for the first time since my injury. I knew how to breathe and I could pray now just by asking for "Mother-Father-God-and-my-Brother, Jesus."

As I look back, I'm aware of how small and helpless I sounded. I spoke with the openness and innocence of a five-year-old. In the past, I would have thought of that as regression, a failure to remain mature in the face of a serious life crisis. Now I see it as a natural result of the "burning-up" of the ego. Pain and fear had overwhelmed my usual defenses, plus any pretense that I could handle my life alone. I was laid bare, open for trust and direction, like "a little child." My prayer had been answered, and I gave thanks every day that a "Gracious Guide" had appeared in the countenance of Jesus, and I felt more secure on the path and more certain of a brighter future.

DRAGON FIRE

ONE EVENING, I watched the movie *Shrek*. Shrek is a huge, green oaf of a giant, actually an ogre, who's enlisted to free Princess Fiona from a castle tower guarded by a fire-breathing dragon. The rescue is completed and made humorous by the dragon becoming amorous with Shrek's donkey sidekick, played by Eddie Murphy. The image that struck me was that of Princess Fiona lying on her bed waiting for a prince to come and save her. When Shrek shows up, she's annoyed that he won't kiss her like she's read about in fairy tales. Repeatedly, she prolongs the rescue by insisting that Shrek act princely. And each time, the trio is nearly incinerated by the dragon's fire.

The princess represents the little-girl self, unaware of the power of her own self-limiting anger. She is unconscious of the dragon-defender she's created, whose fire keeps her separated from love and locked behind thick, impenetrable walls. Shrek liberates the princess from the castle, but she must learn for herself, as she travels the path, about her deep fears of intimacy and of the "true love" she professes that she wants. Fiona, like all of us, lives within the fairy tales we've been told, and she wants her life to unfold according to the story line. She's done her time under the spell of a witch, has been imprisoned in the castle keep, now the spell should be ended, she should marry her prince and live happily ever after.

Instead, Fiona discovers she has fond feelings for Shrek, and she demonstrates an ability for assertiveness and aggressive martial arts that protect her and her comrades from an attack by Robin Hood rogues. She has behaviors and feelings and that don't fit the princess image. Plus, she has a secret. There is literally an ugly side to her. When darkness comes at the end of each day, she becomes an ogre just like Shrek. Her fear of being found out, known and rejected fuels her decision to marry the evil prince.

With a little help from his friends, Donkey and Dragon, Shrek arrives just in time to snatch Fiona from the hands of the prince, and in time to witness her conversion at sunset into a female ogre. Shrek and Fiona acknowledge their love for each other, and the witch's spell is broken. Fiona is then transformed into her true self—a pretty cute female ogre. She no longer has to pretend to be a beautiful, perfect, fairy-tale princess—a caricature of the feminine. She has tamed the angry dragon, and she (yes, it's a girl dragon) is now loving and helpful.

Over the next several years, I would repeatedly be called on to recognize and release my anger toward the men in my life, and hold myself accountable for practicing forgiveness of them and of myself for wanting to remain a girl who would be rescued and cared for by a man. At every turn on the path, in order to keep healing, I would have to learn to bring love to my wounds and compassion to my heart.

MORE COMFORT ON THE PATH

IN MID-APRIL, MY doctor's nurse called me to tell me the results of the MRI. She read the important findings beginning with my head. What seemed like an unending mess of phrases I didn't understand, like "microvascular ischemic change," "configuration of ventricular system" and "9mm cyst at the inferior aspect of the left basal ganglia," finally ended with words I could understand— "normal" and "not of clinical significance." And I felt elated after the final statement: "Diffusion weighted imaging did not show evidence of a recent infarct. No other findings in the brain." Woohoo!

The findings on my neck and back showed narrowing of the left neural foramen at C3-4 and a "central and bilateral posterior disk bulging that slightly indents the thecal sac at C5-6 with some narrowing of the left neural foramen; at C6-7 a small central disk protrusion that slightly indents the thecal sac with some narrowing of the left neural foramen." I got that my cervical spine had suffered some damage.

Regarding my lower back, the nurse said there was a bulging disk at L4-5 and also a small tear of the annulus, whatever that is. To add insult to my injury, Nurse Cathy also pointed out that there was "some facet joint arthritic change bilaterally."

"Oh, thanks for adding that," I teased her. "I didn't need to hear about arthritis. But now at least I know what's causing the pain."

Cathy agreed to fax the report to me so I could share it with my physical therapist and my other body workers. (There would be five altogether, with the following functions: physical therapy, cranial-sacral massage, Rolfing, chiropractic, and acupuncture.) I also had a psychologist, and if length of time in personal therapy is an indication of one's skill as a therapist, I have got to be among the very best. I've had not one, but two psychoanalyses, and many additional years with Freudians, Jungians, Gestalt, and Transpersonal therapists. Since the accident, if I heard about a healer from two people in the same week, I took that as a sign that I was to use their services.

Dr. Cindy, a chiropractor, was one of these talented practitioners. (I'm pleased to not leave a bad impression of chiropractors, since several have now helped to realign my spine.) Dr. Cindy's eastern European last name is hard to remember and impossible to spell, so I felt grateful for her shortened name, and even more grateful for the softness of her touch on my spine that could produce a dramatic easing of my neck pain. At those times, I could give up the sci-fi fantasy of spending the rest of my days flat on my back, still and immobile, my neck not required to hold up my head any longer, but packed instead in a case of numbing ice.

MAGIC MEDICINE

IN LATE MAY, my Rolfer, Dr. Brian Fahey, recommended I receive acupuncture treatments for my head. Brian is seen as a true healer by several of my friends. They swear that his skilled touch put their bodies back to normal function after serious accidents. I trusted Brian. One time I'd complained that the work he was doing on my back was, "*really painful.*" He replied that he was using only "twenty percent pressure." How could he possibly estimate that? Another time he was kneading deep into my left foot. "Why," I cried out, "is that so painful?"

"Because that nerve is connected to your right shoulder, which, as you recall, is broken," he answered. He seemed to know the relationship between every muscle and nerve in my body to every other nerve and muscle, even if they were separated by the entire length of my body or the depth of several organs. Brian said he routinely sends anyone with head trauma to Dr. Wei Zhou (as in Chow) for acupuncture, so I made an appointment.

Dr. Zhou had been a cardiologist in China, and spent over a year doing research at Johns Hopkins, but decided he couldn't commit to the many years required to retrain as an M.D. here in the United States. He had a family to support, so he began to practice oriental medicine and taught at one of the schools in Santa Fe. His wife was a doctor of oriental medicine as well, and worked in the office with him. The photographs of children lining his desk and drawings pinned to the wall seemed to affirm his engagement with family.

After listening to my history and listening to my pulses through his fingers, he told me I had what he called "blood stagnation" in my head. As best I could understand, and it was difficult to understand his words through his thick Chinese accent, the blood stagnation was the result of the brain being bruised and swollen after the trauma. He wasn't surprised the MRI didn't show any acute ongoing problems, but he was glad I had followed through with it. He assured me that acupuncture and herbal tea could increase the circulation and clear the problem. When I shared my concern about my irregular heartbeat, he listened to my pulses again.

"Nothing wrong with heart," he said, but since it'd been recommended that I have a cardiac workup, he suggested I go ahead and do that.

"Yes, yes. Always follow doctor recommends," he said, as he deftly wiped alcohol on various sites on my body.

I had gone for acupuncture following my first accident and the "moxibustion" technique, where a needle is inserted then lit on fire, was the only way to stop the spasm of the levater scapula muscle in my neck. (I never would have come to know some of the muscles in my body so intimately and by name had they not screamed so often for attention.) It was another new experience to have the needles placed on my face and head.

When Dr. Zhou finished inserting the needles and left me alone to relax in the dark room, I fought the familiar panic. My heart felt as though it had suddenly expanded to twice its size, and I was certain its pounding could be heard through the door and out into the waiting room. On that high treatment table I couldn't feel secure and safe in the dark. I managed to hold back the urge to get up, in spite of all the needles sticking out of me, and turn on the light. When Dr. Zhou returned, I told him that for the next session I needed a light on in the room.

I'm reminded of a patient who was telling me about his first panic attack: "I was just sitting in my truck one evening after my mother's funeral, and suddenly I was aware that I was on the earth, and the earth was just a ball in space, and I felt I could fall off, and then my whole body started going out of control." Now I understood that feeling. I had a terrible fear of falling, and even though I knew it was completely irrational, when the panic started there was no way to think it into stopping. It seemed to manifest its own logic from some primitive self deep inside my body.

While I was prepared for the acupuncture needles, the herbal "tea" was a complete shock. Dr. Zhou gave me a large brown bag filled with what looked like scrapings from the forest floor—twigs, bark, nuts, fungi—and complicated directions for preparing the concoction. It took seven hours and the biggest pots I could find in my kitchen. I felt like a witch, working spells into the night, stirring my strange brew. The resulting thick, brown liquid tasted more like some toxic element designed to poison rather than cure. But I was desperate and determined, so I took home my brown bag of forest droppings once a week and cooked up a vat of the foul-tasting, smelly stuff and drank one cup of it in the morning and one cup every evening without fail.

A BAD OGRE

BY MIDSUMMER THE head pain still restricted my life so much that I decided to call the neurologist to ask about the typical course and especially the length of time it would take to heal.

When he returned my call, I told about the accident, MRI results, and current symptoms of pain, memory loss, and vision and sound sensitivity. His answer was short and impacted me like a bullet: "If you still have these symptoms after six months, you'll probably have them the rest of your life." I had a few weeks to go and no sense that I would be symptom-free by the six-month deadline. Even though my doctor friends were irate and each declared, "That's the stupidest thing I've ever heard," I could forget that neurologist's name, but I would remember his words every day as easily as I remembered my own name. He said the brain symptoms could be with me for the rest of my life.

Communications from Spirit

My sister, Judy, sent me a very small book published in 1936 by Eva Bell Werber, called *Quiet Talks With the Master*. It was battered and torn and taped, and Judy said it had belonged to our grandmother. "Nanna" was a Christian Scientist who believed more in the power of prayer than in the efficacy of modern medicine. While she wasn't one of those zealots who opposed vaccinations and all forms of medical intervention, she had a strong affinity for Mary Baker Eddy, who founded the Christian Science religion following a dramatic healing experience.

What I learned from my mother is that Nanna contracted influenza during the pandemic of 1918, known as the Spanish Flu. (Twenty to forty million people died worldwide; 675,000 Americans, 43,000 of them servicemen. It was most deadly for people between the ages of twenty and forty.) My mother was five years old when she heard the country doctor tell the family that Nanna wouldn't survive.

Here the story takes a twist, or at least this is when my eyes bugged: My grandfather, Luther, had apparently left Nanna and my mother, moved away, and fallen in love with another woman. When he came back to ask for a divorce, he brought with him a book, sent along by Eva, the woman who would become his second wife. The book was titled *Science and Health with Key to the Scriptures*, by Mary Baker Eddy. A few months later, after reading the book, Nanna slowly began to walk, put on weight, and re-engage with her life. While she never spoke of these events in my presence, she was resolute in her belief that everyone can control their destiny, and she demonstrated a life of faith in the practice of prayer.

My grandmother's book, *Quiet Talks with the Master*, became my morning and sometimes my nighttime companion. Some of the following quotes I wrote on cards and taped to my bathroom mirror, the kitchen counter, and even the dashboard of my car:

> "I am at the center of your being."

> "You shall find such renewal of strength and beauty and calmness of spirit."

> "I radiate through your being as the warmth of the summer Sun, as cool and refreshing as a mountain breeze, as calm as a starlit night, and as the sweetness of a flowering meadow."

> "I promise you light on the path and help along the way."

> "Turn to the God-Mother within you and find completeness."

> "With my hand on your bowed head I would have you absorb this high glory . . . It is only the fear and

the weight of the burden, the outer wrappings, that
are burned at the altar . . . I can give you in the deep
silence a golden glow which you shall wear as an armor
all the day and which nothing but love will penetrate."

"Love much, bless, and give thanks."

I especially liked the words, "With my hand on your bowed
head . . ." It made me feel that I was being protected and loved,
and that maybe someday my head and my body would heal. I
felt God was speaking these words directly to me, and I imagined a stream of white light pouring down through my head
bringing space, coolness, and comfort.

FINDING THE WAY, FALLING BACK INTO FEAR

TWO STEPS FORWARD, one step back seemed to be my
healing dance. There were hours, and occasionally a full day,
when I felt nearly normal. I could stand for the entire hour at
Gymboree and watch my daughter, Niki, with the baby; enjoy
lunch, and then while Ethan napped, Niki would give me a
cranial-sacral treatment. Her hands gently holding my head
sent me floating to another world, an alternate reality in which
I was perfectly comfortable and free of pain. I was whole and
healthy, secure and surrounded by love. I'd drift into sleep following the treatment, and when I woke up the calm peaceful
feeling might continue for hours, way past the time when the
occipital pain would normally return.

One Friday evening I alone prepared dinner for a friend.
After the meal, Barbara and I went to a movie. We went early
so we could sit in the very back row of the theater to reduce
my fear that someone might hit my head from behind, and I

wore my earplugs to diminish the impact of the sound. Even though the movie, *Kill Bill*, was a bit intense (we couldn't find a comedy that night) and I had to close my eyes occasionally to rest them, I was pleased afterward that the anxious physical feeling of, *Get this body home immediately so it won't pass out or have a panic attack*, never happened. I prepared for bed and slept well that night.

At other times, if I caught sight of Ben in the market or passing by in his car, or if I'd hear about him being seen at some social event with a new woman, my thoughts would go to helpless outrage. *How could he be with someone else?* My head would throb with pain, and as my heart fell into my stomach, any energy I'd contained would drain right out of my body.

One evening, after lying on my bed for three hours, I was very hungry, but unable to even consider getting myself up and fixing something to eat. I was weak and fatigued, and felt so alone, all I could think of was Ben. I needed Ben, I told myself. I let the tears flow for a while and then called my sister, Judy. I asked her if she thought it'd be a mark of failure if I called Ben and asked him to bring me food. I was the one to break up with him, and it took every ounce of fortitude I could muster at the time. What right did I have to call him for help? I asked.

"Do whatever you need to do to take care of yourself," she said.

LOVE WARS

I CALLED AND found Ben at a dinner meeting. He sounded delighted to hear from me. He would order something for me from the restaurant and bring it over, he said.

I was able to be up and in the living room when he came. He gave me a long, warm hug, then held me away and looked at me with those gold/brown eyes and hugged me again. He was wearing a soft tan shirt and a cashmere jacket. I loved the feel of his clothes and the feel of him. I loved his smell, an Hermès fragrance he'd buy in New York or Paris. Our physical presence with one another always felt so perfect, as though we'd been together through many lifetimes. Ben set my dinner out for me and placed dark chocolates next to it, "the only chocolate worth the calories," he quoted me. (He didn't know that in my dedication to regaining a healthy brain, I'd given up every food that might interfere with a calm nervous system—caffeine, alcohol, and even sugar.)

He sat across the table from me and watched me eat. "You should have been with me," he said, referring to my accident. I could only register how ridiculous that sounded, like some line from an old movie, maybe a gangster movie. If I'd stayed with him, it implied, nothing would harm me. Right. My mind was muddled by all the reasons I couldn't be with him. I didn't reply.

"Remember Hawaii and the turtles?" he asked. The most perfect week out of the nearly three years we were together was spent at the Kona Village Resort on the Big Island of Hawaii. That beach is home to a clan of large green sea turtles who sunned themselves every day on the sand just as we did.

"Of course I remember. That week was like our honeymoon. And then the honeymoon was over. We came home and you sent me away—again."

Ben put his head in his hands, a dramatic gesture, which, in the past would have signaled me to apologize and be more understanding.

"I have to get over to the sofa," I said. "My head and neck are hurting." Ben offered to massage my neck, and his hands were gentle and warm. The ropelike tension lessened. I lay down on my side with my head on a pillow in his lap. It was delicious to be on my side for the first time in months, no pressure on my shoulder, every part of my body comfortably supported. I fell asleep with Ben stroking my hair. When I woke, Ben said he didn't want to leave, but he probably should. I agreed, and had a fleeting thought of thankfulness that I was physically impaired. If not, we would have ended up in my bed and passion would have pulled me back into darkness, like a sleepwalker unknowingly stepping off the side of a cliff into an abyss.

I had asked Ben to come over the next evening to put together a traction device recommended by my physical therapist for my neck. He showed up looking nervous and distracted. He said he had something important to tell me. He sat me down and took both of my hands in his.

"What I have to say is really hard." He paused, but continued to look right into my eyes. "All the times I was sick and couldn't leave the house, and you thought I was having trauma reactions . . . well, it was drugs."

"What? What drugs?"

"Cocaine."

As the disbelief dissolved, a wave of ice-blue anger came up and filled my chest. It brought powerful insight, but no sense of power. I couldn't speak. I was observing my feelings—foolish, embarrassed, outraged. I recalled how I had defended Ben repeatedly when others had suggested that maybe his thoughtless and erratic behavior was due to drug use. He had expressed insult that his wife was holding up the divorce custody settlement by accusing him of using drugs. He insisted he would never take drugs or abuse alcohol, that Tammy was just using the claim as a ploy to deny him his parental rights. She was obsessively angry and vindictive, he said.

I had read some of her rambling letters to Ben, letters filled with rage, threats, and descriptions of his faults that would fill the page and continue on sideways up into the margins. Then there were her daily phone assaults on him, which some days numbered up into the double digits. It had always seemed to me that Ben was honest about his failings in the marriage, and straight with me about the several affairs he'd had.

He tried to justify his behavior, however, by stating that Tammy was the one to start the indiscretions. I believed everything he said to me—until I began to see the predictable pattern of breaking his word. He would be enthusiastic and agreeable about attending a concert or planning a trip, and then never speak of it again. If I brought it up later, he'd accuse me of wanting to be with him only for his money and then not speak to me for hours or days. I saw the discrepancy between what he said, and what he did (or didn't do), but I was completely naïve about addiction.

"Cocaine," I said. "So Tammy was right."

"She was right about that. Look, I'm really sorry. I'm not using it anymore. A couple of my friends took me east to a tennis tournament and lit into me all weekend. They really sat on me. I got it, and I've changed."

"You lied to me, over and over. You lied. You told me you'd never use drugs or abuse alcohol because of the history of alcoholism in your family. How could you lie to me like that?"

"I couldn't tell you about it. I didn't want you to know about that part of my life. I didn't want to hurt you."

"Oh, you didn't want to hurt me. That's great!" Now I was up and pacing. Anger raised the volume in my voice. "You could stand me up, throw me out, accuse me of using you, but you 'didn't want to hurt me.' How kind."

"So this is all about you, Gail. What about what I've been going through? I thought you of all people would understand how awful it is to go through a divorce and to lose my kids. What about me?"

"It's always about you. The world is supposed to revolve around you—your losses, your triumphs, your pain. And I'm not supposed to have a life at all. Every time I'd come back from even visiting my family, you'd punish me by canceling any plans we'd made and shut me out of your life for days."

"I'm not taking this shit. I'm leaving."

"Well, I need you to put together this traction thing, and I expect you to do that before you go."

He did, but as I lay on the sofa, I could hear his muttering frustration and resentment. He turned to me before he left and said, "I love you, you know."

"I know. I love you too," I replied weakly. I hadn't enough energy for the usual feelings of fear to take over my body and cause alarm signals to flash in my mind: *He's gone. You'll never see him again. What will you do without him?*

INTERNAL BATTLES

SELF-DOUBT WOULD wiggle its way into my mind after an exchange like this. An inner dialogue started up between my little girl self and my pseudo-adult big girl self: *Maybe he's okay now. Maybe he has changed, and now that he's off drugs he'll be nicer.*

What are you talking about? He was mean as ever. As soon as you say something he doesn't want to hear, he goes on the attack. Have you forgotten how vicious he can be?

But, he's also gentle and loving. He said I'm the only woman he's ever loved.

You are so naïve. He's probably said that to a dozen women. Do you even remember what he said when you broke off with him? He said, "Fine. I'm movin' on."

But that was just his pride. That's what men do. I know he still loves me.

Maybe he does. I'm sure he feels it, but he can't DO it. He doesn't know how to be in a committed relationship. Besides, he says he's off drugs. You can't just stop taking drugs. You have to be in a rehab program, and he would never do that. He won't even belong to a gym, he's so much better than other people.

He doesn't think that. He's just really self-conscious and shy.

You are completely hopeless.

At this point, my true Adult Self, or my Higher Self the Observer, stepped in: "It doesn't matter what he's like," she said. "The two of you are not a good match for each other. You were either wildly happy or wildly unhappy with Ben. Forgive him, forgive yourself, and pray for one another's highest good. If it might help you, talk with an addiction specialist to see about the likelihood of his being free of drugs."

I checked with two substance abuse specialists, and they both agreed that the erratic behavior and the "sickness" episodes I described sounded like addiction to and withdrawals from cocaine. The possibility of kicking a drug habit alone just because one's been caught and confronted, they also agreed, is very small. One psychologist also suggested I "keep in mind that there's often more than one substance being used." He also reminded me that the one consistent behavior of adult children of alcoholics and addicts is deception. "They've spent their entire lives trying to placate and please their parents. They say whatever they think will keep peace. Without knowing it, they become compulsive liars."

The discovery of Ben's drug abuse helped to quiet my mental dialogues. I knew with certainty now that there could be no future with him. But that knowledge did nothing to relieve my heart's persistent longing that somehow, magically, the relationship might be restored. It was as though my heart refused admittance to the wisdom of my head. It kept its gates locked, holding onto its love, aching for its attachment, and preventing any hostile invasion by rational thought.

.4.

HEALING THE BODY, CONNECTING WITH HEART

Yoga for Body, Mind, and Heart

few days after my encounter with Ben, I attended my first restorative yoga class. I lay on the floor with blankets supporting my upper back, and my own pillow supporting my head. The pose, a supported *savasana*, is a "heart opener," designed to relax the body and mind completely. Instead of becoming relaxed, I began to feel anxious and vulnerable. I started to weep, and felt grateful that the room was darkened. Barbara, the instructor, came over and stroked my forehead. A friend of mine for many years, she knew the double impact of my ill-fated love affair and the healing challenges of my accident.

"I'm afraid to open my heart," I told her through my tears. "I'm afraid it will get squashed."

She reassured me that I would be all right and that my heart and my body would heal. "You'll slowly reclaim your heart," she said. "I know you will."

I cried because my heart was broken, but I also cried because even in this class designed for people with physical limitations, I could not do the poses. Too many areas of my body were in pain.

I'd been eager to return to yoga, a practice I'd engaged in four to five days a week for years, since the first skiing accident had ended my participation in high-impact aerobics. I particularly enjoyed the *astanga* classes, which were flowing and fast moving. These classes were so strenuous I could get a cardiac workout along with the muscle-strengthening and the flexibility yoga provides. It was hard to imagine that I would ever again be able to participate in regular yoga classes, let alone the energetic, sweat-producing *astanga* practice.

Hatha yoga, the umbrella term for physical poses, or *asanas*, originated 4000 years ago, but restorative yoga was developed in recent years by B.K.S. Iyengar of India. He created restorative yoga to help people recover from illness or injury. Modified poses using blankets and props are used so that muscle strain or mental energy doesn't interfere with the deep relaxation that restores and balances energy. Restorative yoga is designed to "help the individual feel whole" again. It would be some time before my healing endeavors would come together and result in body parts that cooperated and functioned as one whole and complementary unit. In the meantime, I came to class and did only what I could. My first achievement was to surrender to being in physical limitation, accepting the way I was, without weeping.

I now realize that *pranayamas*, or "breathing purifications," the basic element of all yogic systems, would be the most important part of my learning from yoga at this time. In order to keep faith that I would heal completely, I had to know that I could control and direct my life breath. (At the back of this book, I describe a number of the breathing practices that were helpful to me in this way.)

ANOTHER HEART HELPER

IN ADDITION TO my physical therapy exercises, I began to use the stationary gym equipment to build and strengthen my leg muscles. One day, I sat lifting a bar up and down with my legs, ten repetitions at a time. The bar held fifty pounds of weight, which was the usual amount I'd used before the accident. It didn't seem to require much effort, but I noticed my heart rate suddenly increased and pounded like unexpected thunder. I tried to stay calm, but I was frightened. It didn't make sense. I wasn't upset. I wasn't thinking about Ben or worrying about anything at all. Why would my heart go out of control like that? If there was no emotional reason, what could be wrong?

When I got home, I dug into my desk drawer and found the cardiologist's card that my primary care doctor had given me. Dr. Kathleen Blake. I knew her and also knew of her excellent reputation. I called to schedule an appointment.

Three weeks later, I was in her office, waiting with as much calm as I could muster, carefully counting each breath while she reviewed the notes in my chart and the results of the echo-cardiogram. When she looked up at me she smiled.

"There's nothing seriously wrong with your heart, Gail," she said.

"You have developed something we call paroxysmal atrial tachycardia, but it's not something to worry about. It's fairly common. I'm more concerned about the emotional stress you've been under. You and I both know that depression and anxiety can slow down your healing process."

I told her that the combination of the head injury and the breakup with Ben seemed to have taken me over the edge—all that happening in the context of losing my thirty-five-year marriage left me raw and vulnerable. I'd lost my emotional stability. I told her I couldn't see myself creating any kind of new and happy life. In short, I felt stuck in hopelessness. I also confessed that I had tried numerous muscle relaxants, minor tranquilizers, and sleeping pills to try to quiet my system, but I feared that now they were not only not helping the physical pain, but they might be making my emotional reactivity even worse.

"That can be a problem when you have physician friends who prescribe for you," she said. "I want you to find a psychiatrist you don't know, and see what that person recommends in the way of medication. In the meantime, don't worry about your heart. We used to prescribe antibiotics prior to dental visits to prevent infection, but that's not even done so much now."

BROKEN HEART SYNDROME

I WAS SO RELIEVED to know that my heart wasn't about to explode in my chest whenever it went from a normal beat to a pounding gong that I nearly floated out of the clinic and into my car. I called my sister Judy to tell her the good news. She reminded me that she'd been given the same diagnosis about ten years earlier. I asked if she thought the irregular heartbeat might be caused by stress. She hadn't thought about it, she said, but her first attack of tachycardia took place after an auto accident where she'd been rear-ended. That certainly qualified as stress. She paused for a moment and added that the accident happened right after one of her good friends had been killed in an auto accident. While the first attack occurred in the context of a life crisis, the second attack seemed to occur for no reason at all—she was just standing in the kitchen cooking dinner. Judy couldn't remember what medication she'd been given, but she did recall that after a few months the tachycardia never occurred again.

I thought it interesting that while our first attacks were related to trauma, the ones following had no particular trigger, as though the body was now programmed to randomly react with this new set of alarm mechanisms even when there was no cause for alarm. Although the accident and the ongoing worry about my head injury may have provided the physical basis for my heart's failure to function normally, I knew all along that losing Ben was the emotional trigger for my heart losing its calm, natural rhythm.

I later found that conventional wisdom has been right—one's heart can be broken by lost love. Doctors at Johns Hopkins Medical Center, after studying a group of patients from 1999 to 2003, discovered that some hearts weaken or fail completely in response to fear, grief, anger, or shock. Most all of the victims are women. They do not have blood clots, diseased arteries, or patches of dead heart muscle. They are generally healthy, with no history of heart disease. The victims do have unusually high levels of stress-related brain chemicals and hormones, 7 to 34 times the normal levels, and these adrenaline-like hormones simply overwhelm the heart.

Some of the women studied required aggressive medical intervention to save their lives. But most, like Judy and me, required minor attention and eventually returned to pre-crisis, normal levels of functioning. The good news was that none of the women in the study had repeat episodes. As the stress levels decreased, their hearts returned to normal. The diagnosis given for this newly recognized condition is, "stress cardiomyopathy," or "broken heart syndrome."

FALLEN WARRIOR

A FEW DAYS later, I opened my bedroom door slightly to let in the fresh air on a warm, summer morning. I read some from *Quiet Talks with the Master*, and a few pages of Eckart Tolle's *The Power of Now*. Suddenly I heard a flapping sound. I got up and turned to find a hummingbird inside my bedroom, beating its tiny wings at the large bay window that blocked its way to the trees on my terrace. I was alarmed. I knew it had to get back outside, but I didn't know how to make that happen. I slowly got up on the "banco," or bench-like seat that runs under the windows, and carefully reached up. That little creature with a shiny blue/green neck offered no resistance as I folded my fingers gently around its feathers. I took its warm pulsing body outside. I thanked it for visiting me, opened my hand, and let it fly free. *Sweet freedom*, I thought.

The Animal Medicine book was in the study. I found it and looked up "hummingbird." My daughter Niki had studied Shamanism, both in this country and in the jungles of Ecuador, and from her experiences with this most ancient of healing methods, I had developed respect and curiosity for the many ways that Spirit manifests in my life. I've learned to pay close attention to the animals that show up, and listen for their messages.

The primary power or energy of hummingbirds, the book said, is to bring joy. *Joy*, I thought. *That's exactly what I want in my life—to be "in joy."* I also read that in Aztec culture hummingbirds were thought to be the reincarnations of fallen warriors and women who died in childbirth. I wondered if fighting and "dying in love" counted me as a fallen warrior. If so, maybe I could be rebirthed into joy, like a hummingbird, the smallest creature with a four-chambered heart, a heart the size of a baby's fingernail, a heart that beats ten times a second, a heart that powers this little bird to fly more than five hundred miles without rest, dive at sixty miles an hour, and sip nectar from a thousand flowers in one day.

Now that's a heart—a wild, wacky, racy, voracious, unstoppable heart.

And that was my message—that my heart was strong, and if I wanted it full of joy, I could have it full of joy—that light feeling in my chest like a floatation device that could float me right up off the ground and into the atmosphere, the way I felt on a visit to Bali, so close to heaven I could levitate. Without even closing my eyes, I might simply evaporate into bliss. One day in the rice fields of Ubud, I actually asked a friend to keep an eye on me and if I began floating, to grab my hand and pull me back down to earth. I was light like a feather dancing on the air.

So I gave thanks again for the visit from the hummingbird. I'd been seeing many bunnies each day right near my house, and rather than dwell on the fear that "scared rabbits" represent, I felt ready for the experience of joy. Maybe I could have a great big, happy heart, a strong heart capable of enormous compassion for others and for myself—a compassion that would allow me to accept my body and my life just as they are and just as they will be.

More Assistance on the Path

I should have known that the next healer I needed would materialize without one ounce of effort on my part. I had to remind myself that every time I needed something, it was provided. When my cardiologist recommended that I see a psychiatrist, I thought it might be difficult to find one I didn't know. I'd worked in the mental health field in Albuquerque for over thirty years. But that very afternoon, I saw my friend and colleague Marcia. She told me that a young psychiatrist she'd shared cases with at the VA was now in private practice. She was so pleased because he was skilled in treating trauma victims and "the community needs his services." I told her that, actually, I needed his services. Without blinking, she handed me his card.

Dr. Kevin Rexroad was able to see me the following week in the evening. He met me at the entrance to the building, a big man with a soft voice. He explained that he was using another therapist's office until his practice was established. He showed me upstairs to a rather small space with the usual sofa, chairs, plants, and bookcase. His gentle manner made me feel safe and welcome. He told me he knew me by my reputation for working with trauma survivors and invited me to tell him how he might help me.

I felt like every new patient who comes to consult with me—trying to organize my thoughts, worried that there's too much to say in too short a time, worried that there'll be no coherence in the events that I string together, and mostly worried that I'll be given some kind of diagnosis that translates to "hopeless."

I started with the accident and told him I knew my shoulder was healing, I was familiar with "rehabbing" my shoulders since I'd broken them twice before. I had stacks of illustrated physical therapy exercises. I knew exactly what to do. My neck and back were another story. I'd hoped that the traction would help my neck, but I wasn't sure it was improving. Some days were good, and on others the pain was so intense nothing seemed to help. The back pain made it difficult to sit for any length of time, as pain would shoot down my right leg. My head, though, was a total mystery. Though the MRI showed no need for surgical intervention, I had no assurance that I'd return to normal. The pain made it hard to be upright for long periods of time, and often just as uncomfortable to lay flat.

As I spoke, the usual flow of tears spilled down my cheeks. I grabbed a tissue from the table next to my chair and held it up to my eyes, as though its very presence might staunch the flow. I shared with Kevin the primary thoughts that rolled around in my head: that the pain, fatigue, and memory problems were unbearable; that I was impaired and would never recover; that the doctor who said I could have these symptoms forever was probably right; that I had no control over my emotions, and the final ringer—I'd never get over my love affair with Ben. Even though I knew it couldn't work and shouldn't work, I was devastated that he was gone and I was alone, again.

Kevin asked about my marriage. I'd been married for thirty-four years, I told him, thirty-six actually, because the divorce took two agonizing years to complete. I choked out the words between sobs now. I told him the divorce felt like my life had ended. It hadn't made sense to me, the depth of my depression, because I was the one who initiated it. But I'd tried so hard to avoid doing that. My sister Judy and I had made a pact when we were girls that we would never divorce like our parents had. The word itself was never spoken—we referred instead to "the big D." I had insisted Bruce and I go to couples counseling, which we did for several years, but the important problems couldn't be resolved.

"What were those problems?" Kevin asked. The biggest one for me was Bruce's anger, I told him. I seemed to be the target for his every disappointment. I knew it was rage toward his mother that was unconsciously directed to me, and I tried to not be hurt by it. In the last years, though, he became addicted to day trading and was losing money, even in our retirement account. I was really scared. He wouldn't admit that anything was wrong, and would find ways to blame me for his losses in the market. It felt crazy. He'd sleep in his study instead of with me, drink whiskey at night, and turned down a trip to Greece with me when I went to speak there at a conference. It was as though we'd become toxic for each other.

I'd lost all hope during a therapy session one December. Bruce had promised the previous year to turn our accounts over to a broker, but during this session he admitted he hadn't done that and then denied that he'd ever made the promise. I walked out of counseling and settled into my own anger for eight months until I got the courage to ask for the divorce.

"I wouldn't call it courage, exactly," I restated to Kevin. "I was walking one morning on the bluffs above the Rio Grande River and I had the urge to 'accidentally' fall off the cliff. That got my attention. I knew I couldn't grow old with a man who made me hope that one of us would pretty quickly drop dead.

"I was miserable the last few years of the marriage," I went on, "and then more miserable during and after the divorce. One thing I wasn't prepared for was the social consequences. While people gathered around Bruce, invited him to dinner, introduced him to women—not that he needed that service— I was dropped from invitation lists and marginalized by communities I'd been a part of for thirty-five years." I learned that single women tend to be excluded from social and professional gatherings where couples predominate.

I felt isolated and rejected, just as I did at age eight after the breakup of my family. Loneliness lived with me from that point on, in spite of the fact that, as a girl, I was popular in school and had many friends.

Kevin asked me to tell him more about my family. I explained that I'd grown up in southern California in a family with little education. My mother's family had migrated from Oklahoma to the agricultural community of the Imperial Valley, then to

San Diego. My mother had a tenth grade education, and when my father left, she went to work in an aircraft factory. My father had grown up in a small mining town in West Virginia. After high school, he joined the Marine Corps. When his military service ended in San Diego, he stayed there, met and married my mother, and became a police officer.

"You mentioned a sister?" Kevin asked.

"Yes, I have one sister, Judy. We're really close. She's been married fifty years now and has four daughters and nine grand-children. Her marriage hasn't been easy, but she's committed to this big family of hers." The tears came in a bigger wave as I thought about no longer having my family. I wondered briefly where all that water came from. *How could it be harbored some-where in my head, ready to come pouring out of tiny tear ducts?* "I miss my family," I stammered, "even though my daughter Niki lives right here near me and I have a grandbaby and another on the way. I'm really close to my daughters. My youngest, Megan, is a journalist. She was a foreign correspondent in Guatemala, but now she lives in the Bay Area . . ."

I felt self-conscious, as though I was not only taking too much time, but that what I was saying didn't make any sense. Kevin looked relaxed and attentive, and nodded for me to go on.

"I worked from the time I was twelve years old selling Christmas cards and greeting cards door-to-door," I said, and thought to myself, *Why are you telling him this? You sound pathetic, like a character in a Dickens novel. You want him to feel sorry for you?* But I pushed on.

"Then when I was fifteen I got my social security card and worked Friday nights and on weekends in Mr. A's clothing store. I was intent on getting out of the neighborhood we lived in. It seemed like everyone was either an alcoholic or lived with one. My friend Dee Dee would come to my house when her father was drunk and throwing furniture at her mother, and another friend, Robert, who lived across the street, had parents whose arguments were so loud when they were drunk you could hear them on the street. He and I sat on his front porch once and listened to his parents accuse each other of being frigid. We didn't know what that meant.

"I don't know why I'm saying all this," I said to Kevin. "The main thing is that I don't even recognize myself now. I came so far and accomplished so much. I had a great life for so many years . . . and I've had so much therapy, and now all I do is cry."

Kevin leaned forward in his chair and said, "Gail, you truly did create yourself as an adult. You succeeded in every way. Right now you're suffering from a psychosomatic condition."

This was exactly what I didn't want to hear. The term "psychosomatic" meant that "it was all in my head." My unconscious mind was teaming up with my fearful emotions and making my body symptomatic when there wasn't anything wrong physically. To me it suggested psychological failure, an inability to be resilient in the face of adversity. It meant my past had caught up with me after all, and I was doomed to be a pathetic victim—of my own doing.

He must have seen my face fall.

"I don't mean that in the way you're thinking, Gail. I'm simply referring to a psychosomatic cycling that started with the trauma. With physical pain, there's a natural reaction for the body to tense the muscles in the area of the injury. At the same time, stress hormones like adrenaline are released, causing sensations, like increased heart rate, that you interpret as anxiety. With the anxiety comes more tension, and more tension produces more pain, and it just keeps going. And with this cycling, brain chemicals, like serotonin, get depleted. So I'm going to recommend that you take two medications. One is Seroquel, the other, Lexapro."

This time he saw shock on my face. I knew that Seroquel is a major tranquilizer—that's the good-sounding part. But it's actually an antipsychotic, which made me think I must truly be crazy.

"Don't be upset. I want you on the Seroquel for only one month, just long enough to stop the cycling. But the Lexapro I'd like you to be on for one full year, to make sure you stabilize."

He sent me off with some samples, and said I'd have to get a guillotine at the pharmacy. "A what?" I'd asked. I learned that some pills are so small that when you need to halve them, a tiny mechanism with a blade cuts them for you. I also learned how frightened one can feel at the prospect of taking pills that will alter one's brain chemicals. The first night I took them, I was even more anxious and didn't fall asleep for three hours. I called the next morning and asked if it was me or the effect of the drugs. Kevin said it was the meds, adjusted the dose and asked me to keep on with them.

The third day, I began to feel much more normal. I remembered the patient reports from the first trials of Prozac. I felt just like they did—as though a dark grey veil had been lifted away from my mind. By day four I was amazed to feel like myself again. It was as though, after the accident, my old self had surveyed the damaged body and said, *This is way too painful and depressing. I'm out of here. Let me know when you're half-way normal again and I'll come back.* And somehow, restoring the needed brain chemicals made me feel "halfway" normal again. I was back in my body. It was wonderful. The way I explained it to Marcia was like this: Before the meds I felt like I had become my symptoms, nothing more than a blob of pulsating pain and unhappy feelings, and then in just several days I was myself, a person, a competent woman who was dealing with the aftermath of an accident and a romantic breakup. My physical symptoms and my sad feelings didn't disappear, but I knew I could deal with them and I had real hope for becoming normal, if not mighty.

SNAKE VISIT

ON DAY FIVE after beginning the medications, I woke up, sat up in bed, and found myself looking at a snake. It was stretched out on the bedroom carpet vertical to the bed, looking right at me. My first impulse was to scream, but I squelched that. Second impulse was to call Charlie, my son-in-law, and ask him to come over. I squelched that, too. He would laugh at me. He's the one who originated the term "Mighty Woman," and I used to be one according to him. It would definitely not be "mighty" to call. My heart rate began to come down from a kettledrum to a softer percussion, so I assessed the situation. The snake was probably a garden snake, about five feet long. One instinctively registers a venomous snake by the triangular head, and this one didn't have that. The head was the same width as the body. I also remembered that snake medicine is about transformation, the life-death-rebirth cycle represented by the shedding of the snake's skin. So I silently said "thank you" to the snake for reminding me of my rebirth.

Nevertheless, I began to get nervous looking at the snake. I had the feeling that it could definitely outlast me in a staring contest, so I began to think of how to get it out of my living space. If it slithered somewhere in the house, I'd never sleep again. Because it was lying parallel to the door to the back terrace, I thought I might be able to get my plastic rake from the garage, open the door and scoop it outside. I gingerly crawled out of my bed and tiptoed upstairs and out to the garage, hoping my silence would keep the snake in place. I found my plastic rake and came back down the stairs, relieved to find my snake hadn't budged, but fearful that if I were not completely adroit, the snake could still get away from me and take up residence somewhere in my house.

I walked around behind it and opened the terrace door. Then I positioned myself for what I hoped would be a perfect golf swing (even though I don't play golf). And I did it. I somehow got that snake in the arc of my swing and lobbed it out across the terrace and over the back wall, communicating in some language I hoped the snake could understand, *I hope I'm not hurting you, and thank you for coming, and thank you for leaving.* And as my heart settled down, I laughed out loud. *What else will Spirit have to do*, I thought, *for me to get the message that All is Well, and I am truly on the path to healing?*

I went to my Animal Medicine book and read, "Snake medicine people are very rare. Their initiation involves experiencing and living through multiple snake bites, which allows them to transmute all poisons, be they mental, physical, spiritual, or emotional . . . the transmutation of the life-death-rebirth cycle is exemplified by the shedding of Snake's skin. It is the energy of wholeness, cosmic consciousness, and the ability to experience anything willingly and without resistance. *"That part does not apply to me,* I thought.

"It is the knowledge that all things are equal in creation, and that those things which might be experienced as poison can be eaten, ingested, integrated, and transmuted if one has the proper state of mind." *That's the trick, a proper state of mind.* Then I read, "Through accepting all aspects of your life, you can bring about the transmutation of the fire medicine . . . so that wholeness may be achieved. This is heavy magic, but remember, magic is no more than a change in consciousness. Become the magician or the enchantress: transmute the energy and accept the power of the fire."

There it was again, the allusion to fire. I couldn't say I understood all of that, but it was the first time that I saw fire linked to power instead of destruction. I liked that. Since I'd spent the last five and half months shrinking into preoccupations with my body and my broken heart, emerging from the ashes with greater confidence sounded pretty good. I could see how huge life changes cause a transformation of the energy trapped in the grief of loss and depression into the power of renewed self-expression and capacity to love. Yes, I definitely liked that idea. Thank you Mr. or Mrs. or Ms. Snake.

TRANSFORMING AN OPPONENT

I WAS STANDING in the hallway outside my kitchen after dinner. There were bright headlights shining in through the open front door. That was odd, as I didn't remember leaving the door open and I couldn't imagine how a car could get that close to my front entry. And then a man was walking toward me. He was ordinary-looking, blond, fair-skinned, wearing glasses. He had a coat or a towel over his left arm, and I knew that he was concealing a knife there. I screamed for Jenn, who'd gone downstairs for something, but no sound came from me. I tried so hard to scream and couldn't. Suddenly, strength came flowing into my arms and I wrestled the knife away from the stranger and plunged it into his heart.

Fortunately, I woke up without seeing the gory details of the killing. I simply knew, as my entire body exhaled and relaxed, that that was the last nightmare I would have of a man trying to kill me. I would no longer be vulnerable to men who appeared healthy and loving, but who harbored insecurity and hostility toward women. Most important, my own inner masculine aspect was changed from one that would criticize me and see any signs of "weakness" as deserving of death, to a powerful protectiveness, self-acceptance, and love of life. There need be nothing ugly or hurtful about the masculine. It could now be a part of the wholeness and internal balance that my healing was leading me to.

PROGRESS ON THE PATH

AS THE SIXTH month post-accident milestone approached, I assessed my progress.

1. I was back in regular yoga classes, being very careful to not do poses that put any stress on my neck, shoulders, or head. I thanked my shoulder every day for mending, so that I could use my right hand and arm again. My left shoulder was having "overuse" pain, so it was definitely ready for some relief.
2. I could walk outdoors for longer periods without feeling weak and shaky.
3. I could watch television for longer periods of time, which was good because I still couldn't read the way I'd been used to—a novel every two weeks. And I couldn't spend any time at the computer. The screen hurt my eyes. I noticed I couldn't tolerate regular TV shows or news. My senses felt assaulted by them, so I rented comedy or light films with happy endings. I watched *Under the Tuscan Sun* six times. I liked watching Diane Lane discover new life and love in Italy.
4. The pain was lessening in my back, although sometimes pain would shoot down the under part of my right thigh when I was sitting.
5. I had periods of time when my head and neck felt like nothing had ever happened to them. At those times I felt so happy and giddy with euphoria, I thought I'd been misdiagnosed. Manic–depressive felt more accurate.

All in all, I was improving. Meticulous self-care: eating only organic, healthful foods, keeping every healing/health-care appointment, doing yoga, drinking my foul-tasting tea, taking my medication plus a handful of vitamin supplements every day, getting lots of rest, and learning how to breathe was slowly creating the possibility in my mind of one day being completely well.

WATER, RAINBOWS, AND BUTTERFLIES

THERE WERE STILL the down times when that feeling of emptiness would show up and suggest a bleak future. One after-noon, as I lay on my bed, feeling impatient with the pain in my head and the fatigue in my body, the phone rang. I reached over and picked up the receiver to hear a cheery, "Hi, it's Gloria."

"Gloria Hillard. I haven't talked to you in ages, maybe years. How'd you happen to call me right now?" I asked. Gloria was a CNN reporter based in Los Angeles. After my first book, *Lessons in Evil, Lessons from the Light*, came out in 1993, I became somewhat known for my knowledge of cults, and Gloria had called me about a story she was working on. We'd met for an informal interview when I was visiting Los Angeles, and we quickly became friends. Her affinity for New Mexico brought her through my area on visits to Santa Fe, and sometimes she'd drive down to San Diego when I was there with my family. Although she was known for her celebrity interviews, her pri-mary interest was in sharing stories about people who were con-tributing to society in some way. Plus, she could soften the most intense narrative by adding touches of lightness and humor.

"I'm a mess," I groaned, and gave the details of the accident and my healing saga. "I'm better since I've been on antidepres-sants, but I still feel like a shrunken version of my former self.

I've been on my bed for two hours now and resting or napping has never been my MO."

"I'm so sorry, Gail. I had been thinking of you and got a hit to call. Have you thought about a trip to Hawaii? I think you need to get into the water and have a drink with a tiny umbrella."

"I don't believe this. You are the third person to say that." I told her that my therapist, Mary Rose, was the first to suggest I try to get to Maui because she knows how much I love being there. Then a psychic who doesn't know me at all said the water there would be healing for me. "And now you, who I think of as more intuitive than my psychic, are telling me the same thing."

Gloria laughed. "So, it sounds like there's agreement here that you need to get yourself to Maui. I have a place on Kauai, but it's rented for the next few months, and I know that Maui is your spiritual Mecca."

"That's true, but I can't travel alone right now, and there's no one who could go with me."

"Look, you know that if you're supposed to get there, someone will show up to make that happen." Gloria was one of my most confident, spiritual, and optimistic friends.

I don't know if "Maui on My Mind" is a song or a travel slogan, but it was definitely on my mind for the next few days. I first visited the Hawaiian Islands in the summer of 1977 when Niki was eight years old. Bruce and I took her on a camping trip with the Sierra Club. We slept in cabins and beaches on Oahu, Maui, and the little island of Lanai. That was the beginning of many family vacations, mostly to Maui, with friends from Los Angeles, and then with my sister, who would bring some of her family along. I could usually count on Judy to be a travel buddy. She'd met me in San Francisco at the end of my first book tour, and we went on to Maui for a week. She'd also come to Greece with me when Bruce declined. But now she had two of her grandsons living with her, and they required constant supervision.

I was telling Megan about the three separate recommendations for a healing trip to Maui during our next phone conversation.

"Isn't that wild? I'd love to go, but there's no one to come with me, and I can't even consider going that far alone."

"Uh, mother . . . " Megan only calls me "mother" when she's seriously annoyed with me. "Would you consider asking me to go with you?"

"Well, but how could you get off work? I mean, I'd love for you to go with me." Megan had been a foreign correspondent in Latin America, but after a man she loved died there suddenly, she decided to take a break, come back to the States, and live with friends at Lake Tahoe. The skiing and mountain climbing seemed just what she needed, and she was enjoying working for a small newspaper, the *Tahoe World*.

"I'm sure I can get one of the other reporters to cover for me. There's only a problem when vacations overlap, but my friend, Lisa, is saving her vacation for this fall, when she's getting married."

What joy. My heart felt exceedingly happy. I started making plans for us to stay at Napili Bay on Maui for nine days in July. I was able to use frequent flyer miles to upgrade us to business class, as I knew my body would need the extra comfort. I started swimming laps at the gym two days a week after my yoga class. I used my mask and snorkel to prepare for swimming in the sea (so I wouldn't have to move my neck and head), and I was relieved that the mask didn't hurt my head. I remembered how good it felt to exercise my shoulder by swimming. My fragile head, which I thought of like a slightly cracked egg, was what had held me back. Now, I knew I could relax in the water and enjoy the rhythm of physical movement. My excitement grew each day as I checked off to-do items on the calendar.

Islands, for me, are an immediate transport to heaven. The moist air, tropical flowers, the water, and that other world under the water, all bring me closest to feeling One with nature. Every aspect of that environment is experienced as sacred. I feel immersed in the beauty, and the only appropriate response is gratitude.

Once settled into our room on Maui, Megan and I agreed on a routine. As the early riser, I'd begin the morning with spiritual readings, journal writing, meditation, and prayer. Then I'd practice yoga poses for about a half hour. By then, Megan would be up, and we'd walk (I'd walk, she'd run) up over the hill to the next beach and back. Then we'd get into our bathing suits, masks, and fins and swim out to the end of the bay and visit with the fish. If I felt really energetic, we'd swim the further distance out to the middle of the bay where a family of turtles lived. After showers and breakfast, Megan would work at her computer for several hours, and I would rest. In the afternoon, we'd go back out to the beach and read and maybe swim again. I was filled with joyful appreciation that I could do this much exercise. Except for my need for regular rest periods, I felt like a normal person—a very fortunate normal person.

The next morning, Megan and I swam slowly along the edge of Napili Bay to the end—the opening to the ocean—where black volcanic rock meets the coral and crashing waves signal the dangers of the open sea. On the way, we'd stopped to observe the Picasso triggerfish (Hawaii's state fish), the opaque white unicorn fish, bright yellow butterfly fish, and my favorite—the parrot fish with its iridescent blues, pinks, and purples. As we bobbed up and down in the deep swells, Megan pointed back toward shore, signaling that it was time to swim back in. As she did, a turtle suddenly appeared as if ready to escort us back to the beach. And we dutifully followed it back to the shallow waters, where it quickly turned and disappeared on its way back to the coral shelves and caves in the middle of the bay.

On the beach, as we took off our masks, Megan and I both said the same thing—turtles never appear in that part of the bay. Over the many years we had been coming there, it was common knowledge that if you wished to see a turtle, you had to swim far out to the very middle of the bay. We felt gifted by the appearance of turtle, and I couldn't wait to get back to the room to the Native American "Medicine" book. I read that turtle represents Mother Earth, "the personification of goddess energy." "Like Turtle," it said, "you also have shields that protect you . . . Turtle teaches you to use the water and earth energies . . . to flow harmoniously with your situation and to place your feet firmly on the ground in a power stance . . . You are not a victim, and you are not helpless, no matter how much it may seem like this is the case in your present situation . . . you need only list the things you are grateful for, and from that grateful place in your heart, look for the abundance of alternatives that Mother Earth gives." I loved the perception that I was not a helpless victim, but powerful in the practice of gratitude and abundance. Mother Earth was providing guidance.

Near the end of our trip, one early morning I sat meditating facing the bay. Even though I could hear the water, the stillness was like gray cotton, a soft, surrounding calm. When I opened my eyes, the sun had come up, and there was a rainbow that seemed to take up the whole sky. It extended south from Napili Point and arched up over the bay ending in a place far north of the island of Molokai. I'd seen many rainbows on Maui; in fact Maui is known as "the rainbow island." It's not unusual to see two or three rainbows every day. I'd once seen a vertical rainbow pouring straight down from the sky and into the sea.

Somehow this huge rainbow felt more magical, like a gift just for me. I smiled and thought of how the energy centers of the body, the chakras, each vibrate to a different color, from red at the base of the spine up to purple at the third eye and white at the crown of the head. It was a delightful recognition—that we all have rainbow energy flowing though our bodies.

Megan came out onto the deck, sleepy-eyed in her pajamas. By then the rainbow had evaporated, but I told her how big and beautiful it had been. She began writing in her journal, and I began thinking that I wanted to see that rainbow again. I really wanted the rainbow to reappear. I closed my eyes and concentrated on the rainbow from complete faith that I could manifest it. When I opened my eyes, there it was—that magnificent stream of colors. I touched Megan's arm and said, "Look what I did." With awe and laughter, we observed as another rainbow formed above the first one. "Oh my God," Megan squealed. People began coming out of their rooms to take photos before the rainbows dissolved. "I'm amazed and humbled," I said to Megan. "Just as I'm certain I made that rainbow come back for us, I'm just as certain I couldn't do it again. If I tried it again, it would be from my ego, from a desire to be special or powerful." We sat quietly and drank in the soft beauty of the colors.

And then there was the gift of butterflies. Everywhere we went on our walks, white butterflies drifted in little erratic clouds around bushes of lantana and hibiscus, or beneath the plumeria trees where impatiens and orchids grew. One afternoon as Megan and I were floating on our blue and pink rafts out in the middle of the bay, a white butterfly came by and paused, as if considering whether we were some kind of exotic water plants. I couldn't help but laugh. I'd never seen a butterfly flitting about this far off land, so again, I felt as though

Life itself was poking me, saying, "Hey look at this, and this . . .
Isn't this beautiful, and magical, and wondrous?" And I had to
answer, "Yes. Yes it is."

Back in the room, I took out the Animal Medicine book
and looked up "butterfly," thinking I already knew that the
butterfly represents transformation. Sure enough, I read that
butterfly teaches "the never-ending cycle of self-transformation." The word "self-transformation" struck me. I had been
thinking of transformation as something the world was forcing
on me—I hadn't a real choice in the matter except to suffer
through these difficult life events. That perception made me
a victim. Also, that view was not aligned with my spiritual
belief that before we come into each life, we choose areas
of growth to work on, and that members of our soul families
agree to help us with this growth. If I truly believed that, I had
to acknowledge that Bruce and Ben at the same time sacrificed
and expressed their love for me by forcing me to leave and
grow beyond my dependency on them, grow and engage with
a larger world. My little-girl self would have wanted to stay
safe, secure, and small.

The book also said that sometimes we lose the courage of
the butterfly. I had not associated the word "courage" with
butterfly. The book said we forget that outside the cocoon is
a totally different world and that it takes courage to use our
newfound wings and fly. "This last step involves sharing the
colors and joy of your creation with the world." I wrote this
down in my journal, along with a note to remind myself to
keep gathering my courage and to recognize that I am the
director and manager and co-creator with God of my own personal transformation. I felt grateful for every day, for every
flower and scent and rainbow, for every tropical fish, bird, and
butterfly that appeared to me on Maui.

The first dream I had after returning home was this one: I'm in Rio de Janeiro with Kateri, a friend of Megan's, and lots of other friends. I am so comfortable there that I morph into a giant, resting between two colorful structures that cover the tram cars on the mountain. I feel as large as the mountain. Then I'm my normal size on top of the mountain admiring the views. There's a small lake, and a butterfly—the most gorgeous imaginable. It's floating and flying around the lake. I point it out to the others. It's purple and blue and pink with silver bangles like the most beautiful East Indian scarf come alive. And it's huge, at least three or four feet across. I'm astounded by its size, its beauty, and its unusual shape—much more billowy and three-dimensional and grand than any other flying creature. Then I begin to think that it's getting toward dusk and we should get back for dinner. I then realize that it's only six and that in Latin countries dinner isn't eaten until much later. I'm comfortable with that. The dream ends with me alone on the mountaintop knowing that I'll be back with my friends later.

When I woke up, I wished with all my heart that I were an artist so that I could draw and paint that butterfly. But, more important, I knew that in the gestalt of that dream, I was the mountain, I was the lake, and I was the butterfly—shockingly beautiful, and soft, and free, and happy. I was feeling more comfortable in the world, and I sensed that I would never have another nightmare of being lost and frightened in a foreign land.

.5.

THE JOURNEY CONTINUES

A LANDMARK RESOURCE

*O*tried to retain the image and the feeling of the billowy blue butterfly that floated in my dream. I wanted to be like the butterfly—light, free, a beautiful expression of Spirit, and at the same time, I wanted to be grounded, like the Mayan woman–shaped mountain that contained the power of Mother Earth and was content to rest peacefully as she observed the metropolis below. While I knew I would never again be lost in foreign lands, I did not yet feel like the confident mistress of my own current landscape.

As Thanksgiving approached, all I could think of was the joy of past holidays and the seeming emptiness of the present. In previous years, I'd thrown myself into planning, baking, and organizing the house in eager anticipation of the Los Angeles Feldman family flying in and joining with other family friends for a long weekend of feasting, reminiscing, catching up with now-grown children, and feeling, in all of it, nourished by a deep sense of belonging.

The same families would come together this year, but the out-of-town guests would stay at a bed-and-breakfast, and Thanksgiving would be held at Bruce's new house. It was larger than my townhouse. Bruce's girlfriend would be there, the same woman he'd been with since the divorce. I liked her very much, but it felt strange to be with the two of them, in his house, surrounded by furniture and art that I had picked out and lived with for such a long time. These relocated possessions seemed to announce the dissolution of my family, and, like children of divorce, to quietly puzzle over the new order of things.

While I was always happy to have Megan home and delighted to spend time with little Ethan and the new grandbaby, Adam, I moved through the days like an automaton, knowing how to act, but feeling distant and dull. I missed my family the way it had been, and I missed the deep connection I'd originally had with Ben, a loving partnership that I thought held the possibility for a new expanded and blended family.

During Thanksgiving dinner I observed the comfort and ease in the interactions of our couple friends, and the pure happiness like a force field that emanated from young Jonathan and Laura, married less than a year. Jonathan was born one week after Niki and they had grown up together like siblings. I felt removed from the scene, as though I were watching a film, or peering through a window into the home of strangers, a family sharing a wealth of joyous celebration. I felt separate and excluded. That night when we returned to my place, Megan came to my room as I was getting ready for bed.

"I don't know what happened," she said, "but you're not the same person I was with in Hawaii."

"I know. I think she stayed there. Didn't want to face the holidays . . ."

"Well, I'm committed that you get back to yourself. I'd like you to take the Landmark Advanced Course. I know the Landmark Forum helped you to make the right choices for yourself with Ben. I think the next course might be just what you need right now."

Landmark Education is a global personal growth and development training that both Megan and Niki had participated in over the years. Megan had completed the entire curriculum, including a nine-month Wisdom Course in San Francisco. I had been impressed by the strides she had made in self-confidence and self-expression. A bonus was that she'd identified her life purpose—she would continue in journalism, but she would follow her passion to write, as she had in Latin America, in-depth feature-length pieces about people in the vortex of social crises.

Megan was born nine years after her sister, Niki, when I was nearly forty. She grew up attending adult social and cultural events and participating in conversations with people of all age groups. I was told many times starting at age five that she was wise beyond her years. This was the first time I could remember that she had ever made a clear recommendation to me.

She was right about the Landmark Forum experience. As a result of that three-day weekend, I realized I had not been living a responsible life—a life in commitment to my own well-being. During the relationship with Ben, I'd given myself over to simply being available for him. I'd abandoned myself—my normal routines, my own wishes and desires. I let him be my sun, and I revolved around his schedule, his travels, and his moods. And when I did do something for myself, I allowed his subsequent wrath and resentment to reduce me to tearful depression.

Megan was reminding me that it wasn't just renewed health and happiness I'd sought since the accident (and found in

Hawaii). I also needed to be powerful again, as I once had been through writing, participating in projects, training in new therapeutic techniques, and preparing talks. On Maui, I was happy in every moment. But I couldn't live "on vacation" forever. I needed to learn to be in charge of my real life and create a future that I could "live into." But with that thought, I would go blank. I couldn't imagine a future.

I took Megan's advice. It was time for another three-day course. That Monday morning I called the regional Landmark office in Phoenix and found that the next Advanced Course would be offered in two weeks, early December, in San Diego. I registered by phone.

The second morning of that weekend is engraved in my memory.

The first day of the course we had been assigned a "buddy," to be accountable for that person showing up on time for all the sessions. This reminded me of summer camp and grammar school field trips. As sometimes would happen back then at age nine or ten, I wasn't happy with my buddy assignment. Instead of someone easygoing and compliant, Kathleen was a high-powered attorney in one of the California state offices. She was stressed to distraction by a battlefield divorce with custody of her small son at stake, and she lived many miles away from the conference center. All this seemed to insure her late arrival to each session. This was the second time she didn't appear on time. I was asked to stand and explain why she wasn't there, and I thought it ridiculous that I was being held responsible for her behavior.

"I called her on the phone twice this morning, once when she was getting ready and once when she was in her car," I said. The seminar leader stood, impassive, waiting for me to go on.

"I don't know what else I could do, short of driving to her house at 7 A.M. in my pajamas and supervising her putting on her clothes and feeding her dogs," I said, irritably. More silence. I felt my irritation expand until my chest was filled with anger. And then it seemed to explode right out of my mouth, filling the entire room with protest.

"I don't give a shit about that woman," I yelled. "I don't even know her. And I don't give a shit about anyone in this room," my voice went higher and louder. "I didn't come here for these people. I don't know these people, and I don't care about these people," I yelled directly into the face of the seminar leader, who had walked over and stood right in front of me. "I just don't give a shit anymore," I said, but now in a voice that was lower and trailing off into tears.

I had never expressed anger like this in public. It's possible I never felt intense anger at all prior to this moment. Part of me was shocked at what my mother would have called the "ungodly scene" I was making. Social grace, pretense, professional understanding had all disappeared. Only the feelings that had been holding me hostage were exposed, the deep grief and outrage that had been boiling below the surface.

I'm not surprised now when feelings of upset pop out like a Halloween ghost and yell "Boo!" but then I was shocked. I had been doing so well. After my experiences on Maui, my recovery felt secured. How could I still be this angry and express this with people I didn't even know?

"I really just don't care anymore," I said. "I don't care about anybody." My voice went lower as the angry energy dissolved.

"I've spent my entire life taking care of others," I said, tears spilling down my face. "Growing up, after my father left, I tried to take care of the house and help my mother. Then I took care of my own family and raised two beautiful daughters. We had a great family for over thirty years, then my husband . . . lost himself and I lost my ability to cope, and we divorced. I was never going to be divorced. I never wanted to be a divorced woman, especially at this age."

Now the tears were cascading, and I could hardly force words through my sobs. I couldn't believe I was crying like this—again. *SOS, same old shit.* I was handed a box of tissues, grabbed two and started mopping my face. "But I couldn't go on. I had to divorce, and I thought I would die during the two years it took." I had to stop and get more breath. I noticed then that the room was completely silent. All of these people, over one hundred bodies, seemed to be making a space that my words could fall into. I felt calmer as I continued.

"Then I fell deeply in love with this man who I thought I'd marry, and he turned out to be unstable, unpredictable . . . and then I had an accident last winter and broke my shoulder . . . but the worst is the head injury and the symptoms I'm still dealing with. I can't handle being impaired," I nearly whispered through my tears.

After a few moments, the seminar leader said gently, "You don't want to be alive, do you?"

"No!" I blurted. "I can't see any future. I've just wanted to be dead. I'm so tired of trying to cope with everything and help everyone else, and act like I'm fine. I'm a trauma psychologist, and the kind of brutality people experience is sometimes unbearable. It's just unbearable . . ."

The room was completely still.

The silence had the soft color of blue in it, and time had disappeared into its comfort. The seminar leader placed his hand on my shoulder and looked into my eyes and simply said, "Thank you."

Everyone applauded to acknowledge one of the major teachings for the weekend: that every breakdown prepares the way for a breakthrough. I'd wanted so badly to be well, and I was learning that I was well. I would have to get used to the same phenomenon I share with my patients—that the rhythms of grief come and go in our lives; that our capacity to grieve deeply mirrors the capacity to love deeply; and that as we create comfort with these healing feelings, they bring greater self-understanding, self-acceptance, and self-love, and, eventually, an opening to a self-created brighter future.

That night, I got back to my sister's house at 11:30 to find her and Vince setting up the Christmas tree. Although it seemed completely unreasonable to begin decorating the tree at nearly midnight, Judy encouraged me to join them. The intensity of the day melted as I listened to holiday music and selected ornaments to place on the tree. Nothing mattered during this time except each decision, whether to choose the iridescent red bulb, the gold glittered bulb, the silver snowflake bulb, or the Santa holding a stocking with toys. I carefully placed each ornament on the tree, and then we hung small candy canes on the bottom branches for the children, until the tree was perfect.

We stood back and admired our work. I felt peaceful and happy. *Life is like this*, I thought: When we pay close attention to every act in every moment, all is well. I learned that day about the importance of being present for myself, respectful of every reaction and every feeling. I had abandoned my little-girl self long ago—leaving her alone in frustration, rage, and overwhelming sadness. Maybe now I could nurture and reassure her. I could practice doing what a wise person once said is the purpose of every psychotherapist—Be my own best mother.

The next day at the seminar, Kathleen and I had a chance to visit during the lunch break. She apologized for being late (she'd arrived during my outburst), but I told her it was the best thing that could have happened. Not only did I express a lot of pent-up emotion, I had a breakthrough in perspective. I recognized both the family and the societal contexts for my anger having gone underground. Children aren't facilitated in their grief, and I was no exception. My parents were caught up in their own problems. Plus, I had been socialized to "be a good girl." In the 1950s, a "young lady" didn't get upset or angry. (It wasn't until the feminist movement that "assertive" behavior became acceptable for women, but by then I'd collapsed the concept of "assertive" with "aggressive.") In order to be "nice," strong feelings that might displease the adults in my life had to be disavowed. Accommodation had become my survival mode.

FINDING TREASURE

THAT AFTERNOON, I observed many others "breaking down," sharing their stories of neglect, abandonment, abuse, and physical challenges. I was most moved by the woman who told about her teenage daughter being murdered. I felt my heart drop and I thought, *Clearly, I wouldn't be able to handle that. That's the one thing I'd always told God: If one of my daughters were taken from me, I would cease functioning. The structure and meaning of my life would dissolve. I would be unrecognizable to myself, and I would refuse to work or make any contribution to others.* I resisted any thought of such a thing happening and prayed my insistent prayer of protection. But no amount of prayer can prevent terrible life circumstances from occurring. We live in the world that we live in. Each person in the room had experiences that had dismantled their lives and temporarily destroyed their ability to know how to live. I began to notice that when my tears welled up, they were no longer just about me. They contained a quality, a sense of being part of something bigger—the human condition, I suppose. I began to feel compassion for and connection to everyone in the room, everyone who had the courage to be in this conversation about self-reflection and responsibility. Jungian analyst James Hollis refers to this process, the willingness to go beyond experience and reach for a larger life, as "standing in the transformational fire."

In the past I might have seen this group sharing of tragic drama as indulgent and depressing, a reinforcement of my recent cynical view of life as one long round of inevitable unhappiness. But now, sitting in this place with over one hundred strangers, I felt honored. We had all been wounded by life experience, and we were all being healed by sharing our experiences of being human. Like the Grinch at Christmas, my heart seemed to be growing and overflowing with feelings, feelings I could only call "life-affirming"—the warmth of compassion and love. During an exercise where we took time to look into the eyes of every person in the room, I saw the exquisite beauty, the miracle and mystery of the eyes themselves, and beyond to the life that resides in the depths of each soul.

Creating love, not surviving life, is our only recourse, our only resource for healing. Love is the magic elixir. Love empowers us. Our stories, our hurtful experiences are dissolved in a space of loving understanding and communion. That insight was my treasure, my boon, my blessing.

As I looked around the room, I no longer saw victims. I saw people with the resilience required to share their pain and the commitment to use their special knowledge to make a difference in the world. When the seminar leader reminded us that "Suffering is inevitable, misery is optional," I understood that saying for the first time and knew that a major purpose for being alive is to alleviate misery, our own and others'.

I was jolted by the realization that not caring about life is just the same as being dead. Withdrawing from the world is a constriction of the heart, a shriveling-up inside of oneself into a dark space devoid of energy. Staying in that place would be a form of arrogance, making my personal pain more special or important than that of anyone else.

I was pulled out of my reverie by someone sharing about being estranged from a sister who was now struggling with cancer. Suddenly I was struck by the realization that I had not been keeping in touch with Marcia. My best friend, my officemate, my confidante, the woman who supported me through every life crisis, participated in every family celebration, held me in the highest esteem as the sister she never had, this very special person who was struggling with a very rare form of cancer—instead of staying involved with her care, I had withdrawn into my own physical and emotional concerns.

The next morning, I called her as I walked along the beach at La Jolla Shores. "Marcia, I want to apologize for being so preoccupied over the last months and not keeping in closer touch with you."

"That's fine. It's okay. You've had your own stuff going on. I understand that. Don't worry about it."

"No," I insisted, "it's not fine and it's not okay that I've been so self-absorbed that I haven't been checking in with you regularly like I used to. And I want to apologize. I'm really sorry."

When the call was complete, I could tell that Marcia was touched and near tears. I could feel the love-bond between us strengthened. I had learned, from the Landmark coursework, that most apologies come from the ego—empty words, verbal rituals learned in grade school to quickly cover over misbehavior and "get back to the playground." I was aware now of how much more focus and energy was required for a heartfelt apology, a communication that restores connection and keeps us life-centered in integrity.

Not only was my apology a declaration of accountability, it was a commitment to change, to new actions. That commitment to be responsible made me feel bigger right there on the beach, as though I'd grown a few inches. It was probably my happy heart stretching in calisthenics.

That afternoon, Greg, the course leader, reviewed the elements of the Landmark Education curriculum. He reminded us that the first weekend course, the Landmark Forum, was focused on inventing a life of possibility, possibilities that would call us to be authentic, fulfilled, and powerfully self-expressed. Clearing the past from the present and giving up stories that make us victims are a part of the individual work involved at that first level of learning.

The Advanced Course and subsequent seminars are designed to promote extraordinary relationships, including family relations. We're called beyond the personal pain, patterns, and problems that have captured and held our attention, to a greater capacity to be truly present for others. Skills are developed, such as new ways to listen and to honor others, and the ability to care deeply that everyone we know live a fulfilled life. The course also gives one the freedom to live powerfully in the present and to "generate a vision for your life that is solidly anchored in reality . . ."

These first three levels of learning establish a personal foundation from which we can see opportunities to make a difference—first for ourselves, with friends and colleagues, and for our families. In the fourth level of courses, we're taught community building. The basic community development course is called "Self Expression and Leadership," Greg said. It lasts three months, provides a personal coach, and requires that each participant create a community project. The goal is for the project to serve a specific need and to also provide a context for communication that "calls forth the alignment, cooperation and partnership of others."

Greg was pointing to a large illustration of the Landmark Education levels of learning. As he described the opportunities for development, I was reminded of a rainbow. (Rainbow images came up readily since my experience on Maui.) I could imagine the colors red, orange, and yellow starting at the bottom curves, representing individual, relationship, and family growth, and then the green in the middle representing the community development of Self-Expression and Leadership.

The fifth, sixth, and seventh levels of learning involve the transformation of organizations, and then societies, and then the entire world—all of humanity. In my mind, the rainbow would be completed with the colors of blue, purple, and white at the top. White, the color that contains all other colors, would represent the energy of total transformation, world Oneness.

The purpose of all of these courses, Greg was saying, is to create a world that works for everyone—every person safe, fed, educated, fulfilled—their possibilities for creativity and vitality facilitated from birth by a loving family and community. Even though it sounded utopian and impossible, what better goal could there be? I remembered a businesswoman I knew back home who'd made an "impossible promise" to end child hunger—to provide food for every child in every part of the world, and she lived that commitment. I was moved by the strength of her dedication.

By the end of the weekend I was both exhausted and energized. I was excited by my discovery that through connection and commitment to community I would be creating my new life. I would be living my values. I would be putting meaning back into my life. Before I left the San Diego center, I registered for the Self-Expression and Leadership course to begin in Albuquerque in January.

RETURNING WITH GIFTS

PLANNING FOR THE Christmas holidays felt completely different when I returned home. Instead of the dread I'd felt at Thanksgiving, I felt joy at the thought of each family ritual. My daughter Niki and I began planning for the children's presents from Santa, Christmas Eve dinner, and afterward going to see the lights (luminarias) displayed in Old Town. There would be "smiley-face" pancakes for Christmas morning, and our usual walk to the Rio Grande after cleaning up the living room chaos of torn wrappings and toy boxes.

The holiday was indeed peaceful and joyous. I rested, visited with friends, and resisted the temptation to fret about not being invited to the parties that Bruce would attend without me. In the past, I'd traveled somewhere, anywhere, to be away for New Year's Eve. This year I invited my friends for dinner and a "sharing circle" focused on our personal growth over the year. Megan was there, and so was Sarah Barlow, my "third daughter." She's two years older than Megan, a teacher in New York City, and was struggling with her mantra of, "I'm thirty-three, and I want to be married and pregnant LAST year."

Just before midnight we lit candles and chose blank cards from a pile I'd purchased with beautiful painted scenes or photographs on the front. I'd been doing this exercise in self-acknowledgment for many years, and it was the one part of New Year's I looked forward to. We opened our cards and wrote "Dear (self)" on the left side beneath the date, December 31, 2004. Then we wrote letters of appreciation to ourselves for all we'd coped with, handled, learned, and achieved during the past year. On the right side we wrote "Dear (self)" and listed everything we were anticipating and planned to accomplish, along with all the happy possibilities for the coming year.

Then we opened a bottle of champagne and toasted ourselves and acknowledged the strengths and gifts we saw in each other. At two A.M. we reluctantly gave in to fatigue and headed off for bed. I wasn't alone in the recognition that this had been the best, most love-filled New Year's Eve I'd ever had, and the first time I looked with joyous expectation to the coming year. I knew I would be emotionally stronger and on the move to becoming physically healthy.

A MIGHTY WOMAN

IN JANUARY OF the new year, 2005, I invited a few friends over who were also going through the midlife "mysteries." Jenn, my closest ally, liked the idea. I'd met Jenn in the fall of 1999 when I walked into an evening Spanish class. I noticed an empty seat next to an attractive Chinese woman and sat down feeling immediately drawn to her. Her pager went off, and I leaned over and asked if she was a physician. She whispered yes before hurrying out of the room to return the call. After class, she introduced herself as Jennifer Kwong (Jenn for short), and we discovered we were both in the same emotional maelstrom called divorce. Later, over tea, we agreed that we were studying Spanish to help fill the time and hopefully force information bits into our brains that would push aside some of the obsessive thoughts about our husbands and our fears of the future.

"How long were you married?" I asked her.

"Twenty-one years," she paused. "Well, that includes the last time I divorced him, and we were apart for two years."

"What? You divorced him before?"

"I did," she said with a laugh. "Fell in love with a doc who was willing to go to China with me. Brad never would go. The trip was really good. We took a course with a lot of neat docs, mostly from Australia, to get certified to treat tourists in China. But the relationship didn't work out, and I missed Brad, so I got him to marry me again. I'll always love the guy, but his passivity makes me crazy. He'll work his butt off for his business—loves to work—but then sit and watch television all night."

She paused, thoughtful. "He's been good to me, though, and he's really been Kim's mother. Our daughter, Kim is twenty-two. I was raised in an orphanage, so I was clueless about raising a kid—especially in this country."

"You're an orphan?"

"Not really. My mother's alive. In fact she lives here now." Jenn groaned, comically, and put her face in her hands. "I really have trouble with my mother. After we came to this country— I was seventeen—I looked for a college as far away from D.C. as I could find to get away from her. So I got into University of New Mexico and guess what then? She brings my brothers and moves here." Another groan. "Oh god."

"I'm totally confused. You said earlier you were anxious and fearful about your divorce, but you sound like the mistress of cool. And how did you grow up in an orphanage if you have a mother?"

Jenn giggled and smiled a smile that took up fully half of her face. Her large dark eyes crinkled into a smile as well, and I couldn't help comparing her face to a happy jack-o'-lantern, or maybe a laughing Buddha.

"I know. It's totally weird. My father died when I was five, and my mother put me and my younger brother in an orphanage in Taiwan. Then she left the country and moved to Libya and then Europe. I probably have what you'd call 'attachment disorder.' Brad calls it 'orphan syndrome.' I'm defected."

"You mean defective?" I asked.

"Yeah, defective," that melodious laughter again.

"You're not defective," I insisted. "You just grew up learning certain patterns of behavior, just like we all do."

"Well, I had killer fights with him. Fortunately, he's much bigger than I am, so he got the knife away from me."

"Jesus. Maybe you are defective." We both dissolved into laughter.

"I can't handle relationships. I can be with men, they can take my crazy anger, but I don't have women friends. I drive them away." Jenn looked me straight in the eyes, suddenly dead serious. "I want you to be my friend. Don't let me get rid of you."

"I'm good at handling other people's emotional upsets," I told her. "Just can't handle my own. But, don't worry, I won't let you get rid of me. Just don't come at me with a knife."

Jenn invited me to her house for dinner that weekend. The large, rambling Spanish-style home sat on a hill in what's called the Spruce Park area of Albuquerque near the university. Jenn gave me a big hug and a "Hi, honey," and told me to come look at the house. The large living room window looked out to the west, with views of downtown and the mesa beyond, like a perfect picture frame for the orange-yellow sunset. I was impressed with her taste. Elegant American furniture sat among antique Chinese pieces, large vases, and modern art.

She took me to see the master bedroom and bath, huge pine trees towering outside the windows, and a swimming pool nestled at the bottom of the hill. On her dressing table was a small, rustic structure, like the pole ladders leaning against the outer walls of the territorial houses here in the southwest. There were dozens of pairs of earrings hanging on the little ladder.

"This is so clever," I told her. "And so many beautiful earrings. Did you make some of these?"

"I made all of them. I went nuts into beading a couple of years ago. It was a good distraction. Take whatever you want."

"I'll take one pair," I said, and picked out a pair with rust colored stones and dangling tiny bamboo pieces.

Jenn took me to see the other bedrooms, baths, and guest wing of the house before we ended up in her large kitchen that looked to me like a professional chef's kitchen on the Food Channel.

"This place is so gorgeous, but I'm glad you were with me on the tour. I would have definitely gotten lost in here on my own," I told her.

"I know. It's way too big," Jenn said, as she grabbed pots down from the rack above the food preparation island. "I hate it. I have to remember too many routes. What do call them, escape routes?"

"What do you mean?" I asked, puzzled.

"Like there are too many doors, too many ways to get in. So in every room I have to know how I would get out. Like if I'm coming in from the garage, there are four other doors someone could have gotten in, and if they come at me then I know these routes to get away . . ." she looked over at me and, no doubt, saw my blank face. She flashed her big face smile and laughed. "I know it sounds crazy. But that's why I'm selling the house. It's too big. I want a small house. Small garden. Simple. Easy-to-take-care-of.

"Here," she said, changing the subject. "Would you cut up this celery for the salad?"

Jenn quickly put together a meal of fried rice, vegetables, dumplings, and salad, with pieces of persimmons ("paarsimmons") artfully arranged on a decorative China plate. "This is my favorite fruit. I call the Chinese market to find out when they're getting them in."

"How do you say persimmon in Chinese?"

"*Shouldsa*, probably spelled "she-ze,: or something like that."

"Jenn isn't your original name is it?"

"No. My Chinese name is Suan Ying. It means 'vast intelligence.' But my nickname in the orphanage was Genghis after Genghis Khan, because I was so strong and wild. That's the Mongolian blood from my mother's side of the family.

"How I got the name, Jenn, though, is funny. On the plane to this country they showed the movie *Camelot*. I wanted to have the name, Gweneviere, but it wasn't in my name book. So I went to the J's and picked Jennifer. People call me Jenn Jenn or just Jenn."

"Well, somehow it worked," I said. "It fits you."

Jenn began talking about her plan for a Spanish conversation group to meet at her house, and once we established the date, time and the friends we would invite, she moved on to salsa dancing. Her face got brighter, her smile broader, and her tone more lively as she shared her research on the locations, times, and teachers available for Latin dancing.

It quickly became clear that Jenn would be our social director during the next months of dealing with divorce lawyers, accountants, and court dates. She spoke of hiking, river rafting, crafts projects, and various places to go dancing.

"Jenn," I interrupted. "I can tell you have five times the energy I do right now. I'm just barely dragging myself through this divorce, and I often don't sleep but a few hours at night. You're gonna have to go slower here. Am I getting it that you do activities instead of sad feelings?"

"Oh yeah. I don't do sadness. I go play. And I can't be a patient. I have to be the doctor. I had a double mastectomy last year, and after the surgery I dosed myself up on pain meds and went in to the hospital with drainage tubes hanging out from under my armpits. We were short-staffed at the hospital, and my patients needed attention. I don't sit with pain. I distract myself and go do something."

"That is totally amazing, Jenn," I said. "First of all, I can't imagine going through breast cancer. I'm too vain to lose my breasts. I'd go into some deep, dramatic depression. But going to work after the surgery? My god. Was Brad helpful during that time?"

"That was part of the reason I divorced him. He was furious about the surgery."

"What? How could he be angry about it?"

"It was lobular carcinoma in situ, so they said I could just check it every three months. But there were ten locations on both breasts. Like hell, I would live with a time bomb like that. He wouldn't even go to my appointments with me. He said I should do alternative medicine. We'd have shouting matches about it. Here I'm a doctor and a statistician. I did all the research on the pathology and the prognosis, and I tell him and he says I'm self-destructive. I tell him to go fuck himself, and I take the surgical option. Do you get this?" She looks at me intently.

"I do. I'm sorry you had to go through that, and go through it with no support. Did you need to have radiation or chemo?"

"No. The lymph nodes were negative, so it wasn't indicated. That part was good."

Finding the good in situations seemed to be Jenn's resilience mode. And if the good couldn't be found in a particular situation, she'd find another one to temporarily occupy her mind. I learned that she was a caring and concerned friend when

I'd express worries about emotionally surviving my divorce: "You'll be fine, baby (the same endearment she used with her daughter, Kim). You're gonna come through this with flying colors."

When I had time-related complaints, whined about how long something might take, she'd give a dismissive, "You can stand in a bucket of shit for that length of time, Gail." That was after I'd expressed concern about how long it might take to sell my house: "It'll take less than a year, and you can stand in a bucket of shit for that length of time." A check I had to wait a month for brought the same comment: "You can stand in a bucket of shit for a month." Or dreading two hours in the dentist's office: "You can stand in a bucket of shit for two hours," she said, always with accompanying lilting laughter. The "bucket of shit" always brought perspective.

❦

I viewed Jenn as some amazing, exotic, paradoxical creature. What kind of person could have breast surgery and go to work the same day to care for others? Who could love a man enough to marry him twice and also hate him enough to try to kill him? What woman could be so blasé about divorce she could breeze through it with multiple boyfriends? (Jenn was on her second, while I couldn't stand the thought of even locking eyes with a man over coffee at Starbucks.) Most of all, how could this woman be so happy? While I had to force the appearance of relative cheerfulness much of the time, Jenn seemed to exude pure joy and vitality.

What kind of woman would be extremely intelligent, brilliantly successful at work, intense at play, able to care for others under any circumstances, nearly superhuman in coping with physical pain, but have inconsistent, highly-charged emotional relationships? I knew that kind of woman from my work. It's a woman who has survived multiple traumas, abuse, and abandonment, and thrived by creating a life of resilience, activity, and contribution. Jenn's enthusiasm for life was real, but beneath the bubbly surface, I suspected there was a deep and fearful sadness. It would take time and trust for Jenn to share the darkest parts of her life experiences with me. In the meantime, we concentrated on having fun.

Jenn was my indispensable sidekick for the next few years. She helped me create budgets and settlement proposals, and I helped her create tolerance for the predictable feelings that come with grief and drastic life change. We were both consistent reliable sources of support for one another. But ultimately, we would each have to find our own internal strength to meet the challenges that lay ahead.

.6.

SHARING THE TREASURE

RED TENT WISDOM

During the holidays I reorganized some books in my study, and there it was at the bottom of a stack—*The Red Tent*. This historical novel by Anita Diamant riveted my attention when I first read it nearly ten years earlier. Set in the Biblical time of the Old Testament, one reviewer was moved to say, "It celebrates mothers and daughters and the mysteries of the life cycle." For me, it was less a celebration of women and more a history of the tragedies that befell women as a result of their being possessions of men, totally vulnerable to the violent whims of those who held power over them.

The only oasis in that desert of dependence and oppression was the Red Tent, a place of community for all women during childhood, menstruation, childbirth, illness, abandonment, and the performance of daily domestic duties such as weaving and preparing food.

I read the book again. I was struck by the sense of safety and nurturance that the Red Tent provided for women. The Red Tent was a refuge and also a metaphor for the protection and love that a community of women can create for one another. I wanted that safe space. I felt moved to tears to realize that women are designed to provide a caring, sustaining environment, especially during times of change, turmoil, and life crisis. Over the centuries, however, the structure for that provision had dissolved.

SHARING CIRCLES

I HAD JUST begun the Self-Expression and Leadership course, and my community project came to mind with ease. I wanted women's groups available as supportive structures for women in midlife transitions. I brainstormed one evening with Chela, the course leader, to find a suitable name for my project. I told her I liked "Mighty Women" because Charlie, my son-in-law, said Niki and I were "mighty" whenever we achieved a significant goal. Also, Mighty Mouse was my favorite cartoon when I was a kid, and Mighty Mouse's girlfriend was my symbol of femininity, probably because whenever she got into trouble, Mighty Mouse would swoop down and rescue her in the nick of time.

"Why not make the name, "Mighty Women Unite," Chela suggested.

Yes. I liked that. I realized the Mighty Mouse concept was obsolete. Women have the task and the opportunity to recreate themselves in the world that we live in now. The message to women, the declaration, would be: "A Mighty Woman is aligned with her power—mentally, emotionally, and spiritually. She has let go of all limitations, those invisible chains that held her back from her highest self-expression. A Mighty Woman lives in all possibility."

I talked with Jenn about meeting with other women who were engaged in the same midlife mystery of suddenly being single. She liked the idea. Jenn was game for any kind of new experience, even though she expressed doubts about being able to tolerate an all-women group. The first meeting was held at my house for dinner and a "sharing circle." After that, Jane, Annie, Fay, Elizabeth, Jenn, and I took turns hosting an evening of potluck, meditation, and "sacred sharing." In the Native American tradition each woman would hold the "talking stone or stick" and speak freely about issues facing her on her path. The rest of the women would honor her by holding the silence.

Fay and Elizabeth had just completed long-term marriages and long, drawn-out adversarial divorces. Annie had been ready to ask for a divorce when her husband had an accident that left him physically handicapped. She remained with him while he readjusted to life, but after three more years of no connection and no conversation, Annie had told me the previous year, "If I'm still married at the end of next year, shoot me."

Jane's partner of twenty-seven years had decided to leave just before Christmas. He didn't love her any longer, he told her, and he was interested in a younger woman. When Jane had returned my invitation call, she said the offering of a women's group was a "gift from God. I really need to be with a group of women I can share with right now. I'm feeling completely alone at sea."

Meetings were held in the evening, and each woman brought food to share. We left our shoes in the entry. Before eating, that first night, I said a simple prayer of gratitude. "Mother, Father, God, we give thanks for the healing energy of friends and for the food before us that represents the great abundance we all share." We held hands, "thumbs left," Annie said, so that one hand is down, to signify giving, and the other up, in a gesture of receiving. After dinner we moved to the living room and sat in a circle. I lit candles and put the Angel Oracle cards face down on the coffee table. We selected one of the cards to meditate on during the next ten to fifteen minutes, and then I rang my Tibetan Singing Bowl to sound the completion of the meditation period.

Fay was the first to pick up the small ceramic duck that was serving as our "talking stone." She settled back into the big easy chair by my fireplace and said she'd had a dream she wanted to share. Fay was fingering her Angel Card as she began:

"A door opened into this deep cellar. It was oppressive, like an underground prison. I realized that's where I've been living much of the time—in my grief, but unaware of it. I thought I'd grieved the death of my first baby, but I hadn't. Not completely. Back then I had a pattern of acting out my anger and rage, both about the baby and toward John for his affairs, by having affairs of my own. Needless to say, I didn't feel very good about that. I carried a lot of guilt and sadness for many years.

"In the dream, I got that I can now grieve on the level necessary to make me free. Then, suddenly I found myself floating in a sea of love. I can't explain that. I just know that's what it was. This card, the Angel of Reconciliation, says, 'Let me be fully reconciled with what I have left behind.' That means to me that as I release the past, I can be accepting of the present. I can take myself into my own heart for the first time. And the two wings on the angel make me feel like I'm beginning a kind of spectacular unfolding."

Fay smiled at us and replaced the duck. After several minutes, Jane leaned over and took the duck, holding it in both hands in her lap.

"I've never had any grieving strategies," she said. "I was fine with my divorce thirty years ago. I was young, and Jack and I were so mismatched. Tom was more like the father to my children. For all these years he's been family. When he walked away this Christmas I was so shocked, and then devastated. I could cry and be angry with him, and beat myself up, but mostly pretend I wasn't scared. Now I can say, 'I'm scared.' I've felt so much shame that Tom doesn't love me anymore. Like there must be something wrong with me. I realize I have the choice to love myself. I know I can choose to be independent and creative—and I will. But this feeling of vulnerability is new. I hate it. And I hate crying all the time."

Jane grabbed several tissues from the box on the table and continued. "The card I drew seemed weird at first—the Guardian Angel of Children. But under the picture of the angel it says, 'I honor the precious child within me. I nourish and cherish all new beginnings.' And new beginnings are exactly what I'm looking at. I was thinking of retiring next year and joining the Peace Corps or some similar program. I'm going to start looking into that." She looked around at all of us and said, "I'm so glad to be here. I'm so grateful for this group."

When Jane set the duck down, Jenn picked it up. She flashed her big grin and laughed.

"I got the Wisdom card, can you believe it?" More nervous laughter, then she turned serious. "I think it's telling me I have to stop getting rid of people. At least I get it now. I've had a need to not need anybody. I could never depend on anyone, so I never wanted to. But I have a doctor friend who's dying, and she's young and still has kids at home, and I realize how precious life is. I just don't want to be so angry anymore. I know it's my form of grief, but I want to learn to be able to feel other feelings. I've been so angry with my mother my whole

life, but it spills over to Kim, my daughter, and I get resentment. She's had it so good. She's spoiled compared to me. But
when I see her that way, I don't treat her well. Then she cries
and calls me a bad mother. And I say, 'You're grown up now.
You shouldn't need me.' Then we don't talk for days, and I feel
like a bad mother. Actually, I'm a rotten mother."

Jenn laughed and got teary at the same time. Jane passed
her a tissue. "I love her a lot, but I get so defensive with her,"
Jenn went on, looking at her card. "It says on my Wisdom
card under the angel, 'Wisdom comes from the depths of my
experience.' And in the book—I was reading about it while
the others were talking—it says that 'Wisdom is an internal
awareness' that can help us 'live in peace and harmony.'
That's what I need—peace and harmony. That will really be
challenging for me, but I'm going to work on that."

When Jenn settled back on the sofa, Elizabeth picked up the
duck. With her lovely Australian accent, she began: "I was a
proper little English girl when I married James. He was a very
successful American businessman, and I thought he sat on the
right hand of God. My family was so excited for me to marry him.

"After the wedding, he brought me to the United States.
I must have gotten pregnant on our wedding night because a
few months later, I was quite pregnant, and he went to Asia to
open a new manufacturing plant. He was gone for six months.
And that set the scene for the next thirty years. I don't know
how I survived, except that I loved all four of my children
and devoted myself to being a mother. In these last years,
I've found that I'm actually a very fine businesswoman. And,
what's really new is to realize that I love being on my own.

"My 'inner critic' that started out as my parents and then
was my husband is completely gone. I don't give a rat's bottom
about anyone's approval. I'm out from under all the rubbish and
just aware of becoming myself. I drew the Angel of Being. It

says, 'My soul rests in the truth that my Being is eternal.' I love that. What it means for me right now is that I can bask in self-acceptance and self-love. So, ladies, I'm just going to bask."

"Wow," Annie said, as she picked up the duck. "That's what I hope to get someday—self-acceptance and self-love." She paused. "I've decided I am going to leave my marriage. I've begun to have talks with Ralph about the fact that we need to separate. We have no common interests and nothing to talk about except our daughters. Our house is not set up to handle his wheelchair. He needs a place that would accommodate him better and allow him to cook and care for himself. I told him I'd help him find a place and organize the move. He's made new friends at the rehab center, which is great, and he's still active with his old friends.

"I need to stay at the house because of my horticulture business, the trees and the greenhouse, and my flower beds. My business is growing, and I feel so lucky. For me God is luck—like being blessed. The card I drew is the Archangel Raphael. It says, 'I am strengthened and healed by the power of Divine Love.' I know that archangels aid us in our daily lives, so I'm going to keep faith that I'll be helped to move through this divorce. And that's it for now." She replaced the duck.

It was now my turn. I had been sitting there struck by the brilliance of each woman's insights about her life direction and the knowledge gained from hard experience. Naturally, I related most deeply to Jane's sense of desolation at being left after so many years of connection with Tom and the joys of raising a family together. Even though my divorce was my idea and even though my breakup with Ben was my doing, I still felt defective in some way, a sense of shame that I could not save either of the relationships.

It had been over a year since my accident and the bad ending with Ben. My body and my brain were much better, but I thought I should be completely over the romance and ready to get on with my life. I still needed reminding occasionally that there would be times when I would be "in the impact" of the grief. Rather than berate myself, I could choose to be with those feelings and practice self-acceptance. Only from that space of self-love could I create new possibilities for my future. I knew that truth, and that I could teach it to others, but I wasn't being a very receptive student to the learning.

"I've been closed in on myself this past year," I began. "Cut off from others, except for Jenn and Marcia, my two crutches; just focused on trying to get well. But I feel embarrassed that I haven't kept faith, except for short periods of time. I have to keep realizing that I'm much better and that my prayers are always answered. I still go into breakdowns over Ben, and then I feel like a wimp, really pathetic. And I convince myself that I'll be alone the rest of my life, that I'm too old to have a great love—an old, tottering companion maybe, but not a vibrant, stimulating love. I guess my grandsons will have to do for the time being.

"And speaking of them, I have to tell you what happened with the baby last weekend: Adam had a bronchial infection, and he couldn't breathe lying down. Niki had been up with him for several nights. On Friday at the bookstore he fell asleep in the front pack on my chest. I was sitting in a big rocking chair, and he slept on and on. After one hour, my shoulder and back were aching, but the sleeping angel motivated me to ignore the pain and meditate on comfort and the baby's healing. His little head was right at my heart. I felt the warmth of his head, and the beating of my own heart. The aching in my body continued, but I kept bringing my concentration back to the baby's breathing and my own. And soon I noticed that our breathing felt like we were One Being. It was as though we were breathing in a soothing, all-embracing, golden light. It was magical.

"That night and the next I sat with Adam in the rocking chair in his bedroom, feeling that peaceful, little warm body and the golden light around us, and being aware of the heat generated between my heart and his head. I knew that holding him like that enabled him to breathe and be nurtured and healed. And I knew that this was my healing as well. It felt like we were in space, our breath being fueled by a warm furnace. Holding that baby made me remember what life is all about—love."

During the early sharing circles, my friends and I did not feel particularly "mighty." It didn't seem to matter, however, who had a beautiful insight, who couldn't stop crying, who felt hopeless. We had a context in which to share whatever called to us to be explored from the depths. And we had a format to follow to insure that we were supported both during and after leaving the group. Confidentiality was a given, and judgment, opinions, and advice had no place in this sacred conversation. We would be nurtured by being listened to, accepted, and understood.

In every meeting, I was struck anew by how fitting our cards were. This first night I drew the "Guardian Angel of Service." The awareness that service was my path to healing was the insight, the treasure I'd already discovered. And service, for now, simply meant reengaging and connecting to others. The groups allowed me and the other women to share our stops and starts, support one another in letting go of the past, and open our hearts to the treasure of our own inner wisdom on our challenging journey.

HISTORICAL HEROINE

WHEN MEGAN AND I were in Hawaii, I'd picked up a book called *Six Months in the Sandwich Islands*, by Isabella Bird. It was a travel book written by an English woman in 1873. Miss Bird had become known in England as an intrepid adventurer who sailed off alone to distant lands, sending detailed accounts of her journeys home to her sister. The letters became popular travel books and magazine articles in England.

I was enthralled by this tale of a forty-two year old woman leaving New Zealand on a paddle steamer and sailing (around the cape) to what is now known as the Hawaiian Islands. The poor condition of the ship, the hurricane that blew for eleven hours (noted by the captain as the most severe he'd encountered in seventeen years), and Miss Bird's ability to accept any hardship without judging it so, impressed me no end.

She had grown up with horses, loved to ride, and was delighted and excited to be taken to see every unique aspect of the islands, riding along narrow tracks through the jungles or thirty miles up a "perpetual upward scramble" to see Kilauea, the largest active volcano in the world.

She became known and admired for her expert horsemanship, riding with the Hawaiian cowboys, or "paniolos," at full gallop, for her undaunted courage in fording fast-moving rivers, and for her general indifference to adversity. Sitting in the saddle for ten hours soaked by rain, for example, would not be my idea of a vacation. But after arduous long days, Isabella would spend nights sleeping on the ground of a grass hut, appreciate the hospitality of the natives, and eat exotic food she'd never before encountered.

Impressed as I was by Isabella's adventures in Hawaii, her next book, recounting her trip through the Rocky

Mountains, amazed me still more. After sailing from Hawaii to San Francisco, Isabella traveled by train to Sacramento and then on to Denver. To see Estes Park, Colorado, had been her big dream, her greatest longing. It had completely captured her imagination. Later, she wrote of her experience in the park as being "rapturous . . . in everything it exceeds all my dreams." Isabella explored the Park on horseback, riding alone over seven hundred miles in the freeze of an early winter. She would set out purposely during severe snowstorms, so eager was she to not miss Mirror Lake, or one of the peaks she'd read about.

It was fortunate that her reputation had preceded her to Colorado, because ranchers who made it a practice to not hire out horses even to men during the winter season had read about Isabella, and would trust her to take one of their horses into the snowy wilds for some unknown period of time. If it weren't enough that she (and her horse) survived blizzards, falls through frozen lakes, and thirty-mile rides with nothing to eat but a handful of raisins, this woman climbed Longs Peak in her cotton Hawaiian riding dress and a borrowed pair of some man's hunting boots.

"Come on!" I yelled out loud when I read that part of the journal. "How is that possible?" I don't care that she had help from a desperado called "Mountain Jim" or that she experienced "extreme terror." It was "12 degrees below the freezing point," and she slipped and fell and grasped hand over hand in the ice and snow for hour after hour in complete exhaustion and "tortured with thirst" until reaching the top of a peak 14,700 feet high. Isabella Bird clearly had the stubbornness of a mule and the perseverance of ten mighty angels. If she could overcome fear and follow her fierce dreams and live to tell about it, I could surely get through this period of my life and create some fun in the process.

PAST LIFE ADVENTURES

THOUGHTS OF FUN always brought up images of Maui. I know that my happy past lives were spent on tropical islands. As a hypnotherapist, I'd found that at some point with certain patients, when the suggestion was made in trance to go back to the origin of a chronic physical symptom, they'd find themselves in a past life having been shot by an arrow or knifed in the back, or hanged by the neck. Or, when asked to go to the origin of a current relationship problem, a past life scene of abandonment, violence, or betrayal would show up. Invariably, after feeling the pain, experiencing their physical death and rebirth into this life, the person would be amazed to find the issue resolved and to feel a new sense of physical and emotional well-being.

When this phenomenon occurred in my office fifteen years ago, I accumulated a library on reincarnation and studied regression therapy with some of the experts, like Dr. Brian Weiss and Dr. Edith Fiore. I also spent many hours being facilitated to explore my own past lives. The theme through most of them was of being violently killed by men. After a number of such lives, I apparently tried to avoid that end by entering a convent at the age of fourteen. I was sexually abused by the priests, contracted a contagious illness, and died at age sixteen. My plan didn't work.

My therapist then took me to the most traumatic lifetime of all—I was a ruthless killer in the Middle Ages in England. My father was a feudal lord who I disdained. My mother, I called "The Whore," because she was much younger than my father and married for position. In a time when peasants were thought to have no souls and were considered chattel, they could be disposed of with impunity. I would climb on my huge black horse and ride into the countryside with my henchmen, terrorizing and killing for the thrill of power. I was nothing more than evil. Apparently, in that lifetime, I had chosen to learn about the darkest side of human beings.

While I had to gently work myself through the pain and grief produced by the experiences of victimization in these past life sessions, nothing could have prepared me for the psychic wounding of being the perpetrator of horrifying violence. During that regression, when I looked into the eyes of the last man I killed with my sword, I saw light, and knew I had none. I felt only dark energy and was devastated to realize I had forfeited my soul.

It took me much longer to recover from this session, and to integrate the knowledge that I was not unlike other people—I had the capacity to kill. I was not a helpless victim in any lifetime. I saw a pattern of my soul's evolution—learning about life by experiencing every diverse situation, like a character actor trying on new parts and living them fully. I began to have more compassion for criminals—not for their crimes, but for their deep unconscious pain and isolation from loving connection. I came to feel more balanced and less judgmental of others.

In my last hypnosis session of that series, my therapist gave me a vacation by suggesting I go to a happy lifetime. I was a great big Polynesian woman walking on the beach. I wore little clothing, the day was beautiful, and I felt an indescribable comfort. I was part of every palm tree, every patch of sand, the water, and the air. I was an integral aspect of the world. There was no negativity, no separation. I knew I had a big family— they were a natural part of the world too. I had no reason to dwell in the past, or feel anxiety about the future. The present peaceful moment filled me to overflowing.

Like Shakespeare, I've come to believe that "all the world's a stage." In our interminable drama classes on the earth plane, we get to play all the parts that teach us the nuances of tragedy and love, and hopefully we get comedy roles as well, so that we can learn the wisdom in humor.

❦

That summer I took my kids and grandkids to Maui. My sister Judy joined us, too. She needed a break from "the horde," as she calls her huge family. I swam in the sea and floated through the days in that tropical air, played in the sand with the baby, and helped three-year-old Ethan over his fear of the water. One evening when Niki was bathing Ethan, he let out a blood curdling howl. And it continued. A flustered Niki came out from the bathroom and explained that all she had done was say what beautiful blond hair he had. He'd yelled, "No I don't. I don't have blond hair." And there was no consoling him. The loud protesting, yelling and sobbing continued as his dad, Charlie, wrapped him in a towel and carried him around until he finally calmed down.

Niki flopped down in an easy chair and looked at me inquiring, "What was that?"

"I have no idea. Some might say it could be a 'bleed through' from a past life experience. Until children are seven, they're much closer to those memories. The good part is, kids can let their feelings come through so intensely. They release, and then they're calm again. We adults train ourselves to suppress feelings and suffer with them. Now," I said, looking over at Ethan happily playing, "it looks like the storm is over."

We returned to our evening activities of getting the kids into pajamas, making hot cocoa, and playing games. Ethan still talks about his memories from the trip—the tide pools, sand castles, learning about whales and dolphins, and that coconut we opened. He got to drink the coconut milk. But he never mentioned his horror of being blond again.

Asserting New Power

In August I helped Megan move to New York City. Record-breaking heat drained the energy right out of me after carting boxes up four floors and making repeated trips to the hardware store for clothes-hooks and kitchen utensils. My daughter the journalist was used to moving. During and after college, she'd lived in Spain, the Dominican Republic, Chile, and Guatemala, with trips interspersed to colorful places like Peru, Venezuela, Argentina, Cairo, and Havana. Her longest residence was in Guatemala, and she'd just returned from a three-week visit there to research a book.

As much as I loved being with Megan in any circumstance, after five days of cleaning and organizing her apartment, I was exhausted. That Sunday afternoon, I was relieved and happy to settle into the back seat of the car I'd hired the previous day to take me to LaGuardia for the flight back to Albuquerque. I'd saved half of my sandwich from lunch to serve as dinner, knowing little or no food would be served on the plane. I'd taken several bites when my cell phone rang. I answered and the voice on the line said, "Where are you? This is Carmel Car Company. I'm here outside the apartment."

"I'm in a Carmel car on my way to the airport," I said.

"That's not a Carmel car," the male voice replied. "You need to get out of that car right now. I'll come and get you."

My body tightened and my stomach lurched, constricted and felt sick. I looked up front to the driver and realized he hadn't spoken a word since I got into the car. He'd just nodded when I said, "Carmel Car?" after I tossed my carryon into the trunk. He was a big, broad man, a black version of Odd Job, the Asian hit-man in the James Bond movie, *Goldfinger*, I'd thought when I first saw him. He sat there, mute and motionless, as the voice in my ear kept repeating, "You must get out of that car now. I will come to get you."

My throat closed, and my mouth dried up. I frantically looked out the windows trying to sense where I was being taken. I was unfamiliar with New York City, but it looked as though we were driving through Harlem. I had no idea if that was the usual route to get to the airport highway. I wasn't keen on jumping out of the car, a blonde white woman in the middle of Harlem, and my body felt stiff, unable to move even if I'd wanted to move it. I said weakly into the phone, "I have no idea where I am." The voice responded firmly, "He's going to rip you off." And I thought, "That's fine. Let him take my money. I just don't want to be taken somewhere and hurt."

That was when I observed myself on the very edge of panic. I noticed it was hard to breathe, and my heart was pounding. I knew then the meaning of the expression, "I was beside myself." I was beside and just above myself, aware that I could easily fall into fear and simply fragment into uncontrollable, dramatic emotion. I was also aware that I had a choice and that losing command of myself would be anything but helpful.

"Who are you?" I demanded of the driver.

"Amsterdam," he muttered. I knew that was the name of the next street over from my daughter's apartment.

"How much are you charging me for this ride?" I asked.

"Thirty-five dollars."

"And can I put it on my credit card?" I asked, as I had arranged to do with Carmel.

"No, cash," he said sullenly.

I had not been listening to the voice on the phone, but now I attuned. "I will still come to pick you up," it said. "I can be there in ten minutes."

But now I noticed signs that said, "Airport," and we were getting onto a bridge. "I can't get out here," I told the voice. "We're on a bridge."

"Go to the police as soon as you get out of the car. Be sure to report him," the voice told me.

"Thank you, I will," I said, feeling a bit stronger. "Thank you very much."

I began to plan a quick escape. I got my money out and a pen and paper. I was prepared to get my bag from the trunk and write down the license number as I did so. As soon as he stopped at the terminal, I quickly went to the rear of the car and got my bag. When I finished writing down the license number, I handed him ten dollars and said, "I'm reporting you." Even though my heart was still thudding and I was aware of the effects of the adrenaline shooting through my body, my voice was calm and clear.

As I turned to walk away, the expression on his face looked as though he'd been wounded, and I could tell he had to suppress a protest. His scam had failed and he'd only gotten enough money to pay for a little gas. Once up on the sidewalk, I turned and shouted, "And next time, say who you really are!"

A woman standing nearby began laughing. I realized that no matter how she interpreted the reason for my anger, the aims of a big bad man had just been foiled by a woman. I was mighty, I thought, as I puffed up my chest and went in to report the incident. It took a while for my heart rate to calm down, and as I waited for my plane, I repeated our group mantra: "A Mighty Woman is aligned with her power—mentally, emotionally, and spiritually. She has let go of all limitations, those invisible chains that held her back from her highest self-expression. A Mighty Woman lives in all possibility."

I wondered if that woman could really be me, but now I

knew on a deep level that yes, she was me. But I also knew that the heroine's journey would continue, and that along the way, I might be required to slay more dastardly dragons, my own inner fears, in order to become the strong, outspoken star of my own life story.

.7.

THE LONG ROAD OF RESILIENCE

UNIVERSAL TRIALS

As time went on, creating Mighty Women groups became a major focus of excitement and fulfillment for me. My coach in the Landmark Self Expression and Leadership course guided me through a structured program to develop community awareness and create media attention so that more women could learn about the benefits of forming and participating in sharing circles.

When Megan was in town, the Mighty Women became younger, as Meg and a few of her friends wanted to participate in our female bonding activities. Since Meg had studied goddess rituals during her world travels, on several occasions she led phases-of-the-moon ceremonies for us. At the new moon, we lit four candles, one for each of the directions, and called in female and male energy to assist us in creating a list of intentions for the month. We wrote them down, folded the paper and let faith flow into them. We then closed the circle, giving thanks to all of the mystical powers that work for good in the Universe. At the full moon, we again invoked all sacred energy and gave thanks for the manifestation of abundance in our lives.

I found that single women in their twenties and thirties had the same concerns that we older women did: self-esteem, work, and relationships. They questioned whether they were living their life purpose and doing their life work. Like Megan, they were often in transition from one city to another and wondering if they were living in the right place. They felt they'd lost an earlier confidence and clarity about their life direction. They hadn't found permanent jobs or relationships, and wondered if they ever would.

And the one thing we all have in common, death, visited these women too. Megan's close friend, Kateri, was losing her stepfather to cancer. Rick had been the only father she'd known, as her natural father had died when she was two. Emily, at thirty, was also losing her father to cancer. Her mother had died when she was an infant, so her father had been her primary caretaker and the parent she was completely bonded with. Our sharing circles seemed to be the only place these women could share the deep pain of their grief. And their capacity for zany humor balanced the sadness with hilarious laughter. Like the time Kateri shifted from the bedside sadness of being with her dying father to describing the in-bed sexual acrobatics of a new foreign boyfriend.

If there was any difference between us, it was that the young women brought more humor to the groups. They had a lightness of spirit that I interpreted as being related to seeing a longer future with greater possibilities. Older women, especially in crisis, seemed to need an entire fan club to ignite hope that the future might still hold a handful of dreams.

Reunion with Heart

I was on my way to the second year anniversary of healing my broken body and broken heart. I was pleased to be doing level-one yoga classes, no longer the restorative classes, and my gym workouts were more strenuous. Strength was especially important as my grandsons were growing. The baby was hefty and, at two years old, was like the Energizer Bunny on speed. Between them they required running after, lifting, holding, rocking, sometimes wrestling in and out of clothes, piggyback rides and romps in the park. It felt important to me to be able to help Niki for a few hours on Fridays so she could have time for herself.

Sometimes, my shoulder would yelp in pain, or the lower back of my head would swell and ache, but ibuprofen and a brief rest usually helped enough that I could refocus on the boys, my work, or the Mighty Women project. My memory ability was still spongelike, but it no longer frightened me so much and had become a joke with my friends. They were used to telling me something a second time, or even a third.

I maintained regular visits to my Rolfer and massage therapist, but was happy to drop out of the other healthcare appointments and reclaim time—time for a new patient, a walk along the river, or a break to have lunch with a friend. With Dr. Rexroad's guidance, I weaned myself off of the antidepressant, and used a sleeping pill only occasionally to insure sound sleep on a night when pain flared or stress threatened to keep me up and make me miserable the next day.

It had been three years since I'd written a paper or worked on a book and four or five years since I'd given a talk or presentation. While my clinical work flowed with ease and nourished my sense of being of value, I had "Bambi legs" again when it came to writing or public speaking. My brain didn't seem capable of creating an outline or an overview, and the idea of memorizing material for a talk was in the realm of the impossible.

Marcia suggested I sign up for a writing class for spring semester, 2006. She was taking a class in world religions. We could go to the university together on those Tuesday and Thursday mornings, she said. And what a lovely opportunity that became. I valued time with Marcia. My oldest friend and colleague was surviving her rare disease with daily chemotherapy, but she walked with a cane, tired easily, and needed my physical assistance to walk slowly from the handicapped parking across the campus to her class. We would go early, have tea at the campus coffee shop, and reminisce about trips in our youth—like the academic meetings we skipped once in New York City, in order to sleep during the day and hit trendy art openings, attend plays, and hang out at jazz clubs all night.

I realized that were it not for the accident, I would have stayed on the same treadmill I'd been on—business as usual. Work and more work. I would have missed this time to slow down and be with Marcia. My strategy for life was to do and do and do more. I'd covered over my insecurities with achievement. If I carried a high enough patient load, I believed life would smile on me. If I was a good enough mother and grandmother, I'd be appreciated. If I wrote the next book, I'd be financially safe. If the right man loved me I'd be happy. It was time to simply Be—still, listening, enjoying interactions with friends and family, and allow myself to feel the love that is always available. I began to spend more time in prayer and meditation each morning, and added to my gratefulness list as I gave heartfelt thanks for my healing.

On the mornings with Marcia I felt a peace I hadn't felt since nursing my babies at three in the morning. (When Niki heard me say that, she said I must be nuts.) I felt totally present and complete in that space of love. I knew I was expressing my value of connection with my dearest friend. If I was coming up from the ashes, I wanted to be creating a life in which I would give to others, and also allow the love to flow back into myself. This time with Marcia nourished that flow.

Once I'd get her settled in at her class, I'd go to mine, where the young, engaging professor provided the structure for writing that I'd never learned. We were required to write for two hours each day, produce a paper each week, read each others' papers, and provide written critiques for the class. Professor Martin patiently answered my questions about terms like "narrative structure," plot exposition," and "sequential summary" versus "circumstantial summary," concepts that the other students knew, but I did not. I kept my humor about the fact that I was the oldest student and the most experienced, yet had, by far, the least training and knowledge about the rules of writing. This idea of Marcia's was a good one for me.

That spring two events occurred that caused me to believe I must be looking strong and healthy again. I'd gone to the gym to pick up the boys from day care, where they'd been while Niki taught yoga. A new child-care worker was there who greeted me with, "Your sons are so adorable. I've loved caring for them." When I told her I was the grandmother, she gasped and said, "How's that possible?" I told her how much I appreciated her comment, and that if she'd seen me the year before she wouldn't have thought I could be their mother. But I was elated, floating on clouds, and shared the story with everyone, including little Ethan, who responded with a blank stare.

A few weeks later, I took the boys to Gymboree. Their dad, Charlie, had taken off work at lunchtime to come and participate. He was on the other side of the room watching Ethan climb on a play structure, when one of the mothers nodded in his direction and asked if he were my husband. I laughed out loud, knowing that her hesitancy in asking reflected her sense that if he were my husband, I was considerably older than he. I told her that Charlie was my son-in-law, but any time she wanted to allude to my youthful looks, I'd pay her big money. Again, I was cheered to think I didn't look tired, old, and infirm, the way I had felt for nearly two years.

NEW WORLDS

THE "CREATIVITY AND Madness" conference flyer arrived in the mail announcing a trip to Vietnam in March of 2007. There was a call for papers. The American Institute for Medical Education provides continuing education for physicians and mental health professionals in exotic settings all over the world. I had traveled with them to give a talk in Greece in 1999, and Jenn had attended a conference with me in Australia and New Zealand. To me, these trips were heaven. Stays in luxury hotels, fascinating talks on the psychology of artists, musicians, and historical figures, guided excursions to the scenic highlights of each country, and credits for yearly continuing education requirements . . . What could be better? These trips offered as much comfort and as much adventure as one might choose. Plus, at tax time they were listed as a business expense.

I'd never had a desire to visit Vietnam, but the brochure sent a wave of excitement through me. I read it over three times. The trip would begin in Thailand. I read about each segment: from Bangkok to Saigon, or Ho Chi Min City, then to Hue, and finally to Hanoi, and then home by way of Hong Kong. I read the descriptions of golden palaces, floating markets, the ingenious underground tunnels that housed 10,000

Vietnamese during the war, the wondrous Halong Bay, background for the beautiful film *Indochine*, with Catherine Deneuve, and I wanted to go.

I called Niki's childhood friend, Sandy Buffett, who had lived and worked all over Asia, and asked her if I should go. "If you have an opportunity to get to Vietnam, you must go," she said. "It's my favorite country in the world. And be sure to go early and spend a few days at the beach in southern Thailand." So I made up my mind. But who would go with me, and what about a paper? Could I actually put a presentation together?

A topic did come to mind rather immediately. I had interviewed Michael Naranjo, a Native American sculptor who'd been blinded by a hand grenade in Vietnam, for my book, *From Crisis to Creativity*. His story of trauma and recovery, grief and growth, was completely inspiring. Using him as an example of "determined overcoming" would honor him and gift an audience. Then there was Jacques Lusseyran, a blind French Resistance leader during World War II. I had written about his miraculous survival and leadership skills in the concentration camp. Together, these men would be the basis for a talk I would give titled, "The Light of Creativity, the Psychology of Resilience."

When I began reviewing the material on these two "mighty men," I realized that their own words were so powerful, and often poetic, they could not be paraphrased. I realized I would have to read most of the talk. With relief, I thought, *That, I can do.*

FINDING WISDOM

MY LIFE WAS returning to a normal hum. In addition to my work and the writing class, I'd enrolled in a "Wisdom Course" that would last six months. It required that participants write an autobiography, one page for every year of life, and find pictures (actual photos, or magazine images) to accompany the narrative. Once again, Megan instigated this adventure in personal development. She had taken the course in San Francisco. I told her when it came to the autobiography, it was not fair. She had only twenty-eight pages to write and I had sixty-four. And I had little memory of the past.

It was fortunate that my mother, at ninety, had a prodigious long-term memory and loved to reminisce about the past. I called several times to ask about the first years of my life. I learned that my grandparents lived with us when I was born in 1941 in San Diego. Gas rationing during the war necessitated families moving in with one another closer to town, in order to get to their jobs. We lived in a very small two-bedroom house near Balboa Park. My bassinet was placed in a corner of the dining room, and Nanna and Grandpa Tommy slept in the living room. I cried every night, Mom said, until Nanna found a solution. She placed a clock with a loud "tick-tock" right next to my crib and that soothed me to sleep each night. It did not surprise me that my Nanna, who I counted on growing up to make my clothes and provide me with a new pair of flannel pajamas every Christmas morning, solved my very first problem—calming down to sleep.

With Mother's help, and an occasional conversation with my sister, I learned about the first ten years of my life. Then I filled in junior high and high school from scrapbook class pictures, fieldtrips, proms, and sports events. I proceeded slowly to access memories of college and graduate school, marriage, jobs, and the births of my daughters. The memories stopped once the girls were in school, so I started working back from the present. Using trips, family events, writing projects—I captured another twelve years. Then I was blank for a fifteen-year period in the 80s and 90s. With some embarrassment, I called on Niki and Megan to tell me what they were up to, and therefore, help me remember what I was doing during those years.

"You have to remember when I was living in Spain in 1989," Niki said. "I called you at five in the morning after my passport was stolen. And then I called a few weeks later from Greece where I was supposed to meet Jonathan at the train station in Delphi, but there is no train station in Delphi. I didn't know what to do." Yes, I remembered.

The time commitment involved with the Wisdom course, the weekend travel, the autobiography, and all the other assignments, was so demanding that many times I questioned the "wisdom" of my choice to continue with the program. And yet, the more I learned about my mother's struggles when I was a child—coping with my father's anger, gambling, and womanizing, caring for his father in our home after the other grandparents moved out, going to work in an aircraft factory instead of accepting alimony at the divorce—I began to understand why my inner child self lived in constant doubt, lacked trust in a caring world, and held the belief that women inevitably end up alone.

Consciously I didn't believe that at all. I was all about independence and self-fulfillment. But through the self-monitoring work in the course, listening to my "young conversations," the automatic ways of thinking and speaking I didn't normally hear, I could not deny that the child part of me was running the show in the relationship arena. She truly believed that since my grandmother got left when she was sick, and my beautiful mother got left when she was well, that must be the way the world worked. And I was just the next victim, powerless to change the tides of women's fate.

One way back to the authentic adult self was to simply notice and "be with" the feelings and "false beliefs" conjured up during times of upset. I learned to write about how life "seemed" from that perspective and create collages expressing all of the feelings that came from seeing life as occurring in that sad or unfair way. Writing and visualizing the "seeming" gave me distance from the experience. I would then write a new possibility for life, one based on an empowered adult perspective. When I was stuck in that place of "there are no good men and you can't depend on a man anyway," I pasted pictures of an old ape, a dinosaur, a devil, a dragon, a terrorist, and a herd of stampeding buffalo on the paper. My grumpiness turned to amusement, and I made a new declaration—that most men, among the billions on the earth, are wonderful human beings, and that there is a special man for me that I will meet when I'm ready to open my heart again and be powerfully responsible and loving.

I eventually covered an entire wall of my study with collages depicting sad, angry, violent, resentful, cynical views of the world, along with humorous, joyous, grateful, loving, and optimistic images. As I tacked them on the wall, I saw the humanity, or the "perfection," some would say, about monsters, spiders, and exploding helicopters, being there with fairies, flying pigs, clowns, and eagles. Maybe I could learn to accept all of it—the darkness and fear along with the light and the love, the struggles and the failures along with the successes and victories. I knew that acceptance is the final stage in the grieving process. Learning to accept "what is" could allow me to create and believe in dreams for the future.

During a morning meditation, I found my own definition of wisdom and I wrote it down. "Wisdom: The ability to lovingly embrace the totality of the past, seeing the perfection of life's unfolding, and in the present create a future filled with magnificent possibilities."

WITCH TRIAL

JUST WHEN I'D get to a place where I thought I could float and balance above the cycles of sadness and elation, something would happen to kick me into the dead-end doubt that characterized my inner child self. It happened at a course weekend in Denver.

The topic for this Wisdom weekend was *The Created Self*, based on the premise that we are all capable and responsible for creating and designing the life we desire. This particular workshop was being led by an attractive, vivacious brunette, whom I guessed to be in her late thirties or early forties. I loved the small group of women who happened to be staying at the same hotel where I was. One was from Seattle, one from New York City, one from Colorado Springs. We'd have breakfast and then drive to the meetings together. We were sharing in the excitement of the new material and reviewing the "fixed ways of being" that would distort perception, limit our self-expression, and block our ability to see our potential greatness.

On Sunday morning, the leader, in describing her own journey, alluded to her happy life now with her husband, children, and an abundant supply of money. I stopped hearing what she spoke of next, just automatically wrote notes. At lunch I felt depressed and angry. Silent outrage bubbled within me about the course leader with the perfect life. My friends noticed that I wasn't as engaged and exuberant about the morning session as they were. "What's up?" Joanne asked.

"I'm feeling so mad and so sad," I said. "I feel like sixteen, in high school. Ann's one of the rich kids and I'm thinking she's a witch with a B. Like who does she think she is being beautiful, married and rich? Oh yeah, and young," I added. "As though anyone can be like her. Well, when you're in your sixties, you can't be like that."

"What's coming up for you?" Patti asked gently. "What's this really about?"

I took a deep breath, thought a moment and then dissolved into tears. "I just got it. Today . . . I just realized today would be my fortieth wedding anniversary. Except it's not. It's closer to the sixth year after my shitty divorce."

The women were sympathetic. Two of them had been divorced and were familiar with the wildness of that emotional landscape. One of them had lost all of her financial resources when she left an abusive relationship. It took years to reestablish her life and her self-confidence. These women were supportive and understood the power of anniversary reactions to bring up more of the grief that needed to be healed. At the end of our discussion, Joanne suggested I create a possibility that would restore my integrity, my power as an adult.

"Well, the act I go into reflexively when I'm stopped in fear is, *I can't cope.* And that makes me a victim and puts me back in childhood. So, what I'll create right now is myself as a capable and loving woman, a woman committed to living in joy in every moment. And I'll write it down as a declaration: 'I am capable and loving. I am committed to living in joy.'" And in that new context, Ann, the course leader, could shape-shift for me from a witch to a queen, and I could transform from bitch to inspired woman, the competent woman I chose to be.

I was learning that rather than suffer alone, every "breakdown" could be an opportunity to share, get a different perspective, let others contribute, and in this case, allow a revisiting and an honoring of the graves, the resting places of those who've departed from our lives. And in doing that grief work, we guaranteed ourselves a "breakthrough," a breaking out of old patterns of thinking, bringing ourselves back to the present. At the end of lunch, we acknowledged how far we had all come on our wisdom journeys and what fulfilling lives we were committed to creating.

My sadness didn't evaporate that day, but the experience brought a renewed sense of the natural cycles of grief and growth and the necessity of sharing our pain with others in order to normalize it. Our natural resilience could emerge from this communion, and we could proceed on our path with a stronger step. Trying to handle my angry projections and sad feelings alone would have given them more validity, would have reinforced the notion that sadness and anger were permanent parts of me, a personal defect that I carried like a birthmark.

Instead, I called Bruce when I got home and thanked him for the many happy years we had together. I told him I still had times of making him wrong, in fact I had just had one, but that my strongest commitment was to our family being close and harmonious. I could tell he was pleased. He thanked me twice for calling. Then I e-mailed Patti and thanked her for urging me to "get clear and complete" with Bruce. My soul felt lighter.

I was growing more confident with every dive into the darkness. I knew I would come back up feeling stronger and brighter. As I worked on my autobiography, I began to see that positive, happy, silly, celebratory experiences far outweighed the negative. Even though death, divorce, illness, accidents, and losses of every sort were catalogued, what truly shone from the pages of my life story were smiles, awards, tributes, travels, family, and friendships. This was a life anyone would be proud and grateful to have lived.

CELEBRATIONS

LOOKING BACK OVER the year, I realized I'd created Valentine's Day 2006, the second anniversary of the accident, as a celebration of Self. My friends and I covered the dining room table with red construction paper, white paper doilies, hearts of all sizes, shapes, and shiny textures, and store-bought kids' cartoon Valentine cards. With scissors and glue, and listening to old pop songs on the stereo, we created cards for ourselves. In addition to the mushy love message I wrote myself on one card, I did another from Bugs Bunny honoring my Inner Outrageous Rabbit. Each woman brought a dessert, and we spent the evening emitting orgasmic sounds of bliss while we ate chocolate truffles, flourless chocolate cake, and coeur à la crème.

The Wisdom Course had taught me to celebrate life with "fun, play, and ease." I'd applied that focus to my life in every way that I could, and especially to every holiday. After Valentine's, the delight moved on to Easter. Stuffed bunnies, chocolate bunnies, egg-coloring, Easter-egg hunts, brunch with little and big friends highlighted the beginning of spring. On Mother's Day, I had a special celebration of all the women I knew who had created or nurtured life. After sharing a potluck dinner, each mother was acknowledged by her adult child or a friend who thanked her for her contribution to the world through her mothering.

Acknowledgment became a theme, adopted from the Wisdom Course and used daily with every person I met. Acknowledging my coffee shop waitress for remembering what kind of tea I order, the market checkout clerk for being happy, my patients for their insights and actions, my friends for their power in expressing support, my daughters for their skills and talents, and the easiest to praise, the "babies," my grandsons every time they learned to get food into their mouths instead of in their laps or articulate a new word, like "Grandma." (Although I would have preferred being called "Bamma" forever.)

I learned that people are starved for acknowledgment. Each time I offered it, I could see eyes beam, auras shine brighter, bodies grow a little in height, and I felt my own heart grow a bit more in loving connection every time I shared in someone's light.

Thanksgiving was the perfect holiday for acknowledgment, so we added a ritual after dinner. All twenty-six people shared what they were grateful for about themselves and their lives, and not surprisingly, everyone ended up acknowledging someone else at the table for enriching their life.

What with writing, wisdom, and a trip to Vietnam and Thailand on the horizon, 2006 seemed like a "banner year." The banner read, I AM WELL. I was happy and excited to be fully engaged in my life again. I was on track, and I felt driven to complete my talk by the end of the year. I arranged to meet with Michael Naranjo in Santa Fe and photograph his latest work. My son-in-law Charlie helped me put together a Power-Point presentation of photos, quotes, and research data. When he asked why I needed to complete the talk in December when I had until March, I said I wanted to have January and February to organize and prepare for the trip. I hadn't traveled internationally since Jenn and I had gone to Australia a year before the accident. I worried about fatigue, jet lag, immunizations and illness. Jenn had told me of infectious diseases in Asia I'd never even heard of. Two months should give me plenty of time to get ready.

By mid-December I felt like I did as a girl waiting to get on the Matterhorn ride at Disneyland. I couldn't tell how much of the pounding of my heart was from fear and how much from excitement, and it didn't matter. I was full of energy. I felt proud that I'd learned how to use a laptop computer. It allowed me to take breaks and work at a coffee shop near my office. The talk for Vietnam was nearly complete. I bugged Charlie to be there with me when I'd go over the presentation so that I'd remember how to use the PowerPoint, save it on a thumb-drive, copy it onto CDs as backup, and learn the timing cues for changing slides. What I didn't have in the way of confidence and memory, I'd make up for in preparation.

Megan was back for Christmas and we had a Christmas Eve party with everyone we could think to invite. Sarah Barlow, my "third daughter," was in town from New York, and we invited friends of hers as well. The house rocked with happy noises of adults and children of all ages. Meg and I also planned our usual New Year's Eve party, and I collected cards for our "ending and beginning of year" acknowledgment ceremony at midnight.

BACK IN THE BELLY OF THE WHALE

ON DECEMBER 27, Meg picked me up from work and we headed to a diner downtown to meet Sarah for dinner. While Megan drove, she talked about her day. She was writing her first novel and was having trouble getting the primary characters established. "I think the heroine is too timid," she said. "I need to balance her youth and shyness with her competence. Oh, and I talked to Kateri. She's in town, so I invited her and her new boyfriend to the New Year's party."

It was nearly dark as Megan exited the freeway to cross Martin Luther King Boulevard on the way to Central. The light was green and traffic was flowing. As we approached the middle of the intersection, I glanced to my right and saw a large white SUV coming at high speed. My brief thought was, *No. This can't happen.* I don't remember screaming, but Megan said later that the sound of our screams were all she could remember. She had no visuals. She hadn't seen the car coming.

The crash occurred in slow motion, very loud slow motion. Time stopped, irrelevant to the movement and sound of metal smashing metal. *How could a car fly and turn in the air?* I thought. *Oh, now we've crashed back to the ground. Good thing for seatbelts. We've bounced up onto a sidewalk. I'm covered in white powder. Oh, the airbags. I'm alive. I'm fine. Megan, are you okay? Yeah. Are you? Yeah. I'm all scrunched down to my right. My shoulder and my right ankle hurt. I must have tried to curl up and protect my head. I hurt all over, but I'm alive. How could this happen? Why would this happen?*

We were able to get out of the car, and I dug my cell phone out of my jacket pocket. I called 911 to report our location. "Are there injuries?" the voice asked. "No injuries," I said. I couldn't walk easily and I couldn't think clearly, so I asked Megan to go into reporter mode and interview the witnesses and the other driver. I looked at my beautiful VW Passat wagon, my first new car, a departure from driving used cars until they were passed to one of the girls and I'd find another "new" used car. (This was a tradition I'd learned from my father, who bought my first two cars at police auctions. Looks didn't matter. "You just need four wheels," he'd say. A mechanic friend of my dad's would keep them running.)

It was dark now, but I could see that my silver VW was completely smashed. I looked at glass, metal parts, and debris littering the area and I sat down on the ground and cried. A police officer arrived and I heard him say, "I couldn't even find the car when I got here. Then I saw it and thought, 'There's no way this is a non-injury accident.'"

Sirens, ambulance, Sarah and her mom arrived and started gathering our things from the car and putting them in a plastic bag. Sarah kept asking if I was all right. She'd look at the car and say, "Oh my god." I looked at the wreck and realized that if the other car had struck just inches back closer to the passenger seat, I would have been seriously injured, if not killed.

A paramedic came over and had me follow his finger with my eyes, then asked a series of questions. I passed the test, but he pushed a little for us to go with them to the emergency room. I said no. "I have whiplash for sure," I told him, as I felt my neck, "but I'll just be sore for a few days."

A flatbed truck arrived to load the car for its trip to the wrecking yard. It was too damaged to be towed. I finished up the call to the insurance company, and Megan completed her notes from the other driver, the witness, and the police officer. The officer told Megan the other driver would be cited for speeding and reckless driving.

It had begun to snow, and Sarah asked where we'd like to go. I said we might as well go to the restaurant and then decide. We'd need to eat something at some point. Sarah's mom, a lawyer, said I should keep track of everything in case this became a lawsuit. She too encouraged a visit to the ER. No, no, I said. "I'll be fine. And I would never go into a lawsuit. I like my lawyers as friends."

Sarah said to not worry about a car for a few days. We could use her father's, the one she used when she visited. She drove us to the diner, just a few blocks away, and said her friend, Eric, would pick her up from there and take her to the party she'd planned to attend after dinner. The pain in my ankle became more intense as I walked on it. I realized I didn't feel at all good. It seemed to take great effort just stay upright.

We settled into a booth in the diner, and I called Jenn.

"Oh no, baby. Are you okay? And what about Megan? I'd come right away, but my stepfather's had a heart attack and I've got to stay here with the family. Please go the ER, and be sure to check back with me." Sarah's friend, Eric, arrived a few minutes later, and she introduced him as an ER doctor from Boston. We laughed. "Perfect timing," I said.

Eric was good-looking, outgoing, and generally delightful. After sharing that he'd gone to high school with Sarah here in Albuquerque, but had lived in the east for about ten years, I turned to Sarah and asked, "Why aren't you two married?"

She gave an embarrassed laugh and said, "We talked about that once, but decided we were close like siblings, not like lovers."

Megan groaned. "Mom, I can't believe you just said that."

Eric picked up with questions about the accident. He wanted to know exactly how we were feeling physically, listened attentively, then suggested we go to the emergency room. "Presbyterian is just a few blocks down the street," he said with a grin.

"Okay, you're the third or fourth person. And I have no appetite anyway. What do you think, Megan? Should we go spend the night at the hospital? Right now all I want to do is lie down."

Megan's friend Kateri met us in the emergency room with bags of food, water, magazines, and even a board game. Thank god for friends. She entertained us during the four-hour wait for an exam room. When they called our names, Megan and I gratefully lay down on treatment tables for the remaining hours of the hospital visit.

A nurse technician put neck braces on us, and while we waited for the doctor, we spoke of where we were having the most pain. Mine was right ankle, shoulder, neck, and I had a mild headache. I'd been hit on the same side as my previous accident.

"Bummer," Megan muttered. She said her neck hurt and her lower back. The impact probably reactivated her broken pelvis and sacrum, injuries she'd sustained in a climbing accident in Tahoe two years earlier. Her climbing "buddy" let her drop sixteen feet onto granite. She'd had to be airlifted to a nearby hospital.

"I still can't believe that happened to you, Meg. I will be forever grateful that you didn't have a spinal injury. Whatever happened to the idiot who let you drop?"

"She had to leave Tahoe. Moved to Alaska, I heard. You just don't make mistakes like that in technical climbing. "

We went on to reminisce about long waits at the vet with pets when Meg was a little girl. We had amused ourselves by impersonating animals. She cracked me up with her tongue-waggling, hissing snake, and I did a pretty good Bugs Bunny–like chipmunk.

The young woman ER doc, another Megan, was kind enough, but looked disheveled, as though it'd been a long night. We didn't have the energy to correct her misconceptions—like the assumption that we'd been stopped at a light and didn't look for oncoming traffic before venturing into the intersection. She ordered X-rays on my ankle and shoulder, and another hour and a half later, sent us on our way with prescriptions for pain meds and ibuprofen. The X-rays were negative for fractures, she said.

Megan had called Bruce to come and get us. We'd agreed that neither one of us was in any shape to drive. We were exhausted, and I could barely walk. *I guess bad sprains make for bad pain*, I thought. Megan was annoyed that I hadn't been given crutches. Bruce breezed in, always comfortable in a hospital setting. I thanked him for coming at this odd hour in the morning. He said he was happy to. He and his brother had been up anyway, drinking good whiskey and trading fishing stories.

"Let's see the 'scrips' and I'll take you to get them filled. You'll probably need some pain meds the first couple of nights, and we should get you some kind of soft brace for your ankle."

Outside, the snow was falling steadily, collecting in drifts around the parked cars. Streetlights reflected a golden glow like a second sunset repeating itself for reassurance. The beauty and the stillness contrasted with the pain in my ankle and the woozy feeling in my head. That otherworldly light helped me stay calm and quieted the fear that questioned, *How hurt am I, and will I heal fast enough?* The snow continued falling. When Megan and I awoke to bright sunlight the next day, the snow was deep enough to shut down the entire city.

.8.

FINAL CHALLENGES

MAGICAL ASSISTANTS

As strange as it was to be snowed-in in Albuquerque, sunshine usually showed up in the Land of Enchantment, and the 28th day of December was no exception. It was bright and clear outside. The view of snow draped over the trees along the Rio Grande River and spreading across the city to the mountains looked like a sea of vanilla ice cream rising up into craggy cones. Even though Megan and I were sore and achy, we had to get out in that exquisite scenery. We put on our snow clothes and walked to a restaurant a few blocks away to have breakfast.

The afternoon was planned. Friends who were also Reiki masters were coming to do treatments. Annie, from my Mighty Women group, had called to say she'd be out grocery shopping and would bring us some supplies. She was comfortable driving her four-wheel drive in the snow, she said, and she'd just made a pot of stew. She'd bring us some.

I wore soft, comfy snow boots on our trek, and with the ankle brace my foot felt fine. We carefully set our feet into the deep snow, watchful to avoid the icy ruts beneath the soft snow along the sides of the street where the snow had melted and then frozen again. I felt happy, the way I felt at ski resorts on a walk to the village when taking a break from the mountain activities. I couldn't stop talking about how good I felt, almost euphoric, that my body felt strong.

The pancake house had a festive air. It was full of families and tradesmen, the school and workplace cancellations having created an automatic holiday. The moment I sat down my head felt as heavy as a bowling ball and a dull ache set in at my ankle. I asked Megan to order Swedish pancakes for me and then lay down in the booth using my fleece jacket as a pillow. A feeling of heavy fatigue settled in my head. When the food came, it took much effort to sit up and eat. There was no way I'd be able to walk back home.

Megan called Annie to ask her to pick us up from the restaurant. As I listened to her describe how I looked "done in," I realized I had spent the last twelve hours in post-trauma shock and the 3 Ds of grief: denial, disbelief, and dissociation. The very last thing I wanted to face was the idea that I might be injured and impaired—again.

Our Reiki treatments that afternoon calmed my body and dissolved some of the tension in my head. Megan said she felt better, too. Her neck felt less stiff. After our friends left, we looked straight into each other's eyes, agreed that we would heal with ease and speed, and slapped a high five. Then we agreed that we needed to cancel the New Year's party. We were not up to the preparations, and few people would be able to brave the snow to get to us. Where the snow was not deep, it was now ice. The next days were lost in sleep, soup, and rest. Megan flew out on the second of January, after setting up appointments for chiropractic and massage, and calling in for an extension on her latest feature story.

The first weeks of 2007 I scheduled fewer patients and kept my foot elevated and iced. Fatigue sent me to the sofa between sessions, whiplash gave my head and neck their own language of distress—swelling, aching, and nagging pain. My ankle and leg produced a few of their own descriptors for pain—"sharp," "shooting," and "excruciating." Ibuprofen and Tylenol bottles began to take up space in my makeup bag and appointments with my body workers again filled my schedule book.

I was told of a rehabilitation chiropractor, now in Albuquerque, who had worked with world-class athletes in Colorado, and I scheduled an appointment. When I met with him and complained of the agonizing pain in my calf, he used "deep, myofascial release" to free "three trapped nerves." I stifled the urge to scream obscenities as he dug his fingers through muscle and massaged nerve endings. My eyes closed so tight I saw stars, like a comic book character taking hits from an opponent in a fight to determine who will rule some newly discovered planet. My chest filled with hatred, my lips pursed tight to hold in air that if let go would fly off the walls with expletives.

But when he finally removed his hands from my leg, the tension and discomfort dissolved from my calf. I went limp. The nerve pain was gone. Appreciation filled every part of my body where just seconds before there had been a raging ocean of protest.

I told the story to Niki with great excitement, but added that my head and neck were still complaining, acting like they did after the previous accident. Niki recommended I see her teachers in the cranial-sacral method of massage. And again, I was so fortunate that they could see me quite soon. They were between teaching engagements.

In the tranquil setting of the treatment room in their home, with the fragrance of aromatic oils and skilled, loving hands, my body was able to relax completely, and my mind floated free of pain and worry. Greg and Judy worked on me together, one on my lower body, the other sitting behind me, holding and sometimes massaging my head or neck.

I felt nearly "normal" for days following the first two massages. But then the headaches, swelling, and spasms in my neck returned. During the third visit, Judy asked if I would be comfortable with Greg doing "mouth work," an advanced form of cranial-sacral massage where the therapist places a hand inside the mouth to manipulate the bones of the face. "We typically work on the outside of the head, the cranium, but this work is done to re-adjust the inner bones of the head," Greg explained.

"I'm up for whatever might help me," I said. "Go ahead and do what you're trained to do. It can't be worse than the dentist."

Greg put on thin plastic gloves and placed his hand inside my mouth. My first awareness was that I had no impulse to gag—unlike my last dental visit when several metal gadgets were poking and gurgling, a drill was driving dangerously toward an exposed nerve, and the insertion of a gloved hand claimed all remaining breathing space.

Greg's hand was gentle but firm, as his fingers found the areas to work on. My mouth felt full, but the sensations were of intense pressure on the maxilla, the hard palate, and other bony areas Judy referenced at the end of the experience. After several treatments of mouth work in conjunction with gentle cranial-sacral massage, my head and neck felt like they'd been re-introduced and taught how to live together again, in a little more peace.

Still, my ankle forced me to act like a handicapped person. I could walk from my car to my office, but friends had to drop me off in front of a restaurant, conference center, or theater. Even a short distance of walking sent pain shooting from my ankle up the side of my leg. My soft brace stabilized the foot at night, but as I lay in bed the pain turned into a burning ache, and there was no thermostat to adjust to off. Deep restorative slumber might settle into other people's bedroom chambers at night, but not into mine.

So I found myself back in my friendly psychiatrist's office discussing prescriptions for sleep. I felt apologetic as I explained to Kevin that I'd been in another accident. I listened to myself tell the story as though I were trying to convince him of my innocence, as though I'd already been indicted and found guilty of . . . improper development, immaturity, moral laxity, or maybe hubris? I liked the word *hubris*. I'd learned it in graduate school. Hubris: "the excessive pride and ambition that usually leads to the downfall of a hero in classical tragedy." Maybe I'd begun to feel too good about myself, too enthusiastic and confident about my life. Ambition and excitement had temporarily masked who I would always be—a victim. I'd gone and invited another calamity into my life.

These thoughts bubbled up and troubled me as I explained more details about the crash and the hospital visit. These were the same depressing doubts that came bursting through a door in my mind after the divorce, the previous accident, and the breakup with Ben. Most of the time, I could see them for what they were—my ego parading as truth, my fearful inner child, convinced that the only way to stay safe was to stay small. At other times, like now in another doctor's office, I questioned whether I had any real choice, or self-efficacy, in the matter of health and happiness.

I didn't want pain medication, I told Kevin, but I was

worried about my chances of recovering quickly enough to go to Vietnam. Kevin agreed that medication for sleep was indicated, but then asked if I thought I might benefit from a few months back on the Lexapro. He had heard my inner thoughts driving up anxiety about the trip. Jet lag, exotic illnesses, and immunizations were the least of my problems now. I couldn't imagine being strong, pain-free, and fit. I agreed to take the antidepressant, as well as whatever he thought best to prescribe for sleep. Kevin asked that I go easier on myself, have compassion for the shock and surprise of another injury. He also suggested I monitor the ankle pain.

"Sprains can take some time, but if it doesn't improve, go to your orthopedist and have another X-ray. Sometimes fractures aren't picked up in the ER. And if headaches continue, just for peace of mind, consider seeing a good neurologist."

As with the previous accident, I ignored those recommendations. I continued with rest, bodywork, meditation, and prayer. I was deeply thankful that I'd been compelled to complete my talk before the end of the year. It felt like divine guidance. If I were able to make the trip, at least I needn't worry about the conference. And I was relieved that an old friend, Corky, a substance abuse counselor and photographer, had asked to come with me to Vietnam. "I've always wanted to go there," she said. "I don't know how I'll find the money, but I'll make it happen." So I had a buddy and a roommate for the journey.

SPIRITUAL MUSCLE

IT AMUSED ME to remember that my only access to prayer after the previous accident was cursing. Now, every morning as I sat down to pray and meditate, pleasure and gratitude welled up in me. The five-step prayer outline I'd learned from the study of Science of Mind became the basis for my first "miracle prayer." I found my spiritual muscle hadn't atrophied one bit. The first step is to "recognize" the Oneness, the Allness of God. This is what I wrote after each step:

1. *Recognition:* I know that God is all there is. Everything else is illusion.
2. *Unification:* I am created and have my Being as an expression of God energy. I am God expressing.
3. *Realization:* Therefore I know that my natural way of Being is healed, whole and happy. I am now healed. God energy flows through my body and my mind.
4. *Thanksgiving:* I give great thanks for this grace, this wonder—the beauty of my calm and peaceful life.
5. *Release:* I turn this prayer over to Spirit and to my angels to manifest. And so it is.

If I wasn't pain-free that day, I held the awareness that I would be healed in God's time, not in mine. I had to renew this faith daily for many weeks.

X-ray Vision

ONE NIGHT, THREE weeks after the accident, I lay in bed and cried. The pain in my ankle was impossible to sleep with. I decided then and there that I'd better learn more about the sprain, whether I needed a cast, and what the course of healing would be. The next week, sitting in the orthopedist's office, we looked at the new X-rays together. Even with my untrained eye, I could see the fracture running down along the side of the fibula.

"So here's the break," the doctor said. "And of course you

also have 'stress tendinitis.' We'll put you in a boot and get you going in physical therapy several times a week. Hopefully, you'll be okay by your travel time."

I was annoyed that I was just another "broken bone" to him, and I was more annoyed that "his" hospital didn't find the fracture the night of the accident. But most of all I was relieved that now, with the proper care, my ankle could heal, and I chose to be grateful.

HAWK MEDICINE

I WAS IN "grumpy grieving" mode one morning as I prepared to go to physical therapy. I'd gotten out of my soft brace to get dressed and put on the boot, knowing I'd have to take it off before I got into the car to drive, then put it back on to go into the clinic, take it off again and get into sneakers for the therapy, and back on and off throughout the day. I was also worried about the snow I'd have to trek through, winter having taken itself so seriously this year.

And I was worried about driving—scared as hell about driving. I'd seen five accidents on the freeway one snowy day on my way to work. At each messy wreck, I'd wince, and my heart rate would zoom, especially when I saw one of the occupants being carted away on a stretcher. I was on my third rental car, the first two having felt small and flimsy, not durable enough to withstand a crash. Behind the wheel of these cars, my neck stiffened up at every intersection, and I'd look for new routes to avoid having to cross traffic to make left turns. And I had to shop for a new car, a big car. Test-driving cars on icy roads—ugh. I hated the whole idea.

I grabbed my coat and turned for one last survey of the

kitchen. A glance at the large dining window gave sight of a big hawk sitting on the terrace railing. I gasped in surprise and delight. *Okay, what's the message here?* I thought. Living by the river, I saw many hawks. On several occasions, I felt they showed up just for me, like the time I was sitting on the ground in the garden planting flowers and a red-tailed hawk dove down so close to my head, it sounded a deep "whoosh" and feathers barely touched my cheek as it went by. More often, I'd see hawks, or an occasional eagle, soaring in circles high above the river.

Roadrunners were frequent comic visitors, suddenly zigzagging along in front of you on a path or on the street ahead of your car. One even hopped over the Dutch door and ran around the kitchen of our big house years earlier. Hawks, however, were rarely known to come and sit on your veranda, as though they were waiting to have a long chat.

Native Americans see Hawk as the messenger of the gods. Hawk medicine teaches keen observance and awareness of life from a higher perspective. In seeing the overall view, "the magic of life" is available. This magic is in the power and responsibility to overcome stressful or difficult situations. "You are only as powerful as your capacity to perceive, receive, and use your abilities," I read later in my *Medicine Cards* book. In the book, Hawk's power to see the broad picture is contrasted to the mouse, who lives with its nose to the ground. I got that I was being a mouse, small and fearful. It was time to choose to see the broad picture, choose to accept yet another "initiation into life" and transcend the obstacles that would bar me from freedom of flight. The obstacles were my inner fearful thoughts and judgments.

I nodded in reverence to the noble Hawk, and sent a "thank you" for the visitation and for the gift in the message.

FACING DOWN THE DEMONS

I NOTICED HOW my consciousness bounced between two polar opposites: One side held complete faith in my ability to heal, make the trip and deliver my paper. *I am always guided on my path. All of my experiences are for my ultimate learning. My life is unfolding perfectly for my highest good. All is well.* This was my truth, and I believed it absolutely.

And then the opposite, the lower level, the automatic fall back to fear, the ego in all its negativity, my inner ogres would sneak out of the darkness and take over. In this state, all was lost. *I can't possibly heal in six weeks. I've been walking on a broken bone all this time. I can't stand the pain. Even if my ankle gets better, how could I get through all day tours and maneuver airports? And my head still hurts, and my brain is fuzzy. Why did this happen to me? I heard that if you cause an accident, it's because you're angry; if you're the victim of an accident, it's because you feel guilty. I thought I was free of all that shit. I guess I still feel guilty and unworthy of a great life.*

My ego voice was either that of a small helpless child or a nasty critical adolescent. It promoted cynicism and worry as a way of life, derided thoughts of potential greatness, interpreted self-nurturing as self-centeredness, and self-love as the sin of selfishness. "Stay small. Stay right where you are," it would say. "There's nothing better for you in this world, and everything beyond the house and your own front yard is dangerous."

Hawk's visit inspired me to haul myself back to my adult "voice of reason," my loving Higher Self, my God-Self, my Presence. In order to do that consistently over the next weeks, I sometimes had to call a friend to coach me back to sanity. One said, "Accidents happen. We may never know why . . . or we may learn later on. Feel your sadness about it and keep faith. Keep taking very good care of yourself."

Another friend read a quote to me that she used daily as an affirmation. I later learned that it is from Louise Hay. "Everything I need will be provided. Everything I need to know will be revealed." I printed that quote and added it to the "visuals" I kept in my bedroom, my study, my car, and tucked inside my wallet—my miracle prayer and my message from Hawk. "I see the broad picture of my life," I wrote. "I accept the power and responsibility to remove every obstacle that would bar my freedom to soar."

PRESENCE AND POSSIBILITY

ONE EVENING I watched Tom Brokaw on television hosting a re-enactment of the horrifying survival story of Aron Ralston. This young climber had gone alone to climb in Utah's Blue-john Canyon. As he neared the bottom of one of the crevices, an 800-pound boulder crushed his right hand and pinned him down in a small, cave-like area for six days. No one knew where he was. Suffering dehydration and hypothermia, he realized he was facing death. He tied a tourniquet around his arm, got out his all-purpose climbing tool and laboriously cut off his own hand.

Just hearing the description made me close my eyes and turn away from the T.V. For me, death would definitely be preferable to hacking off one of my limbs. That kind of bravery I couldn't relate to. It was his total commitment to life that pulled me back to watching the show, fascinated by subsequent events. After belaying down cliffs with a bloody stump, he walked miles until spotted by a rescue helicopter. With rest and medical attention, Aron engaged with rehabilitating his body with complete enthusiasm. Now, with a special prosthesis, he is back to all of his athletic endeavors—climbing, bicycling, and paddling.

Aron's book, *Between a Rock and a Hard Place*, is now a feature-length movie 127 hours starring James Franco.

"Insist on yourself," Emerson said, in his essay "Self-Reliance." Aron Ralston insisted on life. Some of my women friends, too, are outstanding examples of resilience: Marcia, in her refusal to be held back from her travels and academic studies, let alone die from her disease; Jenn, in her insistence on being a physician to others in the midst of her own breast cancer surgeries; Diane, in her fight to walk again after paralysis left her in a wheelchair. All of these people insisted on themselves. I would do the same. I declared my intention to be powerfully present for myself, take charge of planning every aspect of my life, and do it all coming from an attitude of joy.

Physical therapy became fun. I pretended I was a real athlete in training for a world-class event. My physical therapist was a young man who'd coached soccer in previous years. He pushed me when he thought I could do more, cautioned me not to overdo when I set a higher weight on the leg lifts or wanted to walk more than fifteen minutes on the treadmill, and while guiding me in my workouts, expressed confidence that I'd be ready for Asia when the time came.

I set up an appointment with a colleague for EMDR (Eye Movement Desensitization and Reprogramming) to get over my fear of driving. The session reduced my fear enough that I was able to test-drive cars even in crappy weather. Son-in-law Charlie researched crash-worthy cars and found one in my price range. With my friend Corky along for moral support, I bought the smallest SUV I could find just weeks before we left for Thailand. I felt safe and high, as in "high up," as I drove. On two occasions, I noticed cars prepared to roll through stop signs until they saw me in my little SUV—they saw me and stopped. Very cool, I thought.

I had a very long to-do list of preparations for the trip, and I delighted in checking off each one: immunization visits, special travel containers for pills and supplements, sun protection clothing, comfort items like neck supports and a pilot-designed inflatable seat for the plane, and the perfect medium-size suitcase for packing. Then there were the e-mails establishing which resort in southern Thailand we would luxuriate in for the first five days before the conference began.

One morning, the quotation at the beginning of the inspirational message I was reading was by Hafiz: "Fear is the cheapest room in the house. I would like to see you living in better conditions." I smiled at the recognition that I was now choosing to live in "better conditions." Fear is not only the cheapest room in the house, I thought, it's often the biggest. No longer. I would renovate, tear down walls, and expand the "great room" of my heart and mind. And I would give my body and mind even more attention in order to be as comfortable as possible before flying off to strange new worlds.

.9.

VICTORY OVER THE PAST

RELEASING THE PAST

As certain as I was of my ultimate healing, I was also impatient. I didn't want my shoulder to hurt, my neck to go into spasm, my head to ache, or my ankle to send out pain signals. I wanted to clear as much discomfort from my body as I possibly could before the trip. Somatic Experiencing was one trauma resolution treatment I hadn't made use of. I had attended a two-hour workshop in Santa Fe five years earlier with Peter Levine, the founder of the method, and was captivated by his films showing animals literally "shaking off" and "breathing out" the tension from their bodies following an attack by another animal. After three deep breaths and a twitch of their flanks, they returned to normal life as though nothing had happened.

I hadn't gone on to take the long and intense training required to practice the method, but I knew a psychologist who had—Carol Hamilton. I was very grateful to find that she was in town and willing to see me on short notice. Her office in an old house in Old Town was filled with family antiques and books overflowing their shelves. After I gave permission for her dog to remain with us, he curled up comfortably by my feet and didn't move for the entire session.

Carol asked me to describe what happened during each phase of the accident. As I did so, she'd ask what my body felt like doing at that very moment. When I saw the car about to crash into me, my right arm wanted to strike out, I told her, to block the impact. Carol had me extend my arm out with as much strength and power as possible in slow motion, over and over. I imagined myself to be a superhero—able to prevent the bigger car from hitting us, able to protect my daughter from harm. I began to cry, realizing that part of the guilt I'd carried was about not being able to protect Megan from another accident. Even though she hadn't been hurt as much as I had, the maternal urge to prevent harm to her had internalized as failure.

My right foot and leg wanted to walk away from the accident unharmed, so I imagined doing that. My neck and head surprised me the most. Remarks had always been made about my long neck, gawky like a giraffe, or elegant like Audrey Hepburn. I preferred the latter comparison, but when my neck spoke, I fell into tears again. It always wanted to be stronger, it said. It felt weak and vulnerable, especially after this third accident. It felt hopeless about ever having the strength to hold my head up effectively, without effort and pain.

My head expressed great sadness that it wasn't smart enough to protect me from so much hurt over the years. If it were only smarter, it thought, then everything would be all right. I was sobbing now, filled with compassion to hear these parts of me expressing their false beliefs and deep fears that something was irreversibly wrong with them. Their only desire had always been to keep me safe and serve me as well as they could. I recognized what I called my "inner child ego states" and what Eckhart Tolle calls the "pain body," and all I wanted was to bring them love.

I felt like an abusive parent, suddenly struck by the insight of how hurtful I'd been toward innocent children. My head and neck needed to know that they hadn't failed me at all. I was always ready to judge them harshly, to expect more—more strength, more stamina, faster healing, greater brilliance. "I'm so sorry," I said to them. "Please forgive me." And since guilt calls for forgiveness, I forgave my adult self as well.

Carol invited me to place my hands on my head and say, "This is my beloved head in whom I am well pleased," just as God blessed creation. I repeated this several times, and then did the same for my neck, my heart, my legs and feet. Carol suggested I imagine my feet and legs together as one, like one tree trunk, strong and grounded. I envisioned divine energy coming up into me from Mother Earth, flowing from my trunk to every part of my body. I felt like I grew a little as I did this, and I automatically stretched my arms out like the limbs of a tree reaching for more air and more light.

I felt somewhat disoriented after the session. I didn't know what to make of the experience, and I seemed to move through the rest of my day on automatic pilot. I loved the idea of blessing my head and my neck, and I did that in the evening before bed. The following morning, I began to cry during my meditation, and I couldn't stop. Tears spilled down my cheeks during yoga class, and I kept tissues out while I drank my tea at Starbucks. I cried as I paid for my office supplies at Staples, and I cried as I picked up my dry cleaning. I turned off the tears that afternoon at my office, but then continued weeping through dinner that evening.

Niki once described to me how massage sometimes unlocks energy that has been held in the body since childhood. She called it a "release." I had facilitated many "abreactions" during hypnosis—highly emotional expressions of pain, rage, and deep grief connected to childhood abuse, but this was subtle, and yet profound. The somatic experiencing had allowed a "release" of old, negative energy—sadness about not being "good enough," not measuring up to expectations—that had lodged in my mind and connected to every part of my body.

On the second day, I felt lighter and pain-free. I blessed my head, neck, and entire body, and I felt so comfortable I almost cancelled my next appointment with Carol. She had re-arranged her schedule to accommodate two appointments, however, so I was back in her office the following week.

"I'm inside my heart," I told her. "It's like a small chapel in the woods—very lovely, but overwhelmingly sad—from so many lifetimes of loss and hurt. It's fearful, not strong. It's afraid of being left—it's always ready to retreat, withdraw and hide." Carol instructed me to look very carefully at my heart and to see it as it had been when it was strong and invulnerable. It took some time, but then I began to see a very old, maybe seventeenth-century, cathedral. It was like a fortress, built of chiseled rock. I was in awe of its beauty, but still aware of its sadness.

"I've had so many lifetimes of suffering," my heart said, "I never want to reincarnate and take physical form." Carol asked me to slowly stretch out my arms and begin to gather all the "past life selves" energetically with my hands and bring them into me. "All of you are One Soul," Carol said, "with all of these experiences. Your heart is the center of your power, aligned with your mind."

I continued pulling the energy with my hands and bringing it to my heart. I felt my chest strengthen. "I can't be destroyed,"

I heard myself say. "I am eternal, always growing in consciousness." I felt that to be true—that my heart, the center of my being, was sacred and indestructible. I felt a sense of awe, and I felt deeply humbled.

After the session I asked Carol how she knew to do that kind of work with me. "Is Somatic Experiencing always spiritual like that?"

"Oh no. I simply follow where your energy goes. And you had important spiritual business to take care of at this time."

There were no tears after that session. I felt free and clear and open to fun. The next afternoon, I took Niki and the boys to lunch at the aquarium cafe. I could think of nothing more enjoyable than to eat New Mexican food, watch sharks, sea turtles, and ugly brown eels swim unselfconsciously in the comfort of their own living room—and see my grandsons in a state of total delight.

MAGICAL FLIGHT

WHEN I FINALLY checked in at the White Beach Resort in southern Thailand, everything about the long plane rides to get there became inconsequential and forgotten. Orchids and exotic plants surrounded the open reception area. The view looked down on a turquoise-tiled oblong pool with eight sculptured elephants sitting cross-legged, sending out fountains of water across the pool's surface. Beyond were palm trees, plumeria, and a broad white sand beach surrounding a small private bay with blue sparkling water stretching out to the horizon.

This area had been hit by the tsunami of December 2004, but twenty-seven months later there were no signs of the disaster. Jenn had gone to Indonesia for one month to provide services as a doctor in Aceh province, where over 200,000 people died or went missing after the tsunami. She would have liked to come on this trip, but was planning another journey, this time to China and Cambodia to set the groundwork for a medical outreach program she was creating.

Each spacious room at the White Beach was like its own small villa. Thai art and silks decorated the bed and walls, and the smooth teak floors invited bare feet. No sign was needed to remind us to leave our shoes outside on the veranda. Corky and I changed clothes and went down to the beach. She disappeared with her camera, and I found a chaise longue beneath a tree and remained there until dinner. At the beach restaurant, over pad thai noodles and fried bananas in coconut milk, we agreed that we had entered a new world—a peaceful world, a world of "no worries," as the Aussies say, and we wondered if it were possible to make that an internal world of contentment and bring it back home with us.

For me, the answer came that very evening. My ankle, swollen from the inactivity of travel, began to ache, and my mind reflexively began to worry about the long days ahead. The worry turned to anxiety, and that fearful ball of tension in my chest was distracting. After a shower, instead of using my small travel hair dryer, I plugged in an electric brush the size of a power tool. A loud explosive pop accompanied flames shooting out of the wall outlet and all of the electricity in the villa went out. I was horrified. I thought I'd wiped out the electricity in the entire resort. The workmen who came later told me I hadn't, and Corky, always calm, said to not let it bother me, but I realized that contentment would require constant monitoring of my ego's fears. I would need to develop the mindfulness of a monk.

Being in paradise made it easier to control my mind-chatter, or "mind monkeys," as Jenn called them, but the "noise" of the ego was always in the background waiting to emerge. I had to acknowledge there were fewer worries here to be caught up in—only three decisions to make each day: should we lie on the beach, should we lie by the pool, or should we eat . . . again? But I wanted to learn to catch my fears and rein in my ego before it hijacked my good judgment. I wanted to live in conscious choice, not unconscious anxiety.

That night I had a dream. I was climbing a ladder. I had to climb very high to reach an old Chinese woman who was giving me a beautiful, intricately wrapped black bag containing CDs. She said she didn't need them any longer. I knew the CDs were Eckhart Tolle's recordings of *The Power of Now*, the messages I'd played over and over after the skiing accident when I was unable to do anything other than lie in bed. The wise "crone" was telling me to stay in the "now" and accept whatever happens. "Nothing stays the same, not even the sea," she told me. "Be flexible, open to learning. Enjoy everything that comes next."

I took her message to heart and realized that one morning meditation was not serving me through the entire day. In my state of vulnerability to fear, worry, and short memory, I needed to support myself by adding two more brief meditation times into my day, as well as several minutes of deep breathing—all in order to keep myself consciously focused on each moment.

REFUSAL TO RETURN

NATURALLY, I DIDN'T want to leave the beach. I never wanted a beach vacation to end. But then I never wanted any vacation to end. I felt I could have stayed forever on one of the Greek islands, or on Bali, or New Zealand. Although I was excited to join the conference in Bangkok, I had a feeling I also wouldn't want to leave Asia at the end of the meeting. And then I remembered the message from the wise woman in my dream: "Nothing stays the same. Be flexible and open to learning." What if I could be present and accepting of every twist and turn on the path, with no evaluations and judgment—what would that make available to me? I wondered about that on the way to the airport. I closed my eyes and took a meditation break. I imagined a wave of relaxation flowing down over me, and when the answer came, I smiled. Acceptance of every "now" moment would allow me to be in a peaceful space from which to simply enjoy the journey.

On the ride from the airport into Bangkok, Corky clicked photos out the window, and I watched the huge city rolling by with its fascinating blend of traditional Eastern buildings and temples, and modern Western skyscrapers. I'd felt pampered at the intimate beach resort, but the luxury of the Shangri-La Hotel surpassed anything I could have expected. I adapted so easily to indulgence that after Corky observed me poolside being served an elegant lunch on a rosewood tray, she took to calling me the "Queen of Sheba."

It did feel queenly and like incredible good fortune to be able to visit the Grand Palace of the Emerald Buddha, the Royal mansion—the world's largest golden teak building—and gardens with streams, lakes, lush flower-beds, and topiaries in the shapes of elephants, rabbits, and deer. And I felt like royalty at every meal—international cuisine overflowing from ballroom-size buffet tables. Fabulous food, stimulating talks, and wonderful tours filled our days in Bangkok.

I felt sad when I brought my bags to the lobby in preparation to fly to Vietnam. But I noticed that it was no more than the natural sadness I had when getting out of my warm bed in the morning, letting go of that comfort and adjusting my mind to look at "what's next." From awareness, I could choose how to Be about the next part of the journey, and I chose to be excited. I looked around the lobby and blew a goodbye kiss to Shangri-La.

MASTER OF TWO WORLDS

HO CHI MINH City (Saigon prior to 1975) brought back memories of living in Los Angeles, participating in peace marches, watching television images of monks setting themselves on fire, and volunteering at the offices of Another Mother for Peace. It was sobering to actually be in this country where the longest military conflict in U.S. history took place. Between 1959 and 1975 fifty-eight thousand Americans were killed and from three to four million Vietnamese lost their lives.

Corky and I were both quiet and subdued that first day. Many of her clients were veterans of that war and were still struggling with drug and alcohol problems. Several had committed suicide. We talked about all this while looking out over the city from our hotel balcony that night. We agreed that our guilt wouldn't change a thing about the past, so we released it to the soft, warm beauty of the night and stood entranced by the splash of neon colors and tiny white lights shining out through the darkness.

The next day I could see why I had been warned before the trip that the greatest danger to tourists in Vietnam was crossing city streets. I couldn't have imagined it—over four million people (of the six million population in this city) were on motor scooters. The streets were clogged with them, everyone honking, weaving in and out, going up on the sidewalks to avoid stops, and then zipping back into traffic. Worse, there appeared to be no rules. When a light turned red, about half the scooters stopped. The rest kept going, plus scooters kept on coming from the other direction so that pedestrians were totally at their mercy. A tour guide gave us one instruction: "Once you start to cross the street, don't stop. Keep going and let the traffic go around you. They're skilled at avoiding pedestrians." I hoped that was true.

I wouldn't cross the street alone. I required someone to be on either side of me holding my arms. The three of us would move as one battle ram (that was the power image I held in my mind) as we marched through the throng of motorized wheels, my heart beating in my ears. From the safety of the sidewalk, I could take in the vitality, the vibrant energy of the Vietnamese people. This young population (so many of the elders having died during the war) are quite literally "on the go," working hard, creating industries, bringing in multinational companies, and growing their rice production to be the second exporter of rice after Thailand.

A visit to the Cu Chi Tunnels was an impressive reminder of how persistent and committed the population of Vietnam was in their efforts to expel foreign occupation in order to unify their country. For much of the twentieth century, they had been fighting China, France, and then the United States. The tunnels, now a unique outdoor "museum," were an underground network of living areas, hospitals, and factories several stories deep that housed up to 10,000 Viet Cong guerrillas and villagers during the war. For the exhibit, there were large dugout actual size models of the rooms and activities that took place below ground.

I watched as one of the tour guides brushed away dirt and leaves to uncover a round covering no more than two and a half feet in diameter. He held it high, straight up over his head as he carefully lowered himself into the hole in the ground, his hands the last part of him to disappear as he neatly replaced the cover. I thought of how clever the Vietnamese were to place pepper around the holes so that the army's German Shepherds couldn't smell the humans below. But then infrared scopes were used by the Air Force to see the trails through the grass that the people made at night to get to the fields. Massive defoliation followed so that the tunnel entrances could be more accurately bombed. Over nineteen million gallons of chemicals were dumped over South Vietnam, 66 percent of which was Agent Orange, a mixture of acids with a dash of dioxin, one of the most lethal poisons to the human body. The area was reduced to dust and dirt for many years, until life won out and trees finally began to grow again.

An old army tank half covered with camouflage netting was back off the trail to my left, and about thirty yards to my right was a still-active firing range. I felt the old sense of pressure on my chest and shortened breath that signaled anxiety. I refused to think of being in those tunnels, and I backed away from the group who planned to follow the guide below. Relief and nervous laughter followed when I almost thumped into several other women who also wouldn't consider the tour of the underworld. Both were much younger than I, and they too had suffered physical injuries from accidents they wished to put far behind them.

I thought of the mythology of the underworld. More than three thousand years before Christ, the Goddess Inanna, "queen of heaven," ruled over Sumerian civilization. Sumerian women are credited with having invented writing as a way to keep track of the grain supplies stored in the temples for impartial dispersal. Dedicated nurturing was inherent in the feminine divine nature. When Inanna's partner, Dumuzi, died and was sent to the underworld, Inanna made the journey to rescue him. She had to pass through seven gates and leave an article of clothing at each one as she made the descent. By the time she reached the land of the dead where her sister was said to reign, she was completely naked. Inanna was told that Dumuzi could return with her as long as someone committed to spend six months of the year in that dark place. His sister volunteered.

Later in history, during pre-Hellenic times, Demeter, the Earth Mother, faced a similar trial. Her daughter, Persephone, was abducted and taken to the underworld by none other than Hades himself. Demeter searched relentlessly in every part of the earth until she was exhausted and bloody. Hecate, the crone, came to her and together with Helios the Sun, they discovered what had happened to Persephone. Demeter was devastated by grief and withdrew into deep mourning, causing the earth to become barren. She refused to allow crops to grow until Zeus intervened and commanded Hades to release Persephone. The earth was restored to fertility when Persephone was reunited with her mother—but only for six months of the year. A balance would be held between the cycles of growth, death, and regeneration.

While there are many variations of these stories, the theme is consistent. Life requires darkness as well as light, struggle and stillness, the sadness of loss and the joy of recovery. Wisdom is gained through experiencing all aspects of life, death, grief, and rebirth. Many of us make this journey to the underworld, and on this journey we are always aided by intuition and by the light of our higher self, our connection to the divine. I saw at the Cu Chi Tunnels that it is our acceptance of two worlds, the dark and the light, the outer and inner, that bring us mastery and a sense of balance.

REAL RESILIENCE

THREE DAYS LATER, I would be giving my talk in Hue, the ancient Imperial City, at a hotel that sits along the meandering Perfume River. On arriving in our hotel lobby, posters and banners announced a festival at the Citadel, the former site of the old capitol. That night after dinner, a group of us decided to walk over the bridge and cross the moat to the palace and the gardens where the festival was being held. Every tree was festooned with twinkling lights, and large areas of the park were taken up with magnificent electrified dragons and phoenix birds. We watched one of the colorful dance performances from just outside an elegant sit-down dinner being served to several hundred people and then wandered among the other stages and pavilions. It was a delightful night. The next morning at breakfast, we learned that we had participated in the annual three-day festival celebrating the defeat and exit of the United States. We had felt no hint of resentment, only a neutral acceptance of our presence.

The morning of my talk, I concentrated on steadying my nerves. This was the first presentation I'd given in years. I was worried about having to read so much of it and of breaking eye contact with my audience. I looked at myself in the mirror and said, "You can do this, Gail." Then I sat down to meditate. I went inward to the beautiful, strong cathedral of my heart. I became aware of a Spiritual Presence there with me, and I asked that divine energy to guide me and to inspire my message so that it would be helpful to as many people as possible. A deep calmness and sense of inner peace suffused every area of my body and stayed with me throughout the day.

That afternoon, standing on the stage of the hotel ballroom, I spoke of two men who exemplify extraordinary resilience— Jacques Lusseyran and Michael Naranjo. I described how each man not only accepted, but embraced his blindness. Lusseyran wrote that soon after losing his eyesight as a boy, he went to a place "deep within. I was aware of a radiance emanating . . . I could feel light rising, spreading, resting on objects, giving them form . . . I felt indescribable relief and happiness so great it almost made me laugh. Confidence and gratitude came as if a prayer had been answered. I found light and joy at the same moment . . . "

Lusseyran maintained his inner "light and joy" after being imprisoned by the Gestapo and throughout his eighteen-month stay in the concentration camp at Buchenwald. He was a beacon of comfort, reciting poetry in different languages for thousands of men as they were dying. Of the 2,000 Frenchmen who entered the camp, he was one of just 30 survivors. All told, nearly 400,000 were put to death there.

Michael Naranjo, blinded at nineteen by a hand grenade in the Vietnam War, told me, "Life is a challenge, a game. If you accept it, it's a gift, and the inspiration and the dreams you have can come true. My blindness is a gift. It has given me a new way of looking at life." Michael returned from Vietnam and re-created himself as a sculptor. Not only has he generated a large body of work, some in museum collections, the White House, and the Vatican, he has taught workshops for disabled groups, high school students, and educators, and has created "touchable" sculpture exhibits, so that other blind people (and sighted as well) can have the pleasure of "seeing" and feeling art kinesthetically.

I told my audience that these two men from different generations and different cultures shared a common bond much more important than their physical blindness. They expressed the primary quality that distinguishes resilient people from others who don't fare as well—optimism, the capacity for positive thinking that allows for hope and causative action in the most difficult circumstances. The other driving force so evident in their lives was compassion.

Jacques Lusseyran called on the last remnants of his energy to soften the pain of his fellow inmates in the camp. Michael Naranjo committed to making a difference for others who are blind. They never gave up, they gave back.

While these individuals no doubt had a natural propensity for positive thinking, the good news for those of us who naturally go negative is that positive thinking, or cognitive restructuring, can be learned. The most important first step is awareness. I presented the four-step "real time resilience" exercise developed by Professors Karen Revitch and Andrew Shatte at the University of Pennsylvania. I had begun to use this for myself and shared it as a "self-coaching tool" with everyone I knew.

1. The first step is to identify the adversity. Pose the simple question, What happened? 2. Next, ask what are your beliefs about what happened? What do you tell yourself about it? What do you make the experience mean? What are the automatic thoughts that take over? 3. Look at the consequences of your beliefs. How do your thoughts and feelings about the event impact you? Negative thoughts are always disempowering. 4. Finally, challenge the beliefs. Go back to the original problem and hear it as a fact of life. See it from a new perspective.

My example was the accident: 1. I was in an accident and my ankle was broken and a previous head injury reactivated. 2. The second step, what we believe about it, what we tell ourselves about it, is where we bring in all the drama. I could go on about how it was the other person's fault and it wasn't fair, and it means there's something wrong with me, and certainly lots of things wrong with that other driver, and I had lots of pain, and I may never recover fully, and so on. 3.The consequences for me to stay in this type of negative thinking would be anger and a slow sink into depression. Whether it's anger, depression, obsession or paranoid thinking, the impact is always emotional and always disempowering. Negative thoughts take us out of our hearts and out of connection with others. 4. To challenge our beliefs, we go back to the event and state it like a news reporter: I was in an accident caused by another driver. I suffered injuries that required months of therapy. And now, I get to choose how to be about it. I choose to be positive and completely optimistic about my healing. And I choose to be grateful that I escaped serious injury, and I choose to believe that I was divinely protected. In other words, we get to move on and create new possibilities for the future.

Many people in the audience came up to me after the talk. They were appreciative and inspired. Dr. Barry Panter, the director of the conference, asked if I would give the talk again the following year in Santa Fe, and he also asked if I would consider letting him use it as a chapter in his next book. He loved the presentation, he said, and he loved the title, "The Light of Creativity, the Psychology of Resilience." I was floating.

The talk had gone well in spite of the fact that I had read much of it. I would give the talk next year to their largest conference (eleven or twelve hundred people attend the Creativity and Madness Conference in Santa Fe), plus, I could invite Michael Naranjo to be there. I continued floating in that happy state of self-appreciation and overall gratefulness through the end of our stay in Hue and through the preparations for the flight to Hanoi. The first day in Hanoi, I would have an opportunity to practice "real-time resilience."

The Ultimate Boon

HANOI WAS HEAVENLY. The lakes, parks, villas, the Old French Quarter where narrow alleyways are still named after the goods that were traded there—Silk Street, Gold Street, and even Fried Fish Street—called for immediate exploration. Art galleries were everywhere and I was especially taken by the lacquer paintings, one small one in particular of a Hmong woman holding an umbrella, with a red and gold brushed background. I decided I must have her and went through the customary bargaining over price. Thirty U.S. dollars seemed more than fair.

That afternoon at the Museum of Literature, our guide, "Tom Hanks," spoke about Confucius. (The tour guides in Vietnam were mostly young, very well educated and good humored. They took nicknames, as it would be impossible for Westerners to remember or pronounce their real names.) He told us what I had learned about Confucius when I wrote about him in my book, *From Crisis to Creativity*—that five hundred years before the Common Era, Confucius taught the Golden Rule: "Do unto others as your heart prompts you. Do not do to others what you do not want done to yourself." Also, Confucius, he said, not Aristotle, was the first to teach balance in life, "nothing in excess."

At the end of the afternoon, in spite of my fatigue, I had to make one last purchase—a duffel bag to pack all the gifts I'd acquired for the trip home. Corky and Toby, my shopping buddies, spotted backpacks and duffels for sale, and I picked one out and went through the bargaining process with the street vendor. A few minutes later, I reached for my camera and realized it had been stolen from my backpack. I was shocked, upset and angry, but most of all I was terribly disappointed. All of my three hundred sixteen photos were lost.

I was in a funk all evening. The next morning I realized it was time to practice what I'd just preached—real-time resilience. Number one: What happened? *My camera with all my photos was stolen.* Number two: What are my beliefs about that? *It shouldn't have happened. People shouldn't steal. Something bad shouldn't have happened to me again. It's just plain wrong.* Number three: What are the consequences of holding onto those beliefs? *I'll be sad, mad and a pathetic victim for the rest of the trip. Ouch.* (Another good question to ask is, What would be the consequences for those around me? *They would have to suffer my irritability and there would be a disconnect in my relationships.*) Number four: What is the challenge to my beliefs? *Shit happens. The fact is my camera was stolen. It's just an object. I'm grateful I wasn't run down by a motor scooter. And the other fact is, I'm traveling with a photographer. Corky's already taken over three thousand photos. I know she'll share them with me.*

After clearing away the negative thoughts, I created a possibility for the day—to live in grace, power, and freedom. At Ha Long Bay, a World Heritage scenic wonder, retaining those feelings would be effortless.

The day was gray and overcast as we got on the bus for the three-hour trip north from Hanoi to Ha Long Bay. The coolness was a welcome departure from the normal 100-plus degree temperatures and 98 percent humidity we'd become accustomed to since arriving in Asia. We'd left the hotel very early, but instead of falling back to sleep, I watched the contrasts in the countryside. New manufacturing plants near Hanoi gave way to donkey carts going to market loaded with pigs and chickens, fields of flooded rice paddies next to fields of waving grasses, bicycles along the road carrying up to three people, at least one of them balancing parcels or baskets of food, and an occasional time-ravaged cemetery, paint gone from the head-stones, grazing cows the only visitors.

I was happily surprised to see the tourist boats at Ha Long Harbor. Instead of the modern boats I had imagined, these boats were old and made of wood. They looked like pictures I'd seen of Chinese junks. Some of the smaller boats had a single bright orange sail. The small "family" boats had an umbrella or a piece of cloth rigged to provide a small area of shade as they plied the waters from village to fishing sites to markets.

As soon as we moved out into the bay the scene became otherworldly. Giant limestone fingers jutted up out of the water like colossal mutated mushrooms covered with moss. I read the ancient legend that had dragons descend from the heavens spitting out jewels and jade which turned into the islets and islands that formed a wall to keep the Vietnamese safe from Chinese invaders. Supposedly, it was a mother dragon and her children who came to protect the people here, and then decided to stay. I imagined them beneath the water, the gentle monster mother with green scaly skin, her wings tucked along her sides, keeping a quiet vigil.

The gray sky turned the bright blue water I'd seen on post-card pictures to a dark green, but the giant limestone islets kept their many shades of olive, emerald, and lime colors. The day remained gray, like the color of ash, but far from dull or dismal, an uncommon peace prevailed, a stillness that felt sacred.

Corky spotted the hawks first. They were slowly circling high above one of the islands, but seemed to stay near the boat for hours—three, four, and then six of these large regal birds, whose singular life purpose was to fly and soar to great heights. I remembered my personal visit from Hawk with the message to see from the broad picture the "magic of life." And I thought of my declaration at that time—"I accept the power and responsibility to remove every obstacle that would bar my freedom to fly." I felt an awesome gratefulness to the hawks for reminding me to stay in commitment to my own life purpose—love and connection, and constant awareness of the "magic of life."

Sometime in the afternoon, after gliding among some of the nearly two thousand islets in the bay, the view opened to a landing dock with a dark cave high above, the opening nearly covered over by bright maroon hanging bougainvillea. We walked winding stone steps, forever it seemed, to enter the caves into another magical world. Limestone stalagmites and stalactites grew out of the cave floor and descended from the ceiling like bizarre forms Merlin the Magician could have created with a wave of his wand. Maybe he created the lighting, I thought—the greens and blues, and an occasional red, illuminating shapes and casting shadows, sometimes blotting out the path, at other places allowing it to show the way.

The ancient, uneven path led down inclines, arched across bridges and curved back up flights of dark stone steps. The darkness seemed to absorb Corky into it, along with the mass of other tourists. I noticed a slight urge to panic when I couldn't find a familiar face, then I reminded myself of where I was—safe in the womb of Mother Earth in one of the most beautiful places on the planet. I continued to move slowly along the path, stopping now and then to gaze at a pool that had become a magic wishing well, coins shining up through the dim water. I passed a gallery of smaller caves with pools at their base, the sound of dripping water echoing off the walls.

When I emerged back into the outside light and took in the sight of the bay below, I inhaled deeply and realized the beauty and excitement of that dark world had taken my breath away. I needed to take several more deep breaths to be back in this world, fully inhabiting my body.

On the boat again, floating back to the harbor, I reflected on this gray, ethereal day with the dark but colorful caves. *Heaven on earth* was the thought that came to mind. I felt as though my Miracle Prayer had been answered. In the fourth step, thanksgiving, I had affirmed "great thanks for this grace, this wonder—the beauty of my calm and peaceful life." This day at Ha Long Bay felt like the ultimate gift—a powerful, loving connection with all of God's creation. I was completely present and aware of my blessed and peaceful life.

The bus pulled up in front of our hotel after dark. We had less than an hour to dress for a formal farewell dinner and packing to depart at six in the morning, as wake up calls would come at 4:30 A.M. As I stepped off the bus, I saw a small antique shop I'd not noticed before across the street. The lights were on, and it looked like it might still be open. I told Corky I had to go there. She raised her eyebrows in a questioning look, but came along.

The shop was very small and very dusty. We looked at carved wooden elephants, bookends, and candlesticks. On a shelf in the very back corner of the tiny room, I saw a female bust. I asked the shopkeeper to please get it down, and before he could remove the dust, I knew that she was the reason I'd come to the shop. The ebony black bronze rendering was of a Hmong woman with an elegant long neck, head with hair pulled back into a knot, and a peaceful expression on her face. The Hmong people are said to have come from Siberia and the high mountain areas of China. For political and economic reasons, over many hundreds of years they migrated into Southeast Asia. The shopkeeper said that when they reached Vietnam, they renamed themselves Hmong, which means "Freedom." I was thrilled to have found her.

The next challenge for this Hmong woman, I thought, as I carried her in a box back to the hotel, would be her migration to New Mexico. My single suitcase was stuffed beyond closing and my new duffel was crammed with gifts and handcrafts from four cities and numerous villages across Thailand and Vietnam. Corky assured me that there were things I could leave behind, and if wrapped in clothing, the statue could safely inhabit my backpack for the trip home.

My bust weighed sixteen pounds, but felt like sixty by the time I'd carried her through the Hanoi, Hong Kong, and Taiwan airports. I created a mantra: "Freedom from the past, joy in the moment, freedom from the past, joy in the moment." The freedom that she represented kept me going until we got to Los Angeles. There, at the airport, a nasty female security guard who was operating the scanner when my backpack moved into view, hollered, "What the hell is this?" When I said it was a piece of art, she replied, "No it's not. It's a bludgeoning item. And it's not going on the plane." So Miss Hmong had to travel in the baggage compartment of the plane from Los Angeles to New Mexico.

She seemed even more beautiful when I removed her from the backpack and unwrapped the clothing to check on her before leaving the Albuquerque Airport. I laughed when Corky said, "You have to suffer for art," but at that moment I felt I no longer had to suffer for anything. I preferred my mantra, "Freedom from the past, joy in the moment."

.10.

FINDING THE FREEDOM
TO FLOURISH

The Keys to Transformation

I wanted to end this story by saying I returned home from Asia and lived happily ever after. But that's how fairy tales end. In mythology and in real life, the most difficult part of the journey ends, but the treasures found along the heroine's path must be practiced. Sharing and declaring the treasures are the magic keys to transformation. These were some of my treasures: support and inspiration from friends; insight and understanding from dreams; lessons in calmness and presence from writers like Eckhart Tolle and Eva Bell Werber; teachings in integrity and connection from Landmark Education; animal visitations with messages to attune to the meanings of life energy; reminders from Spirit to live in faith, to believe in myself and the power of the Universe to manifest my heart's desires. The affirmation my friend shared with me was true—"Everything I need will be provided, everything I need to know will be revealed." I found the source of that quotation when I rediscovered a book I had loved many years ago—*You Can Heal Your Life*, by Louise Hay. Her declaration had proven to be true. Every thing I needed on my journey was provided; everything I needed to know was revealed. I was learning and sharing my treasures with others, and I was filled with gratitude.

Just days after my return from Vietnam, I was scheduled to give the same presentation on resilience at the VA Hospital in Albuquerque. I was pleased that my energy hadn't been reduced to a dribble by the twenty-two hour flight-and-airport marathon that marked our return from Vietnam. Instead of jet lag and exhaustion, I was excited to give the talk again, and motivated to write a piece for my website titled "Reflections on Vietnam." But as I worked at my computer, a rash on my face and neck kept drawing my attention. The pain and itching was especially uncomfortable on my forehead.

The rash had started before the trip, improved in Asia, but now began to flare again. This was not the typical dry, eczema-like rash I'd had in the past, but a painful red inflammation. The very thought of scratching it brought a cringing knowl-edge of more pain, longer healing and bloody scabs. The rash was accompanied by bloating and diarrhea, which I'd easily ignored in Asia. The plethora of wonderful food there kept me eating to distraction, and chewing a few extra Pepto-Bismol tablets to keep my gut calm.

I went to a dermatologist who thought the rash might be a contact dermatitis related to wheat. She told me to stop using shampoos that contained wheat. (I discovered that all the shampoos I normally used contain wheat. There was only one wheat-free product, she said, available though the pharmacy of one of the large Target stores. It had been developed at Johns Hopkins for people with extreme wheat sensitivity.) Despite changing my shampoo, weeks went by, and the rash continued.

I intuitively knew that the irritation was not caused by an outside agent. I believed it was systemic.

A gastroenterologist who knew my history suggested I might
have become sensitive to wheat and should go off all wheat/
gluten. That was easier said than done. Who would guess that
soups like chicken with rice or vegetable would contain wheat?
I began carrying a magnifying glass to insure that I could read
the ingredients list on every product I bought. Off wheat, the
rash improved, but didn't go away. More puzzling was the fact
that taking one bite of salad with vinaigrette dressing or passing
a spoonful of ice cream into my mouth would sometimes cause
my lips to redden and swell.

I made an appointment with a practitioner of kinesiology
and nutritional counseling. Through muscle testing, my body
told her that it had parasites—blood flukes. Hmmm, that
sounded creepy. How would I get blood flukes? And more
important, how could I get rid of them? Janet said they come
through the skin, often when walking barefoot. Since the rash
started before the trip to Vietnam, she said I could have gotten
them from any number of the foreign countries I'd visited over
the years, most likely Mexico.

I remembered that Megan had struggled with skin rashes
a few years earlier. She, too, had gone for traditional evaluations, which included lab tests with blood and stool samples.
Nothing was found. From her work with an energy medicine
practitioner, she was told that she had two different parasites,
one of them blood flukes. Megan's body said the parasites were
contracted during stays in Cuba and the Dominican Republic.

Janet put me on supplements to support my blood and liver,
and suggested that in addition to the wheat, I stop eating all
dairy, soy, sugar, spices, and condiments. That was daunting.
I gave up bread when I found that rice breads with no sweet-
ener tasted like crumbled cardboard. Then I lost my appetite

altogether and dropped eight pounds in two weeks. (The unfairness in this is that I'm a skinny person.) Eating held no appeal. Why would I eat a baked potato with no butter? What's left in Mexican food without flour tortillas, green chilies, and cheese? And what woman on earth could live without desserts—especially chocolate?

Feeling food-deprived was made worse by the fact that the rash continued regardless of eating a Spartan diet. On occasion, after sneaking some chocolate dessert or coffee ice cream, there would be no change in the condition. Janet assured me that three to six months on the diet with supplements would allow the healthy cells to prevail.

Since most restaurants had little that I could trust to ingest, I bought a rice cooker and found special containers to take my own brown rice, fish, vegetables, and fruit along with me when going out to eat. Planning and organizing my food seemed to take tremendous energy and focus, and the food was bland and boring. I was increasingly angry and resentful at having to put so much attention on what I could eat.

*

I practiced "real-time resilience" frequently: 1.What's so? A rash. 2.What do I believe about it? *It's taken all the joy out of eating and out of my life. I worry it'll never go away.* 3. What are the consequences of those beliefs? *Irritability, hopelessness, depression.* SOS—*same old shit.* 4. What is the challenge to those beliefs? *The fact is I have a systemic inflammatory process, likely due to parasites.* (A live blood-cell analysis by a different practitioner gave the same diagnosis.) *It will take time for my body to process the intruders and to re-assert its healthy balance. Learning to eat a diet rich in vegetables and unprocessed foods will support my health and could even help me avoid cancer and live a longer life.*

I was feeling less and less mighty as the rash persisted and the lawsuit I said I would never pursue became necessary. The same insurance company that I had been with for over thirty years also covered the woman who caused the accident. While they took care of her needs immediately, the original agent I talked with left the company and left me to deal with six different adjusters. Finally, I called a lawyer Jenn recommended as being a "hotshot" in personal injury law. I was impressed when I met Mr. Hotshot Lawyer and felt confident that he'd be able to represent me very well.

I noticed, as I put together the information for my case—medical records, police reports and my own lengthy account of the accident—it felt like I was simply taking care of business, like organizing my study or paying my bills. Tension and anxiety, those familiar undercover intruders, were absent. I was calm and efficient. I knew I could handle whatever would be required of me, even if that meant depositions or a court trial. I was stronger and more confident in my behavior than I had been in years.

My thoughts, however, would run off down that old rutted road of worry. The rash seemed interminable and the diet impossible. Headaches had returned, and I was unhappy with the small office I'd moved to after my officemates retired. A taciturn, stingy old man owned the office building. Under the guise of being energy efficient, he wouldn't allow the hall lights to be used. It was unacceptable that my trauma patients should have to come and go to my office through a dark hallway. I made requests, wrote letters, threatened to report him to the city, and complained a great deal to my friends. It was during all of this that I had the following dream:

Megan and I are preparing for a dinner party, and I'm expressing concern that there won't be enough food. I look into the large, empty living room to see ducks and ducklings chasing around the edge of the room while a big gentle lion looks on. I was delighted by this dream. Immediately, I could see how the ducks and ducklings represented my worrisome thoughts—fretful, fast, and going in circles. The lion symbolized power in leadership—strength, grace, and responsibility.

The message from Lion, according to the Animal Medicine book, was "Lead where your heart takes you." I realized that in order to follow my heart, I would have to keep learning to control my mind—herd those ducklings into a safe little pen, so that Lion could focus on the important business of living. Lion would take only positive, well-considered actions.

I had insight, knowledge, and the practices of meditation, prayer, and real-time resilience on my side. And still my ego would seize every opportunity to scamper on stage and yell, "There's something wrong out there. Worry about it!" I knew what I'd said to my patients about those little egos—*"Your inner child ego states need more love and more adult guidance."* But I didn't want to love those inner parts of myself. I wanted them to get the hell out of my life. They were less like cute ducklings and more like little demons booby-trapping my "best laid" plans.

I was talking about this with Ginger Reid, a Landmark Education friend and life coach who lives in Dallas.

"How do I reconcile this love/hate relationship with my ego? I'm like my patients who just want to get rid of those annoying inner kids—throw them out of the house so that I can live my life from my strong adult self."

"The more you resist them, the harder they'll fight you," Ginger answered. "You know the saying, 'What you resist persists.' What if you were to see them as your opponents in a game—on the tennis court, for example? You'd respect them—recognize that they are there to challenge you, keep you in top shape, constantly in training to win each match. You might lose a game occasionally, but in the long run, you'd be victorious. We all need worthy opponents to test our intentions."

I took that metaphor to heart. It was helpful to view my ego with respect and responsiveness. Maybe I could grow to love that part of me that required that I stay alert and attuned to all of my needs—maintain my executive function, be the gentle lion, sure and certain of his intrinsic power. I hired Ginger to be my life coach for the next four months. I told her I needed someone to hold me accountable.

A few days later, I arrived at my office to find an eviction notice on my desk. I immediately called Ginger.

"Can you believe this? I've received an eviction notice from my office," I told her. "I've never been evicted from anywhere." My new coach laughed.

"That's wonderful. You know you made this happen," she said. "What did you plan to do—stay in that office being unhappy and complaining? This is a gift. Now you can move your office to your home as you once said you'd like to do, or move back to San Diego, as you've also mentioned."

As always, Ginger, with great love, didn't indulge my complaints or allow me to be a victim of circumstances. At the beginning of one session, when I wanted to talk about my rash, she said no, she wanted to know what I was doing about my headaches. I'd been sharing my concerns about the symptoms of occipital swelling and eye fatigue that had come back and prevented writing at my computer. During this conversation, I recognized that it was time to take action and not let the ducklings keep running around in fear. I told Ginger I would make an appointment to see a neurologist.

Several weeks later, I was in Dr. Berger's office preparing myself to hear the results of the tests. He greeted me warmly and invited me into his office, offering me a chair next to his computer. As he inserted the CD of the brain scan, he said, "You have a fantastic brain. It's completely normal. There's no reason why you shouldn't be sharp into your nineties, like your mother." That was music to my ears—an entire concert in three sentences.

He showed me all of the normal areas of my brain, then pointed to my neck. "Here's the problem. You have bulging disks here at C 5-6 and C 6-7. These are slightly worse than the neck injury of the first accident. That's why you're having symptoms. There's nothing wrong with your eyes either. But after a second concussion, it simply takes a longer time for the nervous system to recover. There's no reason why you shouldn't recover completely."

I hopped and skipped out of the office to my car. Then I called Ginger and Megan and everyone else I'd sprinkled with my worries and told them the good news.

❦

The next afternoon was grocery day. I'd shopped at the Co-Op, a local organic green food market and returned home to unload my supplies and produce, fruit and a family-sized bag of brown rice. I'd taken the toilet paper and toothpaste downstairs to my bedroom and was coming back up the stairs when I saw . . . a small snake coming down the stairs. It was draped down the middle of three of the stairs and looked directly at me. This snake was much smaller than the one that had visited me in my bedroom. I didn't feel like screaming, but I was definitely shocked and uncomfortable. *At least this time,* I thought, *I left the front door open, as though I'd extended an invitation. This visit is not quite so mysterious. On the other hand, I don't know a single soul who's had a snake lounging in their home, not even on one occasion.*

My thoughts were flitting between how I would get the snake out of my house and what it was I was supposed to learn from the appearance of this small serpent. I chose to believe that this was an emissary from the snake world telling me how pleased they were with my learning. I was continuing to "transmute the poisons" of life, handle problems as they occurred (with a little help from my friends), and help others to do the same.

Yes, I was being validated, saluted, congratulated, and honored. And so, having decided on the purpose of the visit, I could then take action. I tiptoed up the stairs around the creature, went to the phone in my kitchen and called my next-door neighbor, Paul. He was surprised when I named the critter I needed help with, but he didn't laugh. He brought a small box and a stick, and managed to get the now-squirming snake into the box. I took it across the way to a community garden and released it back to nature.

Later, I went to the Animal Medicine book to see if there was more I was to understand from Snake's visit. Of course there was. I gleaned from the reading that I was not embracing "the magician within," that part of me that could truly transmute poisons into the power of creation and rebirth. In order to embody the divine energy of wholeness, the book said, I must stop resisting the release of my "outer skin," my present identity.

Maybe the skin rash is about this struggle to shed my old self, the self that's been living with those well-known roommates, Fear and Limitation, I thought, as I put the book down. Well, I'm committed to becoming all that I was born to be in this lifetime. I will do whatever it takes to be fire energy, the "flame" of passion, personal power, wisdom and wholeness, I declared. And I'll continue praying for guidance, strength, and clarity.

THE POWER OF SELF CARE

I CAME TO see Ginger as two parts angel, one part drill-sergeant. She gave me endless exercises and posed powerful questions. At every phone session, she led the inquiry with, "What are you creating for this week?" And since there were usually a string of complaints at the beginning of our call, she'd ask, "How could you put your stress into what you want to create?" My concerns about moving my office were transformed to a vision for my perfect workspace. Ginger then requested that I list the actions I would take to make my vision a reality.

"You are the designer of your destiny," she'd say. "You get to choose your mission in this lifetime. What are you choosing?"

"I choose excellent health," I told her on one occasion.

"What are you doing to support your 'excellent health'?" She asked. When I told her I did yoga and meditation, and was doing my best with the special diet, she asserted that it was a weak program. What she'd heard in my voice as I described my activities, she said, was resignation, not joy or enthusiasm. Ginger asked me to design a complete "well-being schedule," a document that would show me by the day and the week all of the ways that I was committed to "excellent health."

My health and well-being schedule listed my usual activities, and at Ginger's suggestion, I added a hobby (for me it was drawing), an additional form of exercise (walking was my choice), and time spent with friends. When I told her I was feeling isolated without my colleagues, she requested that I find five new ways to connect with my former colleagues and old friends. In addition to the detailed activities, Ginger asked me to track my attitude—how I was being as I carried through on my practices. Was I positive and upbeat, or negative and resentful? And she asked that I add one event each week that would truly make me happy. In all of this, she advised that I consistently come from the context of "creating" versus "getting through" life. *Great distinction*, I thought. I'd spent the last few years just "getting through."

As the weeks passed, I felt better, stronger, and more responsible. Ginger would say I was being "at cause," rather than "at the effect" of my life circumstances. And I had to admit, in the grand scheme of things, my life circumstances were not a big deal. I had it pretty good. And I'd learned from Jenn that I could "stand in a bucket of shit" for as long as it takes . . .

My Own Crone

IN EARLY JUNE I noticed I was feeling irritated and impatient during family gatherings where Bruce was present. *Oh yeah, the wedding anniversary, I thought.* Discouraging feelings snowballed to other areas, like my imperfect health, being alone with no man in sight, uncertainty about my new office, inability to write with any reliability.

All this pulled me down a rung on my ladder, so I discussed it with Ginger. She suggested I do two things: 1. A "clearing" every morning before I meditated: Write down all the worries and false beliefs that are there as soon as I wake up. Recognize them for what they are—fears of the ego, the opponent. Then create a possibility for the day, a "stand," or an affirmation of who I will be that day and what I will accomplish. Write the affirmation on my planner where I will see it frequently during the day. 2. Write a letter to myself from my self at age eighty.

Ginger said I would find that exercise to be an amazing experience. Somehow, I doubted that.

After clearing away my dinner dishes that evening, I sat at the dining table with my yellow pad and a pen. I took several deep breaths and cleared the misgivings out of my mind. Then I began to write:

Dearest One,

You are a light on the path of so many people. All that you experience is in order to understand life as human being and share this with others. In this lifetime, you have chosen to be a teacher of light and joy. Never worry about the sadness. You have that so that you may know with certainty that happiness is light—the true emanation of Spirit and of who we are. Live more in that joyous light. Allow yourself to feel it. Bathe in it so that you radiate the reason you are on earth.

Open your eyes to your bright future. You needn't worry about the divorce. You and Bruce agreed to this on a soul level. You completed your work together by creating Megan and Nicole. You can continue to enjoy your family. There is someone you are to meet and marry who will be the partner of your dreams. You will aid one another in the next stage of your work on earth.

Wake up to your mission of happiness. Your partner will be a consistent reminder of how simple life can be. Your grandchildren, Ethan and Adam will also be teaching you much about the simple joy of living in creative Spirit. Trust your body and its intuition about how to care for it. Your body will heal. Relax into the awareness that all is well. You can and will have everything you desire.

I put down my pen and thought, *My God, that was me? I am amazed. Ginger was right.* I sat there stunned. My ego quickly jumped in with an attempt to diminish the power of the

message: *You just made that up*. But that's the thing, I replied—
I did make it up. It came from ME. I had to pay attention here.
These weren't the words of a psychic or a channel. They came
from my own inner knowing, my own Wisdom. I quickly wrote
a simple thank-you note:

Dear Eighty-year-old Self,
  Thank you. I'm sure your letter has changed my life.

In mid-July, Jenn came to San Diego with me to celebrate
my sister's birthday. That was the ostensible reason. The true
reason for the trip was to have fun. I took Jenn to Balboa Park
where, growing up, I'd spent many Sunday afternoons by the
huge pond in the botanical gardens, or hanging out in Fern
Canyon at the Zoo between visits to the land of the apes and
the den of humongous snakes. We had lunch at the shaded
outdoor café of the Museum of Modern Art.

That afternoon we visited an old friend from high school,
Steve, and his wife Erin. Steve had retired some years earlier
after a string of successes in the computer products industry.
He and Erin had just adopted a second Chinese baby girl.
Steve and Erin each had interesting tales to tell about the
time involved and the extensive paperwork necessary to bring
these children to the United States. Most of all, however, they
were thrilled to have babies in the house again and their older
teenage daughters felt the same.

Jenn was especially interested in hearing about their travels
in China and their experiences with the people. She was
delighted to speak some words to the little ones in her native
language, being careful not to act like she might try to take
the baby away from her new mother. Erin said that from the

first night they had her in China, Emma had to sleep on Erin's chest. If they tried to remove her, she would cry inconsolably. So for two months, the baby had been sleeping each night directly on Erin's chest, able to hear the beating of a mother's heart. Erin said her own sleep pattern had been interrupted, but it was surely worth it.

Sunday, the last day of our three-day weekend, Jenn and I put on our bathing suits and water sandals, walked down to La Jolla Shores, and rented a double-seated kayak. It was a perfect day—bright, sunny, and warm, but not hot. We waded into the water, got our dry-bags secured in the forward compartment, and carefully, butt-first, rolled into the kayak.

After a few minutes, we were able to coordinate our paddling. We headed across the bay toward the cliffs along the north end of La Jolla Village. Between La Jolla Shores and Cold Fish Point, sandstone cliffs rise nearly two hundred feet above the water. We paddled slowly to take in the topography—reddish sand-colored smooth stone faces interrupted by jagged crevices, rain-darkened and wind-worn. Narrow, pristine beaches lined the bottom of the cliffs here, safe from human visitors, except for the occasional kayaker who might stop by for a picnic on the sand.

As we neared the Point, the numbers of sea birds increased. I expected seagulls and a few pelicans, but I was surprised and delighted to see hundreds of cormorants perched on the cliffside, in spaces from the top all the way down to the water. Jenn and I laughed together at the antics of so many birds in one place. Black and big, they clearly had claimed the neighborhood. We were so busy enjoying the cormorants we didn't notice the seals lounging on the flat rocks at the base of the cliffs.

When we did spot them, though, we squealed with laughter and pulled closer. They didn't seem to notice us. *What a gift,*

I thought, *to be in the natural habitat of all of these creatures.* I felt the energy of life, theirs, Jenn's and mine, and my spirit expanded with joy. On the plane ride back to Albuquerque, Jenn and I agreed that it had been the perfect three-day weekend.

ABUNDANCE

THE SEA, FRIENDS, family, transforming my fears to possibilities, receiving the wisdom of love and acceptance—these must be the reasons why my body was healing. The rash was resolving, and I was slowly adding foods to my diet. The plan to move my office brought the opportunity to organize books, materials, and expenses. It felt freeing to simplify my clinical practice.

In the small basket next to my phone, I had an invitation to attend a fund-raiser in the early fall. Conservation Voters New Mexico was a non-profit organization based in Santa Fe that worked to translate environmental values into state policy. Sandy Buffett, my enthusiastic supporter for the Vietnam trip, was the tireless head of this group. I'd known Sandy since she was a grade-school friend of Niki's, and I'd watched her go from the University at Sea to teaching in Japan, to earning a graduate degree in international economics specializing in the redevelopment of Vietnam, to being the regional financial director of John Kerry's presidential campaign. She lived in San Francisco at that time. Conservation Voters brought her back home to New Mexico. When she was in town and available, she'd come to a sharing group and become one the younger Mighty Women.

Two weeks before the event she called to see if I was coming. I apologized for not returning the response card. "I'll be there,"

I told her, "and I'm really looking forward to it." About once a year there would be a Conservation Voters fund-raiser where many of the guests would be transplanted social activists from the east and west coasts, older now, but still looking like hippies. The social functions Sandy held in Santa Fe were elegant catered garden parties. In Albuquerque, events held in the North Valley were similar celebrations of charm and wealth. This party was being held in the South Valley, where old adobe houses still held the ghosts of Rio Grande wanderers from a succession of indigenous peoples. Instead of fine wines, there would be beer and soft drinks.

At the end of Sandy's call, she reminded me to bring two homemade pies for the auction, preferably my plum pie, she said. *I haven't made my cream and plum pie in years*, I thought. *Here's my opportunity.*

We heard the music long before we got to the house. Cars lined the narrow lane, and I had to park far down the road, nearly in the bushes. Jenn was with me, along with some other friends, and I was beyond happy. Just four days earlier I'd received a call from my lawyer telling me my case was settled. While the insurance company had refused our first offer, they agreed to the second. I would be getting enough money to pay my medical bills and make up for lost earnings and the extra amount it took to buy my new car. Plus, there would be enough left over to help Megan with her expenses. I relaxed into this day truly feeling, "All is Well."

Huge cottonwood trees shaded most of the yard. Dogs and children were weaving through the clumps of adults talking family and politics. Long tables had been set up for the pies the judges and guests would eat. The second pies were inside, safely waiting to be auctioned at the end of the evening. Large pots of *posole* and *carne adovada* sat on a grill next to a table covered with platters of corn and flour tortillas, salads, salsa, and guacamole. Even though I couldn't eat wheat, there was enough food that I could eat that suddenly, I was back in food heaven.

A little Latino man with a mustache and an overflow of personality served as DJ. He played every kind of music from ranchero to salsa to rock 'n' roll, and he cajoled us to get out there on the dirt and dance. We did. Alone, in twos, threes, and fours we bobbed, clapped, swayed, twirled, and finally made a line dance, mimicking the best dancer's movements.

Sandy took the microphone just in time for us to collapse in chairs and rest. She spoke about the successes Conservation Voters had achieved in the past year and the challenges they faced to elect friends of the environment in the coming year, and then she handed the microphone to the auctioneer.

My pie didn't make it to the finals. The "lesser pies" went for ten to twenty dollars. I had planned to go up to fifty dollars as my contribution, so I waited for the fifth-place pies to be auctioned. I bid on Sandy's apple pie, but it sold for seventy-five. I waited out the next two pies, thinking that if the bidding were to go to over a hundred, I'd go for the first-place pumpkin chiffon pie. The third-place lemon meringue went for one fifty, and the second-place chocolate silk brought two twenty-five.

Oh my lord, I thought. *I've never done anything like this before. Am I willing to pay over two hundred dollars for a pie? If you want to stay in the game*, my mind answered. *Besides, you're rich now. Your case settled. Go for it.*

The bidding was a blur of shouting, from my right, my left, and from behind. The numbers went up by tens and then fives. I found myself shooting my hand up and yelling "Two hundred eighty," and then "Three hundred." I expected the pie to be mine at three hundred. My friends and I were laughing and shaking our heads in disbelief. A voice shouted, "Three hundred ten," and another, "Three hundred twenty." Jenn nudged me and said, "Go higher." I held up my hand and yelled, "Three hundred fifty," and there was silence. The auctioneer pointed to me and said, "Yours, for three hundred and fifty dollars."

I folded up into laughter. When I could straighten and stand again, I said, "I just bought a pie for three hundred and fifty dollars," and fell back to laughing. I enjoyed writing the check out to Sandy's organization, and I carried that pie to the car as though it were the queen's diamonds on a velvet pillow.

The Mighty Women group met the very next night, on Sunday. As I prepared for my friends to arrive, I surveyed my living room. I saw art everywhere. On the wall was the lacquer painting I bought in Hanoi. Done in deep reds, the Hmong woman is holding an umbrella, looking as though she's standing peacefully in a golden rain. Also on the wall was a framed print of the Royal palace—a piece I'd purchased in Bangkok to help me remember the walled city with the Emerald Buddha. I looked over at the sculpture bust of the Hmong woman I'd carried home on my back from Asia. She reposed in all her elegance on my rosewood side table. *A sister pilgrim*, I thought. Across the room, Michael Naranjo's bronze, Eagle Dancer, stood on its own pedestal, crouched, wings spread wide as though in the next moment a drumbeat would start the dancer moving, circling and soaring. I looked out the windows across the Rio Grande and the city to the mountains, just beginning to turn soft purple and pink with the colors of evening. *My favorite time of day*, I thought, and I couldn't suppress a smile. My house, that two years before seemed like a cold, isolating prison, was now my home, filled with mementos of my journey and warm memories of new and old friends. And there was something else—I no longer felt alone. I had a sense that Spirit, or God, was nearby, around and within me, available, always accessible with just a word or a thought. I felt the energy of gratefulness flow through me.

As the Mighty Women sat down that evening to the always-perfect-potluck, I looked around the table at the faces of my dear friends and shared a thought. "I think it's time we changed our name. I'd like to call the group, 'Women of Wisdom,' or 'Mighty Women of Wisdom.' What do you think?" The instant agreement came with smiles and nods. My prayer of thanksgiving was longer than usual that night, and each woman added her own prayer of gratitude for the healing taking place in her life. After second helpings of stir-fry chicken, squash casserole, and two different salads, it was time for dessert. I made the fanfare sounds as I carried the pumpkin pie from the kitchen and placed it in the center of the table. "Here, ladies, is the most expensive and the most extraordinary pie you will ever eat. Let it represent the great harvest of our own lives. Enjoy." And then I served the chocolates.

.11.

SUPREMELY SUPPORTIVE
SELF-CARE FOR THE JOURNEY

A Month of Sundays: Daily Declarations
for the Journey

1. Today I accept my life just as it is. I give thanks for all of the ups and downs, and for every bit of the bounteous love that fulfills, sustains, and surrounds me.

2. God is with me. I'm never alone. I'm here on earth to be a Warrior for Love. I am abundantly grateful.

3. As I walk my path, I see that All is Well. Whether I judge the landscape as lush and nurturing or dry and lacking, I open my mind to see the big picture, the expansion and contraction that is life and growth. I know that I am guided and loved on the journey.

4. Today I give thanks for love in every form and every expression. I acknowledge that God expresses through me, and I honor my work, my play, and every person I come into contact with.

5. Anxiety comes knocking, softly at first, then banging, threatening to break down the door. I forgot. It's just my little-girl self being scared of Big Life. She needs to be reminded that she's safe. I hold her deep inside the fortress of my heart. I know how to protect her now—to love her through her fear and bring her back to the light of Joy.

6. Arrogance doesn't even knock. It says, "I'm not doing this work. I'm too busy. Life shouldn't be this hard." I forgot. It's just my little-girl self with her six-shooters on saying, "I'm not afraid of anything." But she really is afraid of Big Life. She needs to be reminded that she's safe and she's very smart, and she's loved enough to be a part of the human community.

7. Today I set my fears aside and look at my soul. I see compassion for myself and for all humans. My heart space loves me dearly and gently helps me cope with disappointment and sadness. I go on, embraced by love.

8. I am grounded in the love of God, inspired to be a light of love for all I meet. With no attachment to outcome, I exercise the muscle of faith. I am blessed to be an instrument of God's creativity.

9. I flow with life today. I move out into the middle of the river and enjoy the current whether it be swift or slow. I love the movement and the light on my face. My river of life takes me to the ocean of all possibilities.

10. Today I elevate, levitate, and transcend the habit patterns of worry and fear that keep me from my highest good and full self-expression. I know that who I am is Energy, Delight, Grace, and Love, and from that Essence my happiness is secured. Thank you, God.

11. Today I allow all of my responsibilities to be acts of ease. I flow comfortably between work and relaxation, always

leaving room for the joyful antics of my inner child to play like the little birds in the trees outside my window.

12. I am clearly and powerfully guided to my highest good, to the expression of my deepest desires, and to the manifestation of my wildest dreams.

13. Today I celebrate myself. I bask in the accomplishment of all that I am and all that I have. God truly works through my life in magical and mysterious ways, and I am thankful.

14. Today I celebrate all of life as a sacred Valentine. All of my relationships are God in love. Everything is sweet because I declare it so.

15. In God there is always enough—enough time, enough wealth, enough love to go around.

16. Great Spirit of Love, God Ocean of Energy, I open my mind and heart to allow the flow of your brilliance to imbue my work and my relationships. I honor every word and deed as an expression of your thoughts.

17. Here in this moment, I am Stillness. I am Love. I am a space from which everything I desire manifests. Thank you God.

18. Today I feel my angels fluttering about in excitement and joy for me. They know the power of God flows through me to the highest good of everyone.

19. Today I am resurrected from all fear, doubt, and limitation. I break out of my shell and live in lavish love—connected to all of humanity.

20. I have all that I need to be everything I am called to be and do everything I am called to do to fulfill my commitment to radiate love and contribution to the world.

21. I live in complete confidence that my mind is the mind of God. God has given me the power to Be and Do and Have all that I desire. My dreams are made manifest and I rejoice mightily.

22. I wrap my arms around that little girl inside. I hold her to my heart and tell her, "Everything will be all right. I'm here now, and I know how to love you and care for you. You're safe." She relaxes inside, and I soften toward myself. I create the possibility of living powerfully, productively and with ease.

23. I have all of my dreams in my arms. They manifest one by one.

24. The Universe is spacious and accommodating. It guides me through its vastness in each lifetime. I love my life and create all that I have come here to create.

25. Today I take a deep breath of love. I recognize that there is one life and that life is God. Divine Spirit breathes me and guides me in every thought and every deed. I organize my schedule so that all is done and all is well. I am loved and guided, and all that I desire is now manifesting like magic.

26. I stay in the present and bring joy to the party.

27. Today I let myself freefall into the comfort of God's love. I am supported and guided on my path to Heaven on Earth.

28. I am full of Joy. My divine energy magnetizes all good to me, and I delight in my dreams coming true.

29. I am always at your side, armed to the teeth with love.

30. I am the beauty of Butterfly. I am the joy of Hummingbird. I am the powerful perspective of Hawk. I am the compassion of the Goddess. I am the strength of God. I am the golden light of Love.

31. I am a brilliant emissary of Father God and the Cosmic Mother. I deliver on the promises I made when I came into this life. I create all that I intended to and share all that will be helpful to others. I love in every way I can find to love.

POWER YOURSELF WITH PRAYER

THIS IS WHAT to do when you don't know what to do—Pray. From time immemorial, in acute crisis, when your very life might be at stake, what words fall naturally from your mouth? "God, help me." Too often, prayer is thought of as a last resort—"The only thing left to do." Known medical treatments may have been exhausted, your own efforts and knowledge-seeking haven't seemed to alter the course, and the help you need seems inaccessible and unavailable. Betty, a fiftyish woman, came to my office a few years ago in a state of panic. Her doctor had said to her that if his latest prescription for a new medication didn't work, "We're dead in the water." Her unconscious mind took that literally. In hypnosis, she connected with the positive thinking of her own Inner Healer, and from that prayerful connection her body mended.

I constantly have to remind myself, as my thoughts are running down some dark, dead-end road, to stop. Prayer is the first thing to do, not the last. It's not only the right spiritual action, it's the right psychological action, because as soon as you begin to pray, you make a cognitive shift from negative thought to positive, from doubt and pessimism to faith and optimism. (And keep in mind that optimism is the key quality of resilient people—those who get right back on their Wisdom Path in the face of setbacks.) In terms of spirituality or physics, in prayer you align with your Higher Power and with the energy of the universe. Remember FEAR as "False Evidence Appearing Real" and realize that the only blocks to your higher good are in your own mind—old patterns of false beliefs about yourself and habits of negative thinking about the world.

While driving on the freeway to one of my doctor's appointments after my second accident, I found myself so worried about the outcome of the visit I began to pray for calmness and reassurance that all would be well. I was fretting and praying, fretting and praying, when I noticed a large sign on the truck in front of me. It said, "Fear knocked on the door. Faith answered it, and there was no one there." I laughed at myself and thanked God, amused that in taking my concerns so seriously, I very nearly missed the quick and direct comforting message. It had to be put right in front of me on a very large sign. There was, indeed, no reason to be fearful.

"Pray without ceasing." Call upon the Source of all life and allow that energy to flow through you and remove the blocks to your trust. Pray and look and listen and receive your response. Allow the way to be opened to your healing, your highest good, and your greatest learning—the learning that will serve you in creating joy and passion in your life. Make every day your first day of faith.

In times of crisis, the creative cognitive mind may not be accessible. After my head injury, I couldn't organize my thoughts, or even remember how to pray, let alone create something lovely and articulate. The following prayers are provided so that you, as I did, can read them whenever you need support in connecting with God, Source, the Universe, and your own inner Divinity.

1. I do this simple prayer every morning when I get out of bed, before I meditate or do my inspirational reading: Stand and face the east and raise your arms up to the sky. Say, "I greet this day with love in my heart." As you bring your hands down in front of you in prayer position, touch your forehead and say, "I bring God's love into my mind," then bring hands to heart, saying, "and into my heart, and into every cell in my body." Repeat this two more times.

2. If I'm fearful about something bad happening to me or to someone I love, I say the first lines of the Unity prayer over and over. "I am in a bubble of white light. Only light can come to me, only light is here." This short prayer was my mantra when my daughters were in their teens, when illness, accident, or some other calamity would jolt me toward worry. I used it recently when my daughter, Megan, a journalist, was covering a dangerous story in Mexico. Whenever I thought of her, I would pray: "Megan is in a bubble of white light. Only light can come to her. Only light is there." And I would know that she was safe.

3. This is a short adaptation of a prayer from the Hindu tradition:

> From the unreal lead me to the Real!
> From darkness lead me to light!
> From death, lead me to immortality!
> May the whole world be peaceful!
> Om . . . Peace, peace, peace.

4. And this is the Metta prayer. Metta is the Pali word for loving-kindness:

> May all beings be peaceful.
> May all beings be happy.
> May all beings be safe.
> May all beings awaken to the light of their true nature.
> May all beings be free.

5. This is one of my favorite prayers to say and to share:

SAINT THERESA'S PRAYER

May today there be peace within.

May you trust God that you are exactly where you are meant to be.

May you not forget the infinite possibilities that are born of faith.

May you use those gifts that you have received, and pass on the love that has been given to you. May you be confident knowing you are a child of God. Let this presence settle into your bones, and allow your soul the freedom to sing, dance, praise and love.

6. I will always love this well-known prayer of St. Francis of Assisi and I use it at times when I'm becoming too involved with my own issues and forgetting my commitment to service. It helps me to remember, from the Course in Miracles, that "the key to God is other people."

Lord, make me an instrument of Thy peace.
Where there is hatred, let me sow love.
Where there is injury, pardon.
Where there is doubt, faith.
Lord, make me an instrument of Thy peace.
Where there is despair, hope
Where there is darkness, light.
Where there is sadness, joy.
O Divine Master, grant that I may not so much seek
To be consoled as to console,
To be understood as to understand,

To be loved, as to love;
For it is in giving that we receive,
And it is in pardoning that we are pardoned,
And it is in dying that we are born to eternal life.
Then miracles shall follow miracle
And wonders shall never cease.

7. Write your own prayer by simply setting an intention for the blessing you desire.

> *Drop into your heart and recognize the one Source of all life. Ask for the realization, the manifestation of your request, knowing that it is already fulfilled in perfect time. Give thanks for the Law of the Universe that is responsive to the evolution of your greatest good, and release your prayer, knowing it must be answered. And so it is.*

8. This affirmative prayer for Choice is from Meenakshi Honig, a yoga teacher in Hawaii:

> *I choose to feel good right now.*
> *I choose to be Peaceful and give Love here and now.*
> *I choose to trust in the process and timing of life.*
> *I am happily married to my own inner peace.*
> *All my needs are always abundantly provided for in a positive, Divinely synchronized way.*
> *I choose to enjoy performing my daily Love missions (tasks, responsibilities).*
> *I choose to have fun . . .*

9. I have a special fondness for this reassuring prayer from Alan Cohen, from his book, *Handle With Prayer*:

> *Today I find God within me. I put aside the distractions of words, and come home to pure peace. Within my heart stands a temple of pure quietude where I am nourished and healed. I rise above human conversation and drink deeply of the stream of my own inner knowingness. I expand beyond all that I have been taught, and I remember what I know. Within my soul is the wisdom of the universe, and I commune with it now. I am one with all that is whole, and I claim peace. Thank you, Great Spirit, for guiding me home to myself.*

10. Start your day prayerfully by giving thanks for five aspects of your life that you are grateful for. End your day by acknowledging three blessings that occurred that day. Ask the question, "Why did this blessing happen to me?" and write the answers in your journal. And again, give thanks. A full and grateful heart has no space for worry and fear.

11. Ernest Holmes was an internationally recognized authority on religious psychology and founder of the Religious Science movement. Dr. Holmes prepared a five-step method or "mold" for prayer. The five steps provide a mold in which to pour out our unique expressions of need and desire in a way that affirms manifestation:

    1—*Recognition:* Acknowledge that there is only one Source, one Energy in all of life—one Divine Reality.

    2—*Unification:* We are all a part of and unified in this one energy Source.

    3—*Realization:* As part of this cosmic energy, we align

our thoughts and feelings to create, co-create, and realize the healing of wounds and the manifesta tion of dreams.

4—*Thanksgiving:* In giving thanks, there is the identification with belief and the feeling of faith that that which we seek is already coming to us. Our vision for good is already in existence.

5—*Release:* We let go in complete trust and turn the process over to Universal Law to manifest in the perfect way and in the perfect time.

12. And finally, a prayer I wrote for my book, *From Crisis to Creativity*:

Mother-Father-God, Angels, and all Servants of the Universal Good. Help lift me out of my grief. Help me to see with expansive vision that I have survived every obstacle in the past. Strengthen my faith so that I may know now on every level of my being that I will survive the present terror. Help me to see clearly the learning from this experience, how I have been guided to my knees, so that when I stand and walk again it will be in the Light and Love of clear purpose.

BREATHING HEALING

THE TRUTH, THAT breath is life, tends to become apparent only when we can't breathe.

After my head injury, I was short of breath constantly, and there were some times that I felt terror because I simply could not get enough air. Then there was that one morning when I got so upset at not remembering how to pray and not being able to breathe that I swore the prayer, Jesus Christ! Why can't I breathe? And a distinct, loving voice responded, "I will teach you to breathe." And He did. So I'll share that again with you here:

1. "Breathe in love," the deep, resonant voice said, "all the way to the top of your head." And the top of my head was where I truly felt I needed the oxygen. Then I was told to "breathe out anger and fear" on each exhale. The irony is that, in spite of my temper tantrum, I hadn't realized I was angry. So I practiced this breathing regularly, and I still practice daily breathing in love, and breathing out negative feelings.

Some of you, like me, will experience lack of breath during a medical emergency, but for most people, not getting enough oxygen to nourish the body is subtle and secondary to the tension of anxiety, fear, depression, resentment, and anger. As we age, the belly-ballooning that allowed air to fill up the lungs as babies is replaced by inner tension and quicker inhalations. Air is drawn from the heights of our chests and not the depths of our abdomens. Richard Brown, psychiatrist at Columbia University, believes that this shallow breathing is responsible for a "gradual fraying of our nervous systems." Another physician, Dr. Sheldon Hendler, has declared an "epidemic of oxygen starvation."

Yoga teaches that the regulation of breath controls the mind and the emotions. Dr. Brown has shown that the practice of Pranayama, the breathing methods taught in yoga classes, and in particular, a technique called Sudarshan Kriya, can effect powerful changes in people with a broad variety of emotional and physical disorders. He has successfully used this method with victims of war, rape, and other trauma in Afghanistan, Kosovo, and Croatia, and with hardened criminals in northern India. He attributes its startling success to the calming of the stress response and the activation of the vagus nerve, a part of the brain that regulates many bodily functions and releases restorative energy through the parasympathetic nervous system. Whatever type of deep breathing you do, it can have the beneficial effects of calming the mind, boosting mood, lowering blood pressure, and improving sleep.

According to B.K.S. Iyengar, peaceful breathing drives away "the two imposters—triumph and disaster," emancipating us from duality. With proper breathing, "The divine fire within blazes forth in its full glory . . . the darkness is banished by the dawn." And this dawn brings integration, wholeness and harmony.

2. Several times a day, consciously breathe into your heart space and breathe out light and love to all others.

3. I like to do the following practice for a few minutes at the end of the day before I start my evening activities. It is very simple and very calming. Lay on the floor in "corpse" position—flat on your back, arms comfortably resting with palms up; surrendering to gravity, softening into the floor. (My yoga teacher calls this "Mama" pose—sinking into the embrace of Mother Earth.) Inhale deeply and think, SPACIOUSNESS. As you slowly exhale, think, RELAXA-TION. Repeat these words with every breathing cycle. As you inhale, imagine creating space in every part of the body and bring air and light into that space. As you exhale, let all the tension from the day flow right out of your body.

4. Another breathing practice to do on the floor is *belly breathing*. Place your hand on your belly and concentrate expanding the belly up into your hand as you inhale on the count of four. As you exhale, let the breath lower the belly to the count of four. Do this for several minutes, then move the hand up to your *diaphragm* and isolate the breath by drawing it into your hand at this position, lowering the diaphragm as you exhale on the count of four. After several

minutes, move the hand to your *chest* and again isolate the breath by inhaling up into your hand, expanding the chest on the count of four. Then exhale, lowering the chest on the count of four or extending to a count of six. Return your hand to the belly and breathe here for a few minutes.

5. *Pyramid breathing* I've found to be effective in coping with fear, anxiety and panic, as well as physical discomfort. Inhale halfway up one side of the pyramid on the count of four, then inhale all the way to the top on another count of four. Pause at the top for a count of four, then exhale half way down the other side on four, exhale completely down to another count of four. Count along the bottom to four and begin again. Do this four times.

6. The following combination of breath-work and prayer helped me to cope with shoulder, head, and neck pain following my skiing accident. Sitting in a chair, inhale God's healing love to the part of the body that is in distress. Let that energy embrace the discomfort and transform it into calmness. As you exhale, share the Grace of comfort by sending it out on the breath to all others who are in need of healing. As you practice this compassionate awareness for yourself and your fellow humans, imagine yourself being in an inner pool of deep comfort that represents your abiding faith in your body and mind healing completely, allowing your body to "remember wellness."

7. If you have sharp, intense pain, inhale a deep breath and send it straight to the pain. Let that powerful breath act like a knife-tip or a laser beam, breaking up the pain into little pieces. On the exhale, blow the bits of pain out and away through your open mouth. Do this three times. On the next three breaths, bring a healing balm of love to that place in the body. On the out-breath, create more space in which to heal.

8. Sitting with a straight back, inhale breath from Mother Earth up along the back of the spine all the way to the top of the head. As you exhale, allow the breath to flow down over the top of your head and along the front body, back down to Mother Earth to be purified. Imagine that when you inhale, the air is aligning the spine and bringing health to all the vertebrae, the nerves and all the organs of your body. When you exhale, the breath is carrying all the toxic influences down through your legs and out the soles of your feet into the earth.

9. Breathing is the foundation for meditation and other altered states of consciousness, so you can use any of these breathing exercises alone as a form of healing, bringing balance to the mind/body, or after doing the breathing for a length of time, you may wish to extend your session with imagery or visualization, going deeper into relaxation. Here is an example: Imagine yourself in your favorite place in nature—at a beach, a river, the forest, a meadow, a mountaintop, a lovely garden. Sit or lie down in that special place and feel the air on your skin, the perfect temperature; the fragrance of salt-sea air, pine trees, flowers. Notice the sounds—of birds, the rippling of water, a breeze moving through the trees. See the beauty in the varying shades of color, like the many shades of green in the plants, trees, and grass. Experience this special place with all of your senses and allow all of the richness of nature to surround and caress you. Let yourself float in that space, becoming one with it, knowing that time has dissolved and disappeared for as long as you choose to be here, drifting gently, like a feather riding the currents of the air, or floating like a leaf on the water . . . And in this space, you are perfect, all is well—all is right with your world. Think: *The breath of God breathes my body.*

10. This grounding exercise is a wonderful way to clear away fear and anxiety and strengthen your core energy. (I learned this from my Feng Shui friend, Sabrina, in Los Angeles.) Use it before going into any stressful situation: Stand straight, legs powerful, posture aligned. Close your eyes and breathe deeply as you imagine your feet growing roots and sending them very deep down into the earth. Then open your crown chakra, the top of your head, and allow light to pour down into your body. Let it stream into you until it fills you completely. Allow a shower of sparkles and diamonds to flow and fall down around you. Step into a bubble and let the bubble contain you completely, zipping it up all around you. Notice that there are mirrors around the outside of your bubble so that all energies from the outside are reflected back and away from you. You are safe and protected by your light and radiate only that light . . . and you breathe naturally, with ease.

GRIEVING FEELINGS

IN OUR CULTURE, we learn that only death requires grief. And even then, there's a proper order for the feelings and we want them done within a short length of time. As we relax our notions of a "right way" and merely learn to recognize our feelings as the "right" ones for the present moment, the energy of unresolved or incomplete grief can be dissolved. Awareness and a deep acceptance of our feelings, regardless of how unfamiliar or uncomfortable, are the key practice.

Along the heroine's journey, the stages of grief show up in the following ways:

1. The first stage, the Call to Change, usually goes unheeded. We simply can't see the need to change a familiar pattern, or grow in a new way, or heal a long-standing wound. We deny the initial indicators and the intuitive signs that we must do so.
2. Being Tossed on the Path following a loss or crisis, we are in new, frightening circumstances with unknown outcomes. We might well be confused, angry, and obsessive about what has happened and what to do next.
3. On the Road of Trials or in the Belly of the Whale, we're abducted into the underworld of emotions—depression, hopelessness, and despair—required to experience and integrate the dark sides of our personality.
4. Returning with the Boon, the gift, or the treasure of transformed awareness, we discover that, not only can we accept what has changed, but we've developed the capacity for greater clarity, strength, and vision for new possibilities and life purpose.

Shocked, stunned, angry, and overwhelmed—these words don't seem to describe grief to most people. Some trauma victims cock their heads and squint their eyes when given the diagnosis of Post Traumatic Stress Disorder, grappling with their own self-assessment of "defective human being." They feel surprise and relief to know that what they are having is a normal, psycho-physiologic reaction to a life-threatening experience, and that reaction is an extreme form of grief. We are all having normal psycho-physiologic reactions to the challenges of change, pain, and disappointment. Big grief or small grief, it's our grief—and it has a special function—to clear the system for gradual renewal and regeneration. To build a new house, we have to prepare the ground.

The simple fact that tears contain stress hormones was reassuring to Mary, a forty-seven year old woman in one of my seminars. She felt "silly" for being so upset when her only child, a daughter, went off to college. "It's such a good thing for her to do and I'm happy for her, but I miss her so much, and my husband and I don't have that much in common," she told the group. When Mary saw that feeling weepy and sad was a way of being in the energy of change, and of allowing that energy to move through her, she also saw that the growth opportunity for her now lay in recharging the relationship with her husband. A smile spread across her face as she said, "That sounds like a very important thing to do."

As part of the heroine's journey we learn to honor our feelings as sacred, to be "with them," and to know they are "metabolizing" our difficult experiences and preparing us to emerge from the darkness stronger in intuition and direction. Glenna, fifty-three, spoke of being "depressed" during the recent years in her marriage, resigned to her husband Larry's drinking and lack of interest. When she mustered the courage to throw him out after he confessed to an affair, she felt empowered, but also anxious. She questioned her decision and mentally reviewed a long list of fearful outcomes. During the seminar, Glenna realized that her anger toward her husband was impacting her children and taking a toll on her health as well. She decided and declared that she would bring compassion to everyone in her family by expressing her commitment that love be present among them regardless of the outcome of the separation. "This feels so much better," she said, taking a deep breath, "because this is what I stand for——Love, Commitment, and Contentment."

Glenna shared during a follow-up group that as soon as her heart softened, she suggested that her grown daughter re-establish contact with her dad. After a long conversation between them, Glenna was surprised when Larry called her and announced he was going into rehab. Two months later, with successful family counseling to guide them, Larry is back home, working the daily AA program, and "being the man I married years ago. It's nothing short of a miracle."

When we choose "conscious grieving," we can observe our denial and disbelief, our anger and obsession, and our depression and resignation. From there, we can know that insight and acceptance of the situation as Reality is right around the corner. Then we can choose to re-create ourselves, just as Glenna did, in line with our values and our integrity. We can also know that we will receive guidance along the way. I was spiritually guided, and even reassured by animals like snake, hummingbird and hawk during my journey. Glenna felt that she was divinely guided to the seminar—"I knew I had to be here as soon as I saw the newspaper announcement," she said. "I knew I had something to learn." The learning involved letting go of her anger and opening her heart to the possibility of forgiveness. As a result, her entire family was transformed by rediscovering their love and their commitment to one another.

Here are some ways to turn your grief into growth through conscious self-awareness and self-nurturing. When you feel deeply wounded and completely stopped on the path, use these steps for encouragement and compassionate self-care:

1. Acknowledge the event that has triggered grief and brought "breakdown" to your life. Know that this is preparation for a "breakthrough," even if, at this time, any positive outcome seems impossible. Stay present for yourself and feel fully. Humans are conditioned to resist feeling fully for fear of being overwhelmed. Gently observe your feelings without any judgment. Let your heart open up in compassion.

2. What pattern of grief may be coming up, and when in childhood did it start? Every experience that produces grief

brings with it the possibility of healing earlier hurts. Take this opportunity to dive deep, go vertical, straight back to the original wounding. You couldn't process hurtful events when you were a child, but now you can. What feelings tend to cycle back on you? Is it anger, resentment, sadness, depression, obsession, anxiety? Where is the location of the feeling in the body? Give the feeling a shape and a color. Give it a voice and let it speak to you about its purpose. What age is this voice? What is it teaching you? Listen and thank this part of you for helping you survive. Say, "I release you now. I'm ready to thrive and embrace new life." As the old energy dissolves and flows out of your body, fill yourself up completely with the energy of love and the beautiful soft light of your favorite color.

3. Take every opportunity to feel peaceful—and when the grief comes up, allow it, feel it, write about it. Take charge of your story and tell it completely. Write every bit of it down. Leave nothing out and don't diminish the impact. See every bit of the victimization. Know that as children we are victims of trauma, misperception, abandonment and abuse, and as adults, we experience crises on that same painful and frightening level. Be aware of that small child who still lives within you in order to bring light and dissolve the darkness, and be the cause of your healing. How did your early experiences strengthen you and prepare you for your life's work? What might this current loss be preparing you for? Would you consider that your soul created this situation for your growth, for your highest learning?

4. Ask yourself what you need at this time. Find at least five things to do for yourself that will support you during this time of growth and recovery. Treat yourself with the same nurturing you would provide a convalescent. In Latin, to "convalesce" means to grow strong and recover your health.

What do you need? Who do you need time with and how often? What spiritual practices will help sustain you? What well-being practices can you bring to your regular schedule that will nourish your body and mind? Find as many ways as you can to bring compassion to yourself.

5. Is there someone you need to complete with in order to feel acceptance of this new reality, more contentment, and inner peace? Are you holding on to negative feelings about yourself or someone else? Debbie Ford writes in her book, *Spiritual Divorce*, "You may want to consider forgiveness as the ONLY solution to becoming a whole, complete, and free person." In Aramaic, the word "forgiveness" means to "untie a knot." Grievances keep us tense and tied up to another person or keep us in internal knots. Float up onto a fluffy white cloud and look down on the situation with new eyes. Feel empathy and open your mind to a new understanding. Gently untie the dark, rough, gloomy knot in the rope, feeling relief and release as that energy smoothes out into relaxation and peace.

6. If you need more strength in your forgiveness muscle, do the following exercise: Write a letter to the person who hurt you and list every detail of the violation, every way that their behavior impacted your life. Let the feelings of devastation anger or outrage be completely expressed. When you're finished, take three deep breaths into your heart center and begin a new letter. This one is a letter that comes back to you from this person—the soul of this person—the words of heartfelt apology that you always wished for; expressions of deep regret that you were harmed, that they caused you pain; a realization that your communication (even if that person is no longer physically alive) is transformative for them. This person asks for your forgiveness, and that act redeems them, releases them from condemnation. Your

choice, to respond with forgiveness, releases you back into
the life flow of love.

7. Ask, "What is my commitment?" Beyond the current circumstances, what is my long-term commitment? Ask, "When I
have metabolized and am complete with this event, when I
accept that all of my life is unfolding perfectly, who will I
choose to Be? How, through this experience, am I tapping
into my own sacred Intuition? How am I creating a ground-
swell, a "body-swell," of self-acceptance, joy, wisdom, and
possibility—the real treasures at the end of the rainbow?

MEETING YOUR OGRES

IN THE TRANSFORMATIVE forest of midlife, we meet the dark,
needy, and manipulative parts of our personalities. If we were
aware of them before, we thought they were occasional quirky
thoughts and feelings coming from the authentic adult self. What
we can distinguish now is that every negative thought, every
angry impulse, every feeling of worrying self-pity is spoken by a
small voice from childhood. At those young ages, we are overwhelmed by circumstances and feel victimized when our aims are
thwarted. At what age do you first remember saying, "But it's not
fair," then feeling the urges to fight back and insist on "my" way?

As children, we constructed defenses, roles, and identifica-
tions to cover over our fears and to give us ground to stand on
and grow, to believe in ourselves and have a sense of safety and
security. The inner voices we refer to as the Ego helped us to
survive, they gave us street-smarts, and they gave us the drive
to succeed. Now, like a boomerang, they come back with disempowering conversations, destructive behaviors, and beliefs
that constrict and limit our relationships, and block us from
pursuing a grand vision for the future.

When I was in grief about my multiple injuries—sad and mad about physical incapacity, pain, and loneliness—I'd hear a monologue inside my head, droning on about all the things that must be wrong with me in order that I would have these accidents and be without a man to care for me . . . *You are really pathetic*, it would say . . . *A pathetic loser.* Or sometimes, when my mind stayed blank and the memory button was off, or I was disoriented in a parking lot unable to find my car, the voice would add, *Stupid. You are a stupid, pathetic loser!* And that's what I believed about myself at those times. I was vulnerable and couldn't see how abusive, even sadistic I was being. Needless to say, I would never speak in that way to another human being, let alone a "Precious Child." Later on, with help from others and with prayer and meditation, I could say, *Thank you for sharing. Now, go in the other room and take a nap. I have healing work to do.* Then I could pay attention from my Authentic Adult Self and with compassion for my needs, I could choose to create responsible actions for self-care.

How could harsh, critical, demeaning, and demanding internal voices help us survive? This is how it works in Ego State Theory: When our personalities begin to develop, we exist as a precious innocent baby/child, vulnerable, in need of love and total "care and feeding." We will always have this Inner Child part of us. Around ages five and six, in order to live in society, we develop a conscience, a very rigid structure of beliefs in what is right and what is wrong; what it is to be bad and what it is to be good. These judgments serve us in steering away from danger and in being self-protective. This new aware-ness of the world also teaches us to survive by pleasing parents and by seeking validation through performance in school and placing high in competitions with others. Now, in addition to the love-seeking Inner Child, we've created an "Internalized Parent Child," what we now call the Ego—critical, blaming, hyper-vigilant to any perceived threat, and intent on personal attainment. The thing is, this part of the personality often masquerades as the adult. It is so focused on having what it wants that it can divert us from the path of growth and good. It can be a clever and cunning con artist, turning us against ourselves and our natural inclination to be socially inclusive and caring.

Without the capacity for abstract thought or reasoning as children, there is no ability to temper our judgments and our reactivity with understanding. As in fairy tales, the "mother" who first sought to protect us, as Ego, now takes the form of the wicked witch who is threatened by our achievements and prepared to throw us to the wolves if we cross her. The strict, overzealous father, intent on having us fulfill his vision of success in the world, now becomes the evil king, ready to banish us if we don't abide by every one of his dictums. Siblings or friends, correcting and directing us from their view of what's "right," become competitors or "archenemies" who would destroy us in order to be chosen for a certain position or relationship. It seems implausible that the condemning, insistently self-loathing ego helps us on the path, and yet, its job is to disallow weakness. Its motto could be, *Do it, and do it right or die trying!* The *ego* gives us the drive and motivation to grow. The problem is, we can never "get it right." We can never do "enough."

On the transformational journey we learn to distinguish the Ego, or the egoic thought forms and feelings, from the authentic Adult Self, our Intuitive Intelligence, Creativity and Choice—our access to the Divine. I believe this Core Self, or Essence, the Queen of our being, is always with us. I like to draw three circles in the shape of a triangle to represent the three primary ego states. The bottom two circles are the Precious Child and the Parent Child, the Ego. The top circle is the Authentic Adult or the Queen. I also like to draw an oblong circle, like a halo, above the Adult, to represent the Observing Self, Higher

Power, or the Divine Feminine that we have access to in this state of being. We all have the capacity to observe ourselves and evaluate our performance with neutrality. While at work, relating to others, during exercise, preparing for a talk, notice how you have your own built-in observation tower equipped with Loving Guidance.

At times on our journey, we may forget about the presence of our Adult Self and the Higher Self when we feel betrayed, trapped, angry, depressed, or poisoned by the pain of deep grief. Plus, wounds, connected to current losses, can also bring a flood of feelings from the past, breaking through doors, latched and locked for decades. The unresolved energy from every experience of hurt comes up now to be healed—but not easily. The inhabitants of this unsettling new territory on the heroine's journey, the shopkeepers of our ego, dig in their heels, post signs, issue threats, sabotage our health, and try to terrorize us to remain who we've always been—small and obedient, or small and rebellious, but certainly not someone who sees their greatness and perseveres to realize their dreams of being a contribution to the world.

Our Ogres, Trolls, Devils, or Demons, however you wish to think of them, emerge whenever the Inner Child feels frightened. They represent the automatic reaction of the Internalized Parent from survival instinct: *Stop crying; Don't be a baby; Get mad; Get even; Run away; Don't even try; You'll be sorry; Kill the bastard!* Anything to present a façade of strength or a sense of control. Shela, a fifty-two year old woman in one of my seminar groups, told of the "murderous rage" she felt toward her husband when she discovered he had another wife in a foreign country. "It scares me to feel this way," she said. "I'm not that kind of person. I did take out my wedding dress and cut it to pieces, but I wouldn't really kill him. I sure feel like it, though." Shela was asked to observe herself as the Queen of her life, able to be in the depths of her feelings, be informed by them, and allow that energy to move through her without a need to Do anything. She could then take time later to consult with her Higher Power before making choices and taking actions.

1. Like Shela, distinguish who you Are from the negative behaviors you Do or wish to Do. Know that who you Are is the Queen of your life, the Authentic Adult. What you Do automatically and reactively comes from Ego, those child parts of you that can act like excited or anxious puppies, or vicious attack dogs.

2. Make a long list of qualities you associate with the Essence of your Being, your nobility, your Higher Self, your Divinity. Select three of these qualities or values that truly resonate and reflect who you are committed to being at this time for yourself and for others. Write in bold letters: Who I am is (and declare the three qualities). For me, the following declaration supported me at one time on my journey through recovery: Who I am is—Healing, Happiness and Contribution. Shela declared: Who I am is—Wisdom, Generosity, and Power. "I won't kill my husband," she said, "but I will banish him from my kingdom for the time being. I'm going to be generous with myself and use my wisdom and power to handle this situation—with lots of help."

3. Begin to monitor your thoughts and your speaking so that you can change unconscious disempowering belief systems. For example, I noticed I was in the habit of answering the question of, "How are you?" with, "I'm really depressed," or "I'm anxious and forgetful," as though depression was Who I Am, or anxious and forgetful was Who I Am. The ego would have us believe we are nothing more than our fluctuating feelings. I changed that response to "I'm **doing** depression today," and "I'm **doing** anxiety today," or "I'm **doing** my grief

today"—making clear that the essence of my Being is always intact and supports me as I unfold my feelings and uncover old programming.

4. Notice the inner voices of your cast of ogres, villains, unsavory, seductive characters, inviting you to listen, conspire with them, or care for them. Remember that, up until now, they've been responsible for your survival, and they are hell-bent on having you be comfortable—at any cost. That means, paradoxically, encouraging you to do ANYTHING to relieve feelings of fear, doubt, or worry. We are compelled to do our habits and addictions to feel less pain and more comfort, less fear and more confidence. Until we're not.

5. Invite Awareness into the room. See these disowned, shadowy characters for who they are—children, some dressed in adult costumes, trying to manage your life. They've been rehearsing and performing their roles for a very long time, but what do they really need? They need the presence of your Adult Self, the Queen of your Being, to take the throne and establish order.

6. Get to know your Ogres. Only when you recognize them can the power of your firmness, your clarity, and your love dissolve their influence.

7. Practice making the healthy, worthy choices that bring balance and integration to all parts of yourself, for this is the transformative goal for your journey.

GENTLE SELF-COACHING ALONG THE WAY

TO REALIGN YOUR heart-mind and get back on the path when temporarily sidelined by fear, sadness, disappointment, anger, or hopelessness, ask yourself the following questions and write down your responses in a special Wisdom Journal. Most of us have patterns we fall into, behaviors that consistently block us from achieving our goals, shadow voices that tell us we can't possibility do or have what we desire. Our "inner trolls" would waylay us, have us hide under the bridge, stay in the darkness and not come out. The place I'm pulled into at those times, we call depression and anxiety. When I notice that energy in my body, I use the following coaching questions as a gentle method of processing and dissolving leftover negative energy. Use the questions to guide you from the darkness of the past to the light of the present, knowing that grief is growing you on your journey of creating wellness.

1. What's happened? What is the event that has occurred? I'll use my divorce as an example. The fact is that I was divorced after thirty-five years of marriage.
2. What do I tell myself? What do I believe about that? What story have I made up? It shouldn't have happened. He did so many things wrong. He should have been able to love me. He was mean and thoughtless. But then I'd turn on myself: I wasn't patient enough. I don't really know how to love. I'm not good enough. I'm not loveable and if he couldn't love me, no other man can. I'll be alone the rest of my life. Write it all out, everything that happened, every interpretation you've invented. Make the story as long as it needs to be to "speak your truth," document every hurtful event, list the violations, acknowledge your suffering, honor your experience. Then look at how you also blame yourself—if you do.
3. What is the impact of that story? For me, the story immediately produced a feeling of being small and stuck in the concrete of negativity—names like "Stupid Loser" or "Pathetic Jerk" popping up in my mind like a Jack-in-the-Box. I'd become depressed and very anxious, hopeless about

my future. I also felt shame, the term "failure" would come to mind, as in a "failed marriage." I'd be angry with Bruce and heap blame on him. The feelings would fuel more negative, limiting thoughts and then those thoughts would reignite the bad feelings creating a vicious cycle. Our stories are always dramatic and imply a frightening future. They are completely disempowering.

4. How can you challenge your story? What I came to see is that my marriage was successful for thirty years. We raised two beautiful daughters and were blessed with two grandsons. We'd supported one another in growing our careers, and we had wonderful family travels. But the marriage had stopped working. The relationship was no longer viable no matter how many ways we'd tried to resuscitate it. I found that I could choose to declare that our work and our learning from one another in this lifetime was complete.

5. What is the opportunity now? From this fresh perspective I could see that my strongest commitment is to the family. When I recognized my commitment to have a happy, loving family life, Bruce would be included as my friend and co-parent, and his partner would be included in our family as well. I shared with Bruce my commitment that we have an extraordinary friendship. From that commitment, we've given ourselves, our daughters, and our grandsons the gift of ongoing comfortable family get-togethers and celebrations.

6. What will you have to give up? Your inner child selves, your inner ogres and little trolls, will not go away. They will require consistent attention, love, reassurance, and firmness. Every time they say that I've been abandoned and will never be happy again, I have to give up that story—notice it, release it, and re-create myself from the essence qualities I say I am: Energy, Love, Grace, Compassion, and Joy.

7. Declare WHO YOU ARE and be the conscious creator of your future based on your most important values.

And here is a shortened version of the self-coaching questions to guide you as you as you use your Wisdom Journal:

1. **What's so?** What's happened? What event triggered you?
2. What do you tell yourself about it? **What do you make it mean?** What are your automatic thoughts, judgments, and complaints? What story have you created?
3. **What is the impact** of that story? How does it affect you? What emotions come up? After writing about the impact on you, write about the impact of your story on those who love you.
4. **Challenge** your interpretations and assumptions about the event. Describe what happened as a reporter would—with only the facts. What is a different perception? What is a new understanding?
5. What is the **opportunity** for you and for your life? What is the gift, the possibility from this new perception? Can you find it in your heart to accept what's happened as a simple fact of life? From **acceptance**, what personal qualities can you allow to come forth that inspire you? How will you Be with this situation? What new, empowering story will you create for you and for your life?
6. What will you have to **give up** to maintain this new way of being?
7. What three **actions** can you take today to support you in making this shift in consciousness and behavior and create new possibilities for your future?

Positive Psychology's ABCs of coaching are the super-short way to remember the steps in processing difficult experiences and bring yourself back to your Essence, your Higher Self, and to Possibility. Notice, this is basically the same process as above.

1. Adversity—what happened?
2. Beliefs—your story about it.
3. Consequences—the negative impact of your story.
4. Disputation—dispute and challenge your story.
5. Energize—refocus energy; generate possibility; create a new vision; be your own fan club and take actions that support you in moving in this new, self-created direction.

Guiding Metaphor—Becoming a Warrior for Your Life

Recognize the limiting childhood metaphor that has guided your life to this point and realize the true, polished, shiny, divine version—the one that describes your life purpose. This is one of my favorite examples: My young friend, Sarah Barlow, was the only Anglo child born on the Navajo Reservation in New-Mexico. Her parents were there working for the Public Health Service. At birth, she was given the Indian name Girl Who Walks up Hill. As she grew, Sarah came to believe that she didn't belong and that her life was just one long uphill struggle. And it seemed to be that way—until the many years of personal development work she engaged in paid off. Now she realizes and has declared her adult guiding metaphor as Warrior for Transformation. She has coached hundreds of people through Landmark Education to claim the myriad possibilities for greatness that are available to them in their own lives, and to her as well.

I realized that my guiding metaphor was Girl Alone on Dirt Road. That's what I remembered—feeling lonely growing up on the only unpaved street in San Diego. The sign on the fence along the canyon said, DEAD END. I internalized a belief that my life would be a dead end, that I would inevitably be abandoned and left alone. And when my father moved out and my parents divorced, I buried that belief even deeper inside. Your guiding metaphor is like a static snapshot of yourself at a young age looking awkward, weak, or even victimized. In the basement of your mind, that photo is the only one posted on the bulletin board. The pictures of you clowning and being the star at your eighth birthday party, crossing the finish in a relay race, getting an A on a science exam, being praised for an essay, looking adorable at your dance recital, placing in the spelling bee, or feeling special in your prom dress may be vague memories or even documented somewhere in an album, but they don't exist next to the photo in the basement.

We need to take that picture down—that embarrassing snapshot that up until now has been a source of shame and fear. We need to bring it upstairs into the light. We need to look closely into the eyes of that little girl and see how much love she needed and still needs, and then we must find ways to give her that love and sense of security. We must also recognize the paradox that the same adversity that made us shy and sad also provided the experience and drive for us to achieve success in certain areas of life. Warriors are trained through hardship, and we can acknowledge ourselves for having survived and thrived because of this training. Now we can choose to be warriors for life, warriors for love.

Woman Who Makes Rainbows is my new guiding metaphor— the truth of who I am. I've always seen rainbows, and as I shared in my story, I was able to create two of them on my healing trip to Maui. I take time now to feel the energy of each color of the rainbow as it flows from the different chakras in my body. You might wish to record the following Rainbow Meditation, have it read to you, or purchase the Rainbow Your Life Meditations CD. As you listen, concentrate on allowing the flow of energy from the various colors to transform your wounding metaphor into your guiding metaphor—the symbol of your vitality, power, and purpose.

RAINBOW YOUR LIFE-A CHAKRA MEDITATION

GENTLY CLOSE YOUR eyes; just let the eyelids meet; and imagine yourself standing beneath a beautiful rainbow. Feel the colors flowing down throught you and around you as a wave of relaxation pours down over you from above, . . . turn your face up to receive the colors as the waves softens, releasing the muscles in your scalp, smoothing away worry lines in your forehead. . . . it relaxes the tiny muscles around the eyes . . . and flows down into your face, your jaw releases, tongue rests ati its root . . . And now this lovely wave flows down into your neck and shoulders, releasing the tension held there, melting it away, dissolving it . . . and now flowing down through the arms, the forearms, the wrists—flowing into your hands, bringing greater warmth; all the way down to the finger tips.

This wave of relaxation is flowing down along your back, like warm or cool liquid, releasing, relaxing every muscle and tendon, every nerve and fiber—completely peaceful . . . And notice the deep, even, natural rhythm of your breathing . . . allow the wave of relaxation to flow down through your chest, aware of the breath breathing you, lightening you . . . loving you . . . bringing health and well-being to every organ in your body . . . now the wave is flowing down through your abdomen . . . allowing all physical system to function with ease, harmony, and natural health. . . . The wave flows down through the pelvis and into the legs—the legs released and relaxed, heavy and relaxed . . . the wave flowing now through the ankles, washing any remaining tension right out the soles of your feet . . . down into mother earth, received and transformed by love . . .

And, in this place of peace—an exquisite sanctuary, of safety, of privacy . . . a garden of visual beauty . . . there is complete stillness, sacred stillness—you may hear sounds of nature-birds, water, a gentle breeze . . . feel the air on your skin—the perfect temperature.. and notice the fragrance of this garden . . . breathe in deeply, and focus your attention completely on standing strong, grounded, rooted to this spot, your legs like one tree trunk roots extending down through the soles of your feet, deep down into the moist earth . . . and now notice, become aware of energy-flowing up through your feet and legs, flowing up to the base of the spine . . . and notice that this energy is the color of (1) red . . . the color of the energy of the first chakra, the energy center at the base of the spine. Feel this color of birth, of blood, of connection and complete care . . . grounded in Mother Earth, a deep sense of belonging, of loyalty and devotion . . . feel the intensity and the love of this energy . . . and feel your innate ability for self care, for standing for yourself in perfect health . . . completely supported . . . you are One with All that Is. . . .

(2) And now, energy flows up higher and notice the color of this energy-orange—a vibrant, physical power the power of movement, the element of water . . . the center of sex and survival¬orange . . . . the color of creativity.., of manifesting all abundance . . . feel this color of orange circling and filling your lower abdomen . . . with clarity, commitment, and total confidence . . . It's time now . . . there's so much time . . . always enough time to allow your creativity to be birthed, to come forth naturally and easily . . . your own signature self expression. . . .

(3) Allowing the life energy now to flow up into your solar plexus—filling that entire area with a beautiful golden glowing light . . . your own inner Sun . . . luminous yellow light. . . . And

see that light flowing to every part of the inside of your body . . .
illuminating, and now radiating out in all directions forming a
lovely shield of light . . . encircling you and keeping safe and
sure the self esteem, the inner power that resides here. . . .
The power that fuels your essence . . . energy that honors you,
that allows you to be fully responsible, in this moment, to your
unlimited potential. . . . The fire energy of the Sun, bringing
you into alignment with joy, optimism, and inner wisdom . . .
let the concept of greatness grow, germinate, and move you . .
. to inspire others to let their light shine as well. . . . You are a
beacon of light . . . your courage growing huge, like the biggest
Sunflower . . . knowing, in this moment, that your full intuition and creativity blossoms as you honor yourself, believe in
yourself . . . bask in the energy of yellow and gold . . .

(4) And now notice energy filling your chest . . . expanding
your heartspace, aware of the beautiful color of green, the many
different shades of green like the many aspects of growing love-
compassion, kindness, appreciation, generosity, the grace of forgiveness, the caring for oneself and others. . . . The "radical love"
that calls to us during times of extreme loss. . . . Your heart growing
ever stronger in its capacity for luscious love- the central power
of human energy . . . feel the green, moss green, forest green . . .
let it flow through you and around you... divine feminine energy,
healing every hurt, every wound from the past . . . growing, letting go, and allowing a new intimacy with yourself. a balance that
grounds you and supports you in the present . . love flowing up from
the Great Mother, flowing down from God the Father, meeting in
the heart center and then flowing out of your outstretched arms to
all of our brothers and sisters . . . an eternal flow of lovely loving
energy . . . healing yourself and healing everyone around you . . .

(5) Feel the energy flowing up into your neck, your throat
and know the color of this energy center is a beautiful blue
. . . deep sea blue, sky blue, light blue, aquamarine. This

energy embodies the power of self-expression . . . the ability to communicate your deepest truths . . . it was not possible as a child. . . . Now you're free . . . trust yourself . . . speak your truth . . . all blocks are removed. . . . It feels so good- in touch with your intuitive knowing no more swallowing lies, half-truths, manipulations this body, this world is yours to express your will Have faith in yourself .The throat and the neck vibrate to the dazzling and divine color of blue... you are engulfed in a sea of inspired self-expression. . .

(6) And now, energy flows up to the center of your forehead . . . the colors of soft violet, indigo... the vibrational force here is of higher knowledge and great vision. . . . Let the soft color of indigo blue fill your mind, reflecting the light of your divine, true essence. . . . Serenity and peace . . . the violet flows around and within you, bringing insight and clarity .Your 'third eye' the energy center of wisdom and contribution; living fully in the present moment . . . in trust . . . knowing all is well . . . your life is unfolding perfectly in this soft, beautiful light.

(7) Be aware of the top of your head, your 'crown," your 'crowning glory,' is your connection to Spirit, spiritual wisdom, the transcendent dimension. . . . Divine energy, white light, is flowing down from above now, mixing with the colors of each energy center . . . all possibility for expanded consciousness, of spiritual awakening . . . living life as a prayer . . . the perfect balance of red and blue resulting in the color of purple . . . royal purple- the color of wisdom, strength to endure any dark night, knowing the truth that the night ends with a light that illuminates a new path . . .

Know, you are a rainbow of light. . . . Be the rainbow you are . . . let your light, your colors flow up and out of you like a celestial fountain, showering you with courage, creativity, confidence, and great love .you are a prism of possibility, attracting and reflecting only light. . . .

.12.

. MIGHTY WOMEN UPDATE .

JENN continues to be the guru of social and outdoor activities. She leads the pack at hiking, kayaking, dancing, and, definitely, dating. She's present for play and dedicated to work. Following her service as a physician in Indonesia after the tsunami, she became increasingly aware of the many medical needs existing in Asia. After visits to Cambodia and her home country of China, she created a non-profit organization, REACH-International, to serve the people in rural areas of Cambodia. As I write this, Jenn is working for the Indian Health Service as a staff physician at the Pine Hill Health Center on the Ramah Navaho Reservation east of Albuquerque. She lives there during the week and comes home for the weekends—ready to party.

FAY sold the gallery she owned for thirty years, remodeled her house, and completed the rigorous training to become an Introduction Leader for Landmark Education. Through her work with Landmark, she met the man of her dreams. She and David had the first "fractal" wedding on the planet. Scientist Jonathen Wolfe, has combined his genius for math, science, art, and technology to create a fractal show for the planetarium of the Albuquerque Natural History Museum. "Fractals are infinitely complex patterns created by repeating a simple process over and over in an ongoing feedback loop of colors and dimensions." The first Friday of the month, Jonathan's "freaky fractal" show is projected on the ceiling of the planetarium to a sold-out audience. During the private showing for Fay's wedding, he'd added special touches and selected music. The guests settled back and were drawn into the images as though we'd been telescoped to the inside of a kaleidoscope. It was a wild three-dimensional ride, punctuated by laughter, yips of delight, and a steady stream of "Oh my God," coming unbidden from my mouth. It was a psychedelic experience without drugs. After the show, Fay and Dave exchanged vows in that beautiful darkness beneath the stars.

JANE found a Peace Corps like program in Belize where she could use her social work skills to help indigenous women. It took more than a year to make the preparations to leave, but she did it. The directorship of the family clinic she had led for many years was turned over to someone else, her belongings were put in storage, and she leased her house. "I'm not sure I'm going to retire and I'm not sure where I'll go when I come back. I'm completely open."

ELIZABETH discovered that her ex-husband had taken a job in Sydney and was moving back to her home country. "How dare he move there!" she fumed, but then realized that what she wanted to do was to move to the Midwest and live close to her grandchildren. Angry grief surfaced again when she found that James had a lover waiting for him in Australia. "There's no fairness in this. I should be the one to have a lover. The hell of it," she declared. Elizabeth came to accept her ex-husband's plans, as well as her own. She saw irony and humor in his moving to live near her family of origin and her staying near his. Acceptance and excitement took over when she discovered her move would present an opportunity to use her newfound business skills. Her daughter was opening a cupcake bakery, and Elizabeth would handle the accounting.

ANNIE divorced Ralph over a carefully planned six-month period. She helped him find a house that worked well for him given his handicaps, and one of their daughters moved in with him for the first few months. He adapted readily and is now in a serious relationship with a woman who joins him in outdoor activities and travels. Annie wears a smile as part of her dress nowadays. She's pleased with her plant and flower business, teaches horticultural therapy, and is moving to Costa Rica to work for a year. "I love my life," she told me the other day over lunch. "I never thought I'd be this happy."

> This is the true joy in life, the being recognized by yourself as a mighty one . . .
>
> *George Bernard Shaw*

FORMAT FOR MIGHTY WOMEN OR WOMEN OF WISDOM SHARING CIRCLES

SMALL GROUPS OF women meet once each month, or bimonthly, in one of their homes. Six to eight seems to be the best number—more than that makes it harder to share intimately as it requires much more time for the sharing circle. Using the following format, there is no need for a facilitator. (It should be stated, however, that confidentiality will be expected, and that only support is offered, never confrontation, advice, or judgment.) Each woman brings something to eat. Shoes are left in the entry. Meeting time is often in the early evening; dinner is served and eaten in first hour. Before eating, we hold hands and say a blessing. Thumbs point left to signify one hand giving, the other receiving. Any simple blessing will suffice, such as, "We give thanks for these friends, this food, and for all of the abundance in our lives." Following dinner, the women move to the living room and sit in a circle. Inspirational cards are placed facedown on the coffee table. (The Angel Oracle cards by Ambika Wauters have been the favorite of many groups followed by the Crystal Ally Cards, by Naisha Ahsian.) Each woman draws one or two cards and a short meditation period follows. A bell or a Tibetan Singing Bowl may be used to signal the end of the meditation.

According to Native tradition, a "talking stick" or stone is placed on the table. Whoever feels moved to speak first takes the object and holds it while she shares. Most women speak of the obstacles they've overcome and the issues they are still addressing. The metaphysical message of the card drawn usually relates to the topic. The group actively listens and holds silence until the last person has talked. This silence is sacred as it honors each person's innate ability to access their own sacred power and inner resources to process and transform problems into possibilities for creative and inspired living.

When the sharing circle is complete, the women stand and again bless the group, give thanks, and affirm that their lives are unfolding perfectly. Sometimes the women stay longer and invite discussion of the sharing. Or some may stay, while others need to leave. A reminder is given of the next month's meeting date. Other activities or fieldtrips may be planned.

From time to time, the sharing circle becomes a prayer circle. At these meetings, each person says what they would like a prayer for and then ten minutes is spent with everyone focused on prayer to manifest the needs of that person.

"You are a prism of possibility,
A rainbow of energy—of colors—
constantly flowing through you;
Creating health, positive thought
and Love that heals the world."

Gail Feldman

ACKNOWLEDGMENTS

The "school" I've been privileged to swim with in this vast sea of people we call the world has grown me in every way. My big sister, Judy, is a solid rock reminder of who I am, what I'm here for, and what I'm capable of. Not that she uses words necessarily to express her belief in me—her presence, the sound of her voice, makes it clear that she stands for my total worth, my complete self-expression, my contribution to the world. And everyone in the "big fat Italian family" she somehow manages would agree with me that she takes the same stand for them. I thank her for her emotional support, her physical care during my down times, and her willingness to join me in playfulness and occasional "laugh attacks" to lighten our lives.

Marcia Landau, my "sister by choice," has loved me unconditionally for forty years—through graduate school, marriage, child-rearing, career development, divorce, deaths—all of the joys and "catastrophes" on our heroine's journey. Marcia's readings of the early drafts of this book were crucial for the book's evolution. Her insights, writing skills, and knowledge of the intricacies of my life helped pull the important events together. I thank David, her husband, for generously sharing Marcia with me.

If life has a jackpot, I hit it by having Niki and Megan for daughters. I am consistently inspired by their commitment to fun, family, and excellence in work. I acknowledge Niki for introducing me to yoga and for expanding her yoga instruction to pregnant mothers and children. And I kiss her feet for bringing my grandsons, Ethan and Adam, into this world. Without Megan's dedication to me and to the world of writing, this book would not have come into being. As a journalist, she understands the need for quick edit calls at any time of the day or night. The same goes for emotional support. "Clearing" calls help both of us clean up negative energy and create a positive stand for the day or for a difficult situation.

My Mighty Women friends continue to be lifelines throughout these midlife years on the journey. To Jenn, Fay, Jane, Becky, Annie, Bobbie, Leah, Emily, Kateri, Deborah, Carmen, Barbara, Suzanne, Joan, Diane, Mindi, Winnie, Mita, Claire and many others who participated in creating a space for healing, I have deep gratitude. I give thanks for open hearts, trustful sharing, and always coming back to possibilities for greater love.

Landmark Education courses taught me much about transformation and brought richness to the lives of my family members and my friends. I honor the Landmark leaders for their commitment to creating a world that works for everyone, and I thank them for introducing me to the extraordinary benefits of life coaching. I thank Accomplishment Coaching for the excellent training I received during the year I attended their program. Many times on the "descent into darkness" or in the "belly of the whale," Patrizia, Jim, and my dear Ginger got me off the shoals and back into the water where I could keep paddling and looking forward to what's next. I credit Elizabeth Ward, one of my coaches, for making this book a reality one year ahead of schedule. Her patience, training skills, and her belief in me allowed energy and focus I didn't realize I was capable of. And Janis Pullen, my current coach, supports me in every way.

Writers need teachers, and mine was Greg Martin. His patience, requirements for performance, and genuine concern for his students' success touched and motivated me. Author and friend Lisa Lenard provided editing and sound advice on the manuscript. Randy Peyser's knowledge of proposals, structure, and the inner workings of the business was an invaluable contribution, and Nina Amir's timely editing brought richness to the storytelling. Sarah Barlow saved me by writing chapter summaries when I needed a quick overview of what I had written. I thank David Nelson, my former agent, for his wisdom and support during the last years of this book's creation, and for his introduction to David Lamb at Vantage. I also wish to acknowledge my first agent Jim Levine, for setting me on the path so many years ago by encouraging me to write *Lessons in Evil, Lessons From the Light*. It was after the publication of that first book that I was honored to share the podium one afternoon in 1993 in Los Angeles with Marianne Williamson. Her book, *A Return to Love*, and her subsequent writings and lectures have provided ongoing inspiration to live the spiritual life—to ground myself in meditation and prayer, and when I've fallen into despair, to ask God to remove the fear and doubt from my heart that I may be strengthened and enlightened and moved to rejoin the delightful "fray" of family, work, and friends.

Ultimately, all gratitude goes to Spirit, Source, God, the Divine—all the names we use to address the Cosmic Energy that creates, grows, breathes us, and brings us to awareness of our greatest gift, the ability to love.

REFERENCES

Ahsian, Naisha. *The Crystal Ally Cards*. Marshfield, VT: Heaven & Earth Publishing, 1995.

Amen, Daniel. *Change Your Brain, Change Your Life*. New York: Three Rivers Press, 1998.

Bird, Isabella. *Six Months in the Sandwich Islands*. New York: Putnam's, 1981. (First published 1881)

Bird, Isabella. *A Lady's Life in the Rocky Mountains*. New York: Barnes & Noble, 2005. (First published 1879)

Borysenko, Joan. *A Woman's Book of Life*. New York: Riverhead Books, 1996.

Bowman, Carol. *Children's Past Lives*. New York: Bantam, 1998.

Brooks, Robert and Sam Goldstein. *The Power of Resilience*. New York: McGraw-Hill, 2004.

Campbell, Joseph. *The Hero With a Thousand Faces*.

Cohen, Alan. *Handle With Prayer*. Carlsbad, CA: Hay House, 1998.

Doidge, Norman, M.D. *The Brain that Changes Itself*. New York: Viking, 2007.

Domar, A., and H. Dreher. *Healing Mind, Healthy Woman*. New York: Dell Publishing, 1996.

Dyer, Wayne. *Ambition to Meaning* (film on DVD). Hay House, 2009.

Farhi, Donna. *The Breathing Book*. New York: Henry Holt, 1996.

Feldman, Gail. *From Crisis to Creativity*, 2nd ed. Bookpartners, 1999

Feldman, Gail. *Taking Advantage of Adversity*. London: Time Warner, 2002.

Feldman, Gail and Katherine Gleason. *Releasing the Goddess Within*. Indianapolis, IN: Alpha Books, 2003.

Flach, Frederic. *Resilience*. New York: Fawcett Columbine, 1988.

Ford, Debbie. *The Dark Side of the Light Chasers*. New York: 1998.

Ford, Debbie. *Spiritual Divorce*. San Francisco: Harper, 2001.

Ford, Debbie. *The Right Questions*. New York: Harper, 2003.

Gordon, James. *Unstuck: Your Guide to the 7 Stage Journey Out of Depression*. New York: Penguin Books, 2008.

Harris, Thoresen, Lopez. "Integrating Positive Psychology Into Counseling." *Journal of Counseling & Development*. Winter 2007: Vol 85.

Hay, Louise. *You Can Heal Your Life*. Carlsbad, CA; New York: Hay House, 1999.

Higgins, Gina O'Connell. *Resilient Adults*. San Francisco: Jossey-Bass, 1994.

Hollis, James. *Finding Meaning in the Second Half of Life*. New York: Gotham Books, 2005.

Katie, Byron. *Loving What Is*. New York: Harmony Books, 2002.

Lipton, Bruce H. *The Biology of Belief*. Carlsbad, CA; Hay House, 2008.

Lopez, Suzanne. *Get Smart With Your Heart*. New York: Putnam's, 1999.

Lusseyran, Jacques. *And There Was Light*. New York: Parabola Books, 1987.

Lusseyran, Jacques. *Against the Pollution of the I. Idaho*, Sandpoint, ID: Morning Light Press, 2006.

Lyubomirsky, Sonja. *The How of Happiness*. New York: Penguin, 2008.

Murdock, Maureen. *The Heroine's Journey*. Boston: Shambhala, 1990.

Myss, Caroline. *Anatomy of the Spirit*. New York: Harmony Books, 1996.

Nelson, Mary C., *Michael Naranjo*. Minneapolis, MN: Dillon Press, 1957.

Nelson, Mary C. *Artists of the Spirit*. Sonoma, CA: Arcus Publishing Co., 1995.

Newberg, Andrew & Waldman, Mark. *How God Changes Your Brain*. New York: Random House, 2009.

O'Malley, Mary. *The Gift of Our Compulsions*. Novato, CA: New World Library, 2004.

Osborn, Claudia. *Over My Head: A Doctor's Own Story of Head Injury*. Kansas City: Andrews McMeel Publishing, 2000.

Ralston, Aron. *Between a Rock and a Hard Place*. Atria Books, 2004.

Randolph, John. *The Abundance Book*. London, USA: Hay House, 1987, 2005.

Reivich, Karen & Shatte, Andrew. *The Resilience Factor*. New York: Broadway Books, 2002.

Richardson, Cheryl. *The Art of Extreme Self-Care*. USA: Hay House, 2009.

Salzberg, Sharon. *Lovingkindness: The Revolutionary Art of Happiness*. Shambala Press, 2002.

Sams, Jamie, & Carson, David. *Medicine Cards*. New York: St. Martin's Press, 1998.

Seligman, Martin. *Authentic Happiness*. New York: Free Press, 2002.

Sheehy, Gail. Passages: *Predictable Crises Of Adult Life*. New York: Bantam, 1976.

Sheehy, Gail. *Sex and the Seasoned Woman*. New York: Ballantine Books, 2006.

Shellengarger, Sue. *The Breaking Point: How Today's Women are Navigating Midlife Crisis*. New York: Henry Holt, 2005.

Shimoff, Marci. *Happy for No Reason*. New York: Free Press, 2008.

Singer, Michael A. *The Untethered Soul*. Oakland CA: New Harbinger Publications & Noetic Sciences Books, 2007.

Siebert, Al. *The Resiliency Advantage*. San Francisco: Berrett-Koehler, 2005.

Stone, Tom. *The Power of How Great Life Technologies*. Carlsbad: CA, 2008.

Taylor, Jill Bolte. *My Stroke of Insight*. New York: Viking, 2006.

Taylor, S., Klein, L., Lewis, B., Gruenewald, T., Gurung, R., & Updegraff, J. "Female Responses to Stress: Tend and Befriend, Not Fight or Flight," *Psychological Review*, 107(3), 41-429, 2000.

Tolle, Eckhart. *A New Earth*. London: Penguin/Plume, 2005.

Tolle, Eckhart. *The Power of Now*. Novato, CA, New World Library, 1999.

Trussoni, Danielle. *Falling through the Earth*. New York: Henry Holt, 2006.

Virtue, Doreen. *Archangel Michael Oracle Cards*.

Weiss, Brian. *Many Lives, Many Masters*. New York: Simon & Schuster, 1988.

Werber, Eva Bell. *Quiet Talks With the Master*. Marina del Rey, CA: DeVorss, 1964. First published 1936.

Williams, Mark; Teasdale, John; Segal, Zindel; Kabat-Zinn, Jon. *The Mindful Way Through Depression*. New York: Guilford Press, 2007.

Williamson, Marianne. *A Return to Love*. New York: Harper Collins, 1992.

Williamson, Marianne. *Enchanted Love*. New York: Simon & Schuster, 1999.

Williamson, Marianne. *The Age of Miracles: Embracing the New Midlife*. Hay House, 2008.

Zander, Rosamund, & Benjamin. *The Art of Possibility*. New York: Penguin Books, 2000.